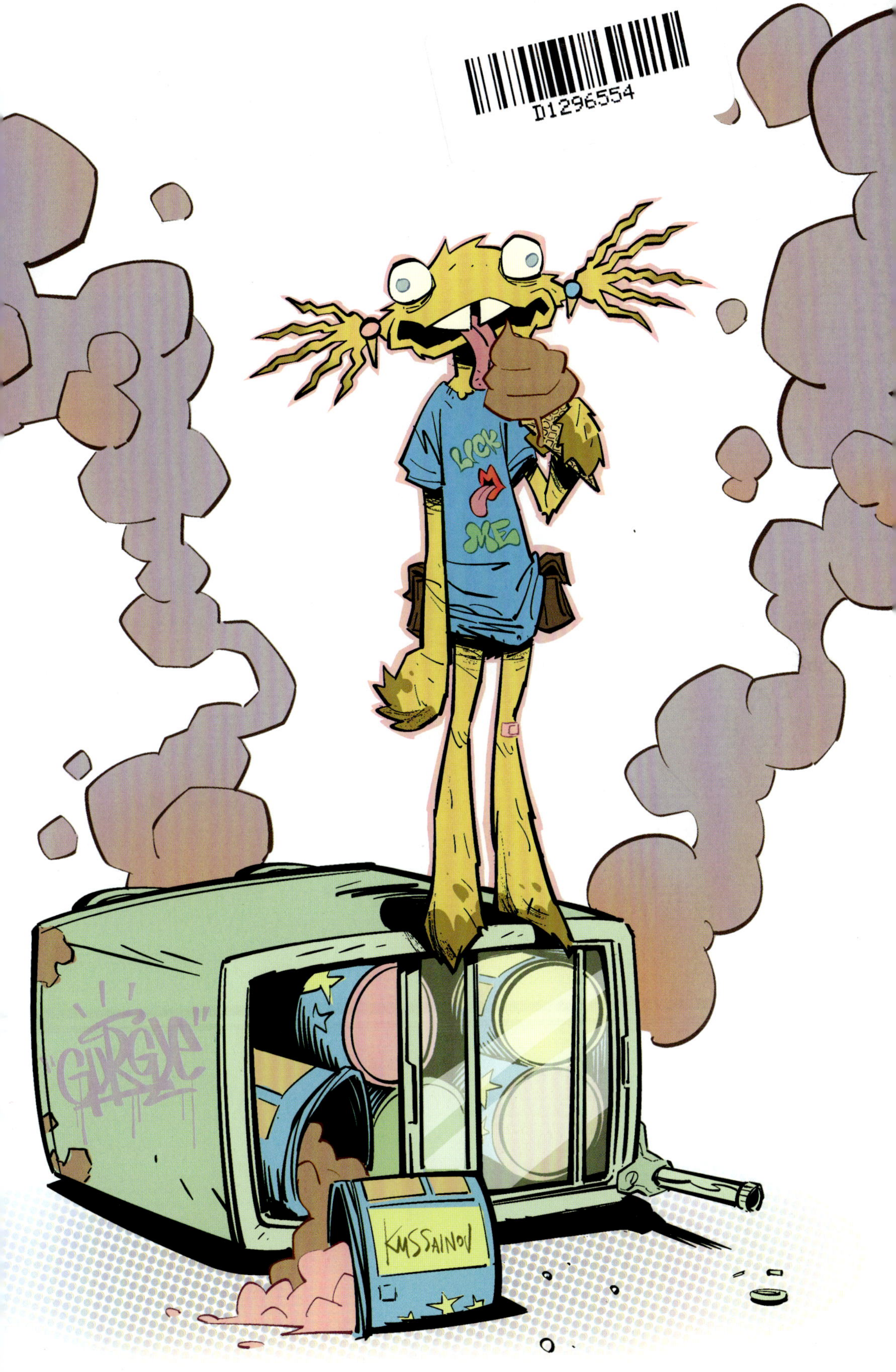

LICK
M
ME
"GURGLE"
KMSSAINOV

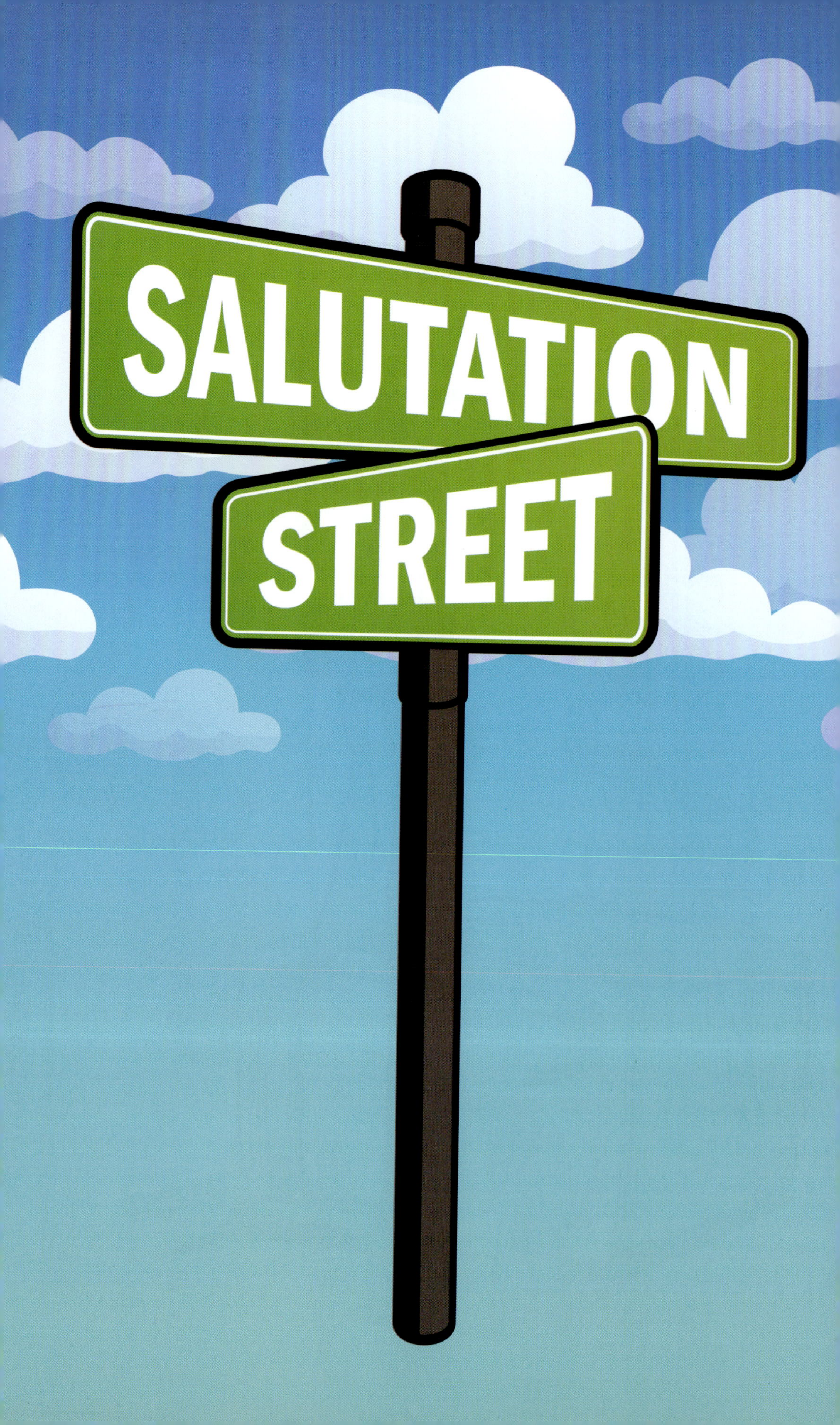
SALUTATION
STREET

script
JAMES ASMUS & **JIM FESTANTE**

art
ABYLAY KUSSAINOV

colors
ELLIE WRIGHT

letters
TAYLOR ESPOSITO

chapter breaks
ABYLAY KUSSAINOV with **ELLIE WRIGHT**

character illustrations
JACK GOODMAN

cover
BENJAMIN DEWEY

Survival Street created by James Asmus & Jim Festante

Dark Horse Books

president and publisher
MIKE RICHARDSON

editor
DANIEL CHABON

assistant editors
CHUCK HOWITT-LEASE and
MISHA GEHR

designer
JIM FESTANTE

digital art technician
JOSIE CHRISTENSEN

Collects issues #1–#4 of the Dark Horse Comics series *Survival Street*.

Published by
Dark Horse Books
A division of Dark Horse Comics LLC
10956 SE Main Street
Milwaukie, OR 97222

DarkHorse.com

To find a comics shop in your area, visit comicshoplocator.com

First Edition: April 2023
Ebook ISBN 978-1-50673-115-5
Trade Paperback ISBN 978-1-50673-114-8

10 9 8 7 6 5 4 3 2 1
Printed in China

executive vice president
NEIL HANKERSON

chief financial officer
TOM WEDDLE

chief information officer
DALE LAFOUNTAIN

vice president of licensing
TIM WIESCH

vice president of production and scheduling
VANESSA TODD-HOLMES

vice president of book trade and digital sales
MARK BERNARDI

vice president of product development and sales
RANDY LAHRMAN

general counsel
KEN LIZZI

editor in chief
DAVE MARSHALL

editorial director
DAVEY ESTRADA

senior books editor
CHRIS WARNER

senior director of marketing
CARA O'NEIL

director of specialty projects
CARY GRAZZINI

art director
LIA RIBACCHI

senior director of licensed publications
MICHAEL GOMBOS

director of custom programs
KARI YADRO

director of international licensing
KARI TORSON

director of scheduling
CHRISTINA NIECE

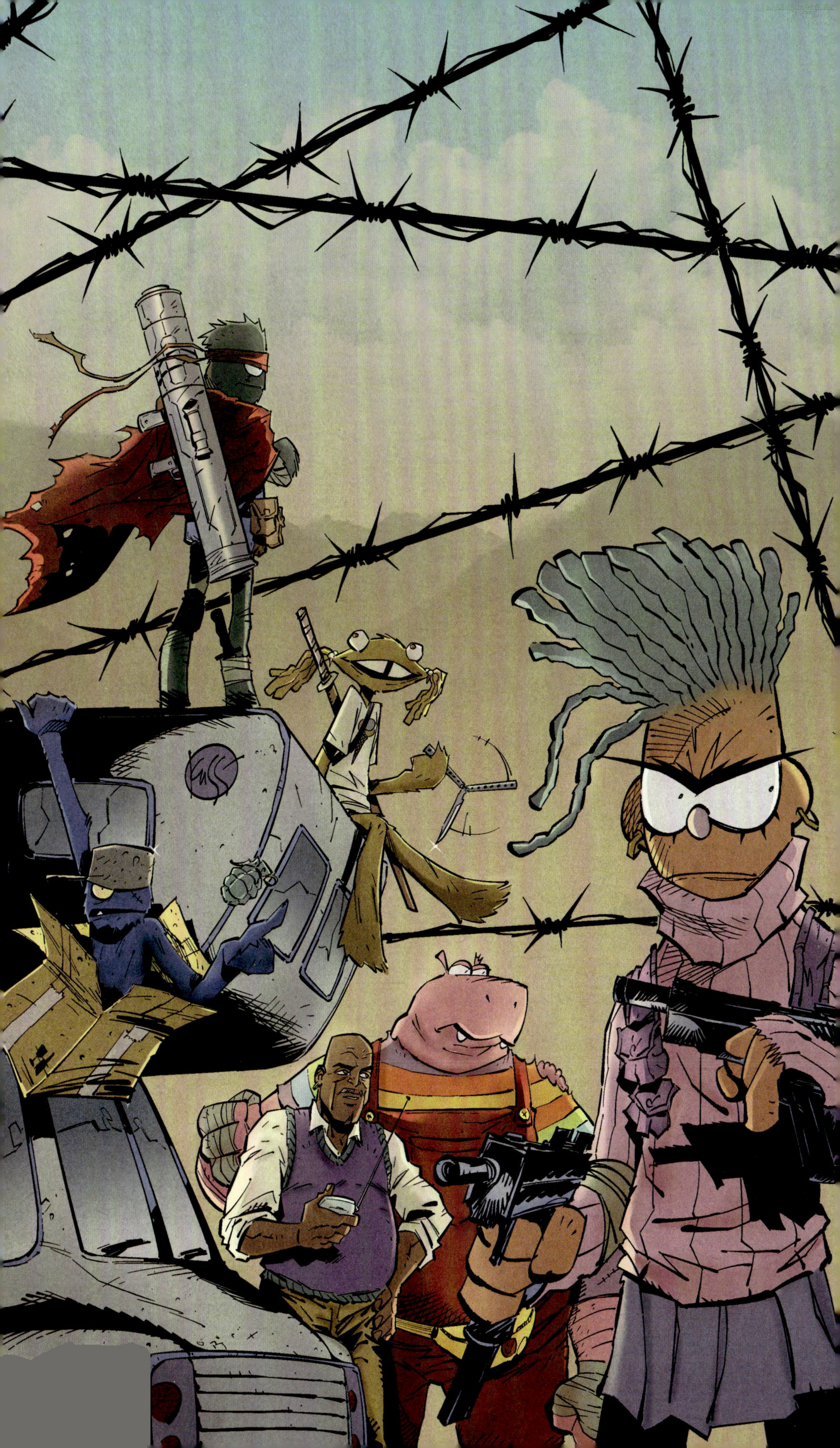

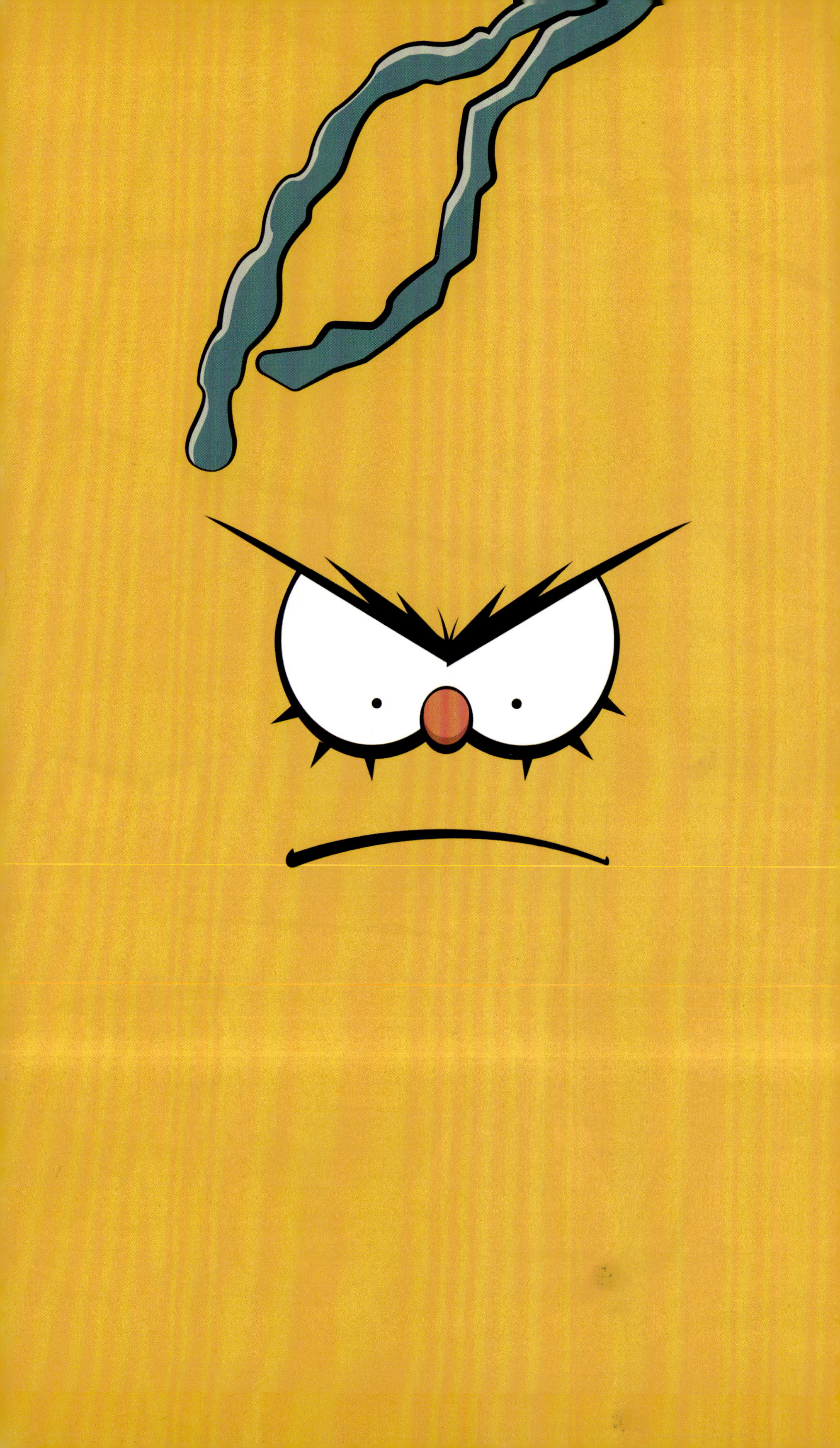

AMERICA: A TIMELINE

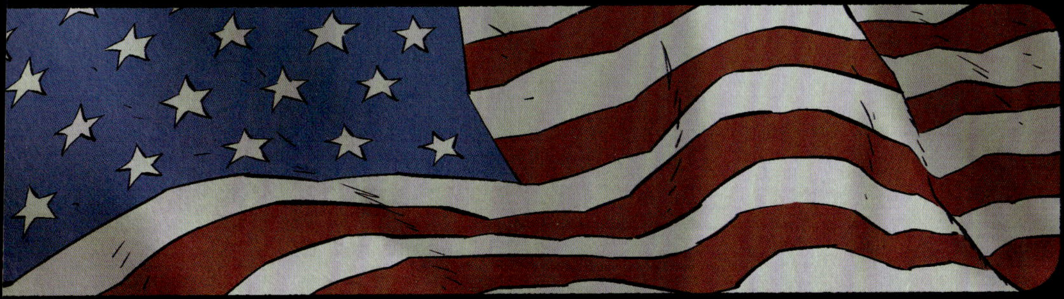

2025

A newly minted 13-to-3 Supreme Court expands their previous ruling that granted CORPORATIONS the same "freedom of speech" rights as citizens to now allow them to run for PUBLIC OFFICE.

2026

COMPANIES large and small pull all money from individual political candidates, instead SPENDING TRILLIONS of dollars securing themselves 83% OF ELECTED POSITIONS contested that year including ALL STATE AND NATIONAL CONGRESSIONAL SEATS.

2027

In under a year, the new legislatures PRIVATIZE OR TERMINATE EVERY PUBLIC SERVICE, LAND, and UTILITY, transferring those assets to their own businesses and running them for profit.

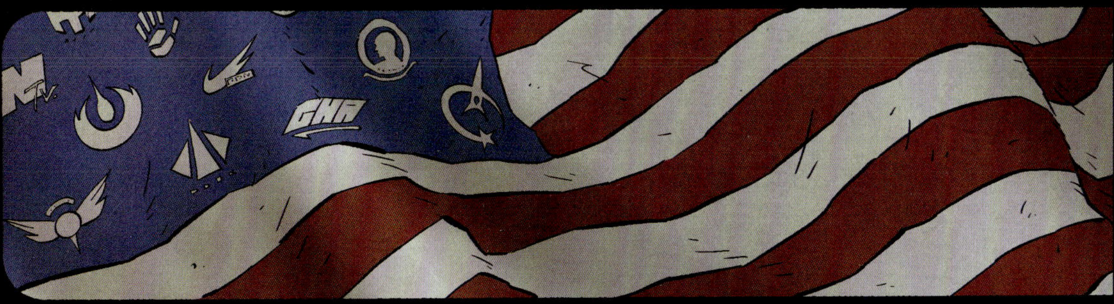
GNR

2028...

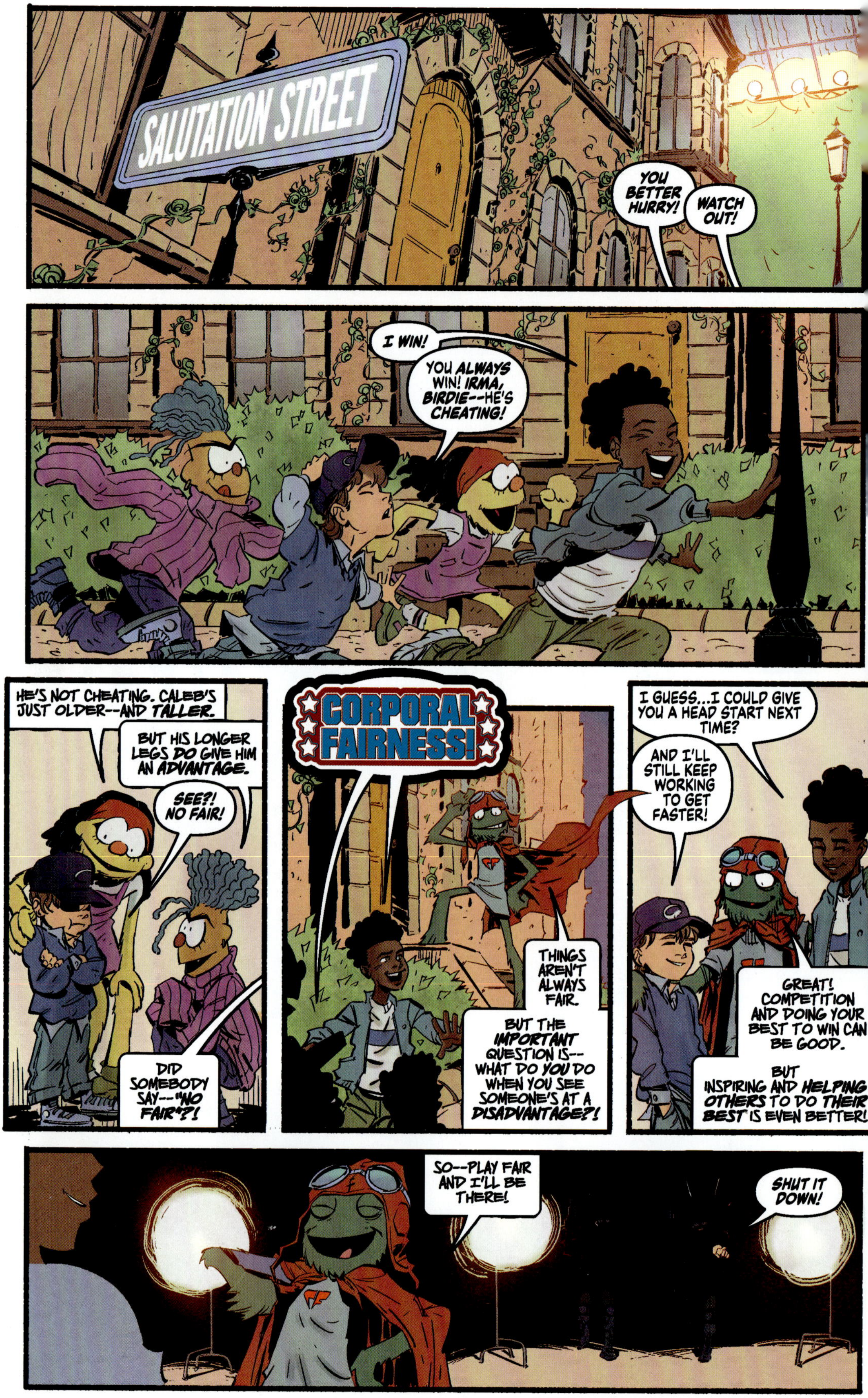
SALUTATION STREET
YOU BETTER HURRY!
WATCH OUT!
I WIN!
YOU ALWAYS WIN! IRMA, BIRDIE--HE'S CHEATING!
HE'S NOT CHEATING. CALEB'S JUST OLDER--AND TALLER.
BUT HIS LONGER LEGS DO GIVE HIM AN ADVANTAGE.
SEE?! NO FAIR!
DID SOMEBODY SAY--"NO FAIR"?!
CORPORAL FAIRNESS!
THINGS AREN'T ALWAYS FAIR.
BUT THE IMPORTANT QUESTION IS--WHAT DO YOU DO WHEN YOU SEE SOMEONE'S AT A DISADVANTAGE?!
I GUESS...I COULD GIVE YOU A HEAD START NEXT TIME?
AND I'LL STILL KEEP WORKING TO GET FASTER!
GREAT! COMPETITION AND DOING YOUR BEST TO WIN CAN BE GOOD.
BUT INSPIRING AND HELPING OTHERS TO DO THEIR BEST IS EVEN BETTER!
SO--PLAY FAIR AND I'LL BE THERE!
SHUT IT DOWN!

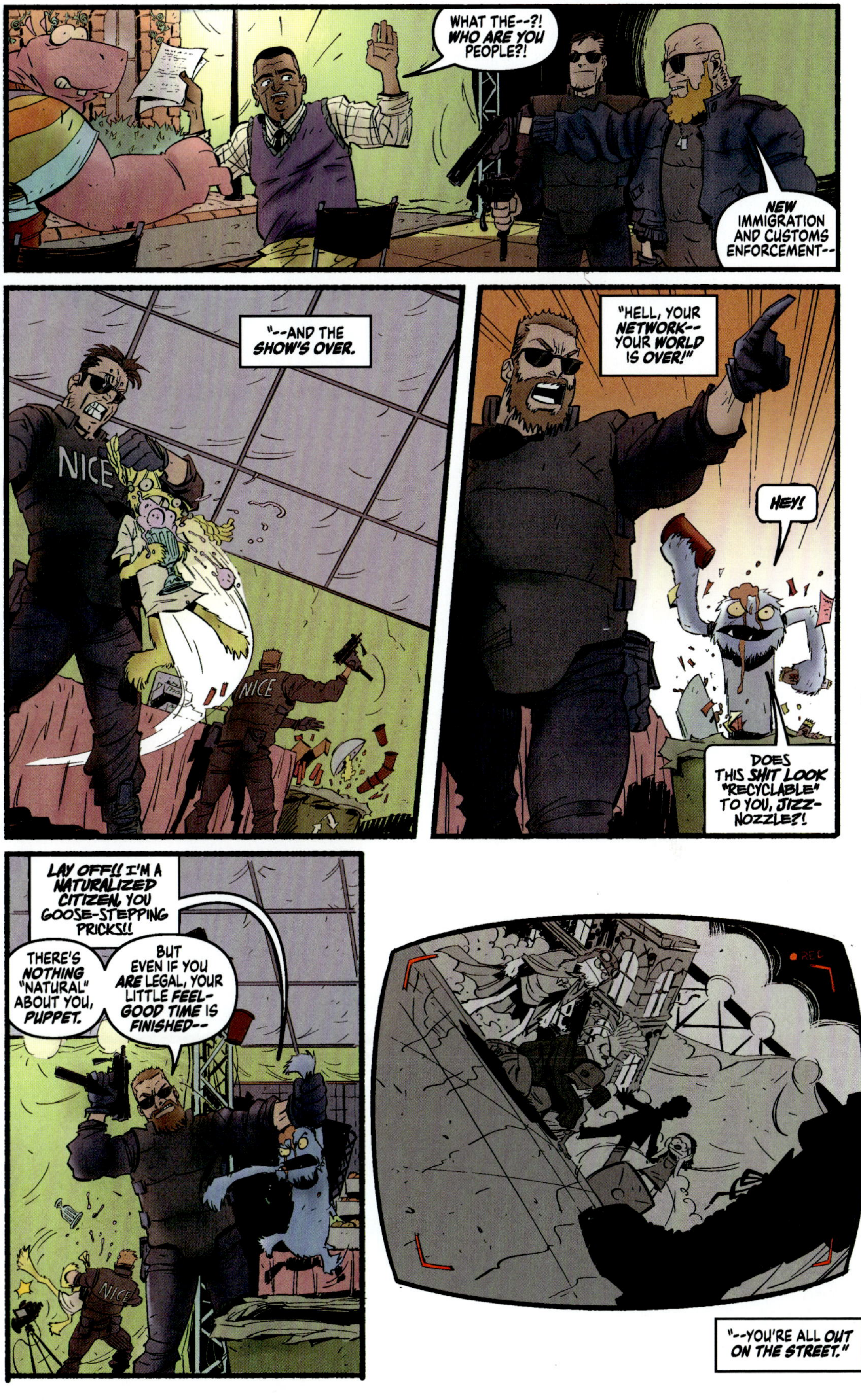
WHAT THE--?! WHO ARE YOU PEOPLE?!
NEW IMMIGRATION AND CUSTOMS ENFORCEMENT--
"--AND THE SHOW'S OVER.
NICE
NICE
"HELL, YOUR NETWORK--YOUR WORLD IS OVER!"
HEY!
DOES THIS SHIT LOOK "RECYCLABLE" TO YOU, JIZZ-NOZZLE?!
LAY OFF!! I'M A NATURALIZED CITIZEN, YOU GOOSE-STEPPING PRICKS!!
THERE'S NOTHING "NATURAL" ABOUT YOU, PUPPET.
BUT EVEN IF YOU ARE LEGAL, YOUR LITTLE FEEL-GOOD TIME IS FINISHED--
NICE
REC
"--YOU'RE ALL OUT ON THE STREET."

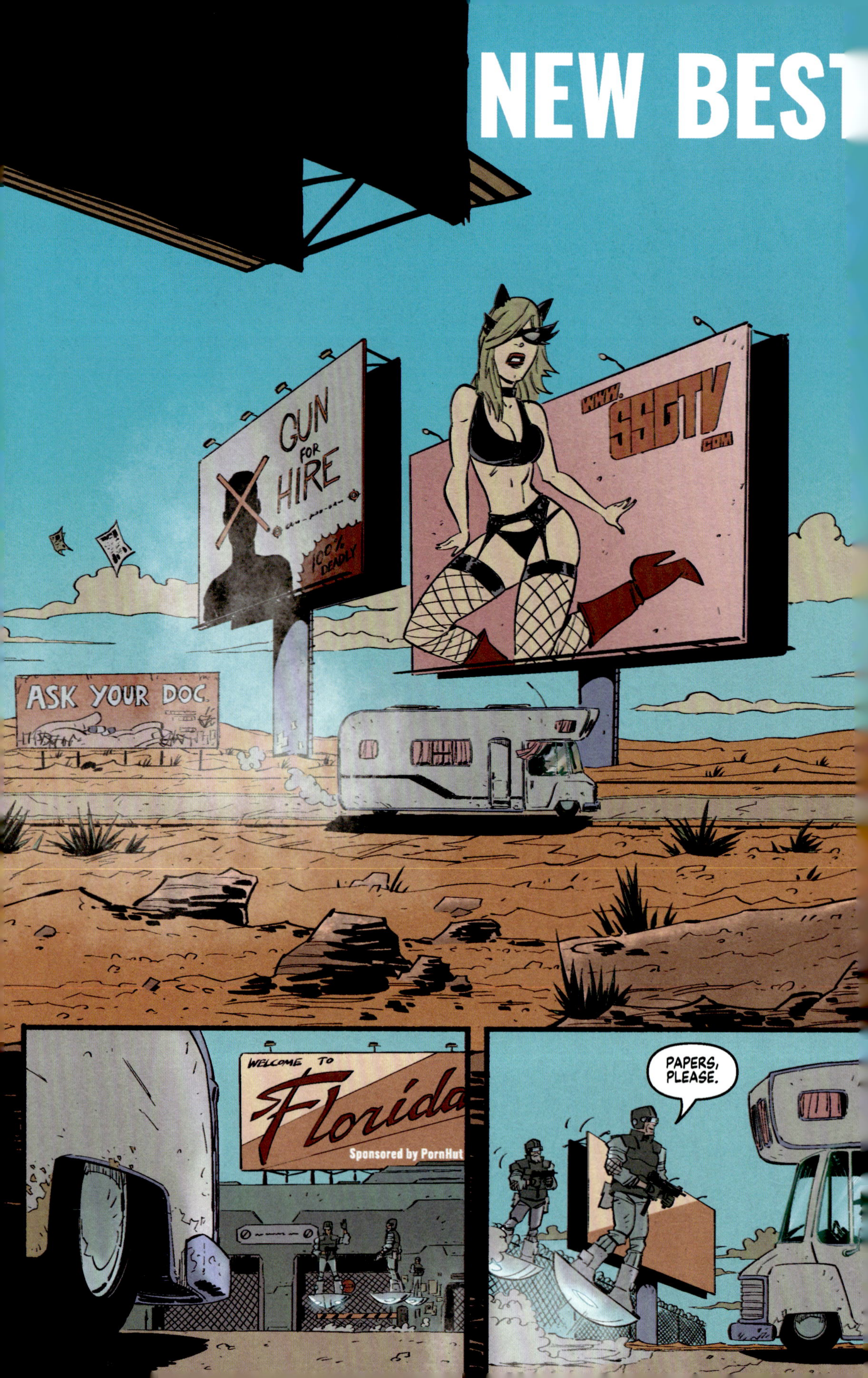

NEW BEST
GUN FOR HIRE
100% DEADLY
WWW. SSGTV .COM
ASK YOUR DOC
WELCOME TO Florida
Sponsored by PornHut
PAPERS, PLEASE.

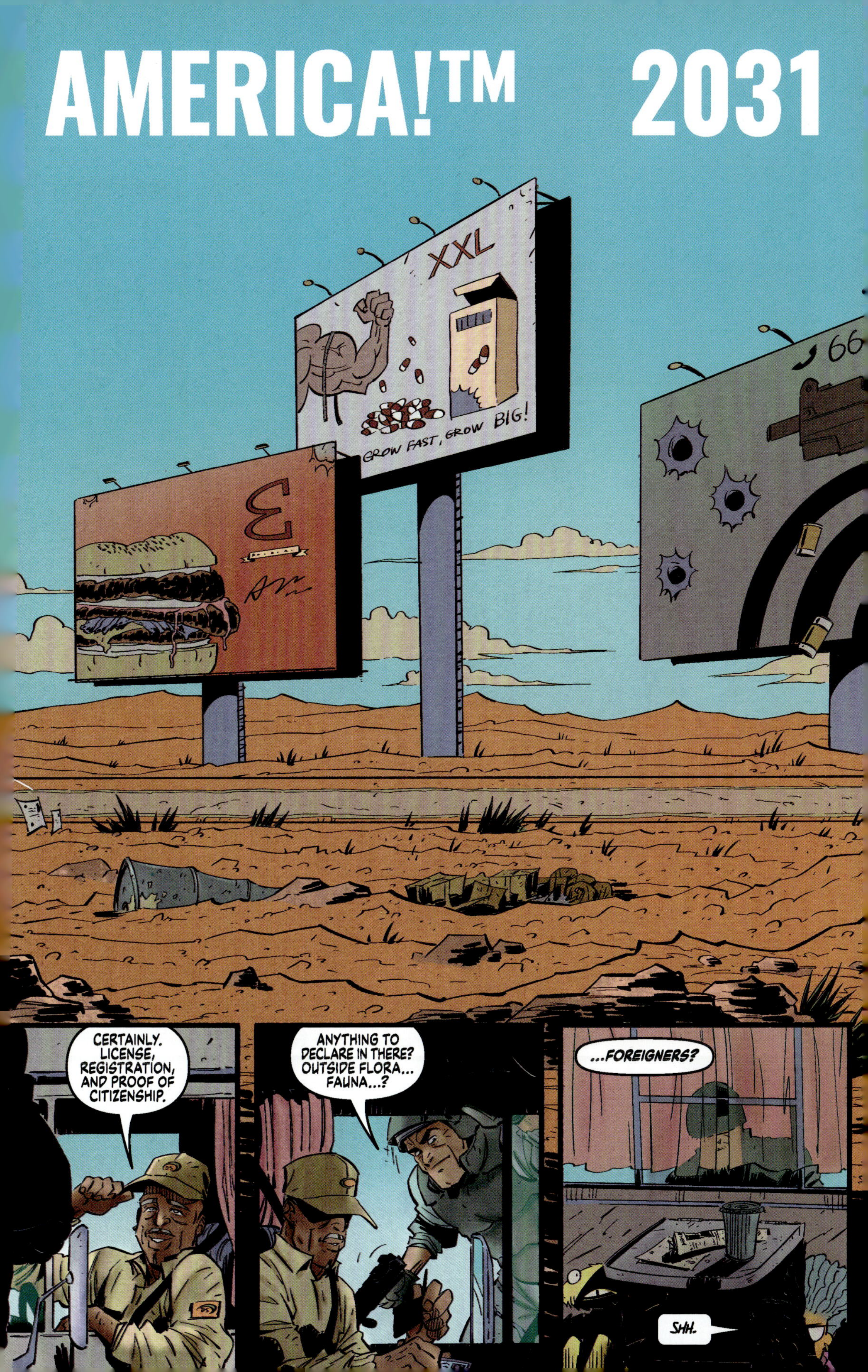
AMERICA!™ 2031
XXL
GROW FAST, GROW BIG!
66
CERTAINLY. LICENSE, REGISTRATION, AND PROOF OF CITIZENSHIP.
ANYTHING TO DECLARE IN THERE? OUTSIDE FLORA... FAUNA...?
...FOREIGNERS?
SHH.

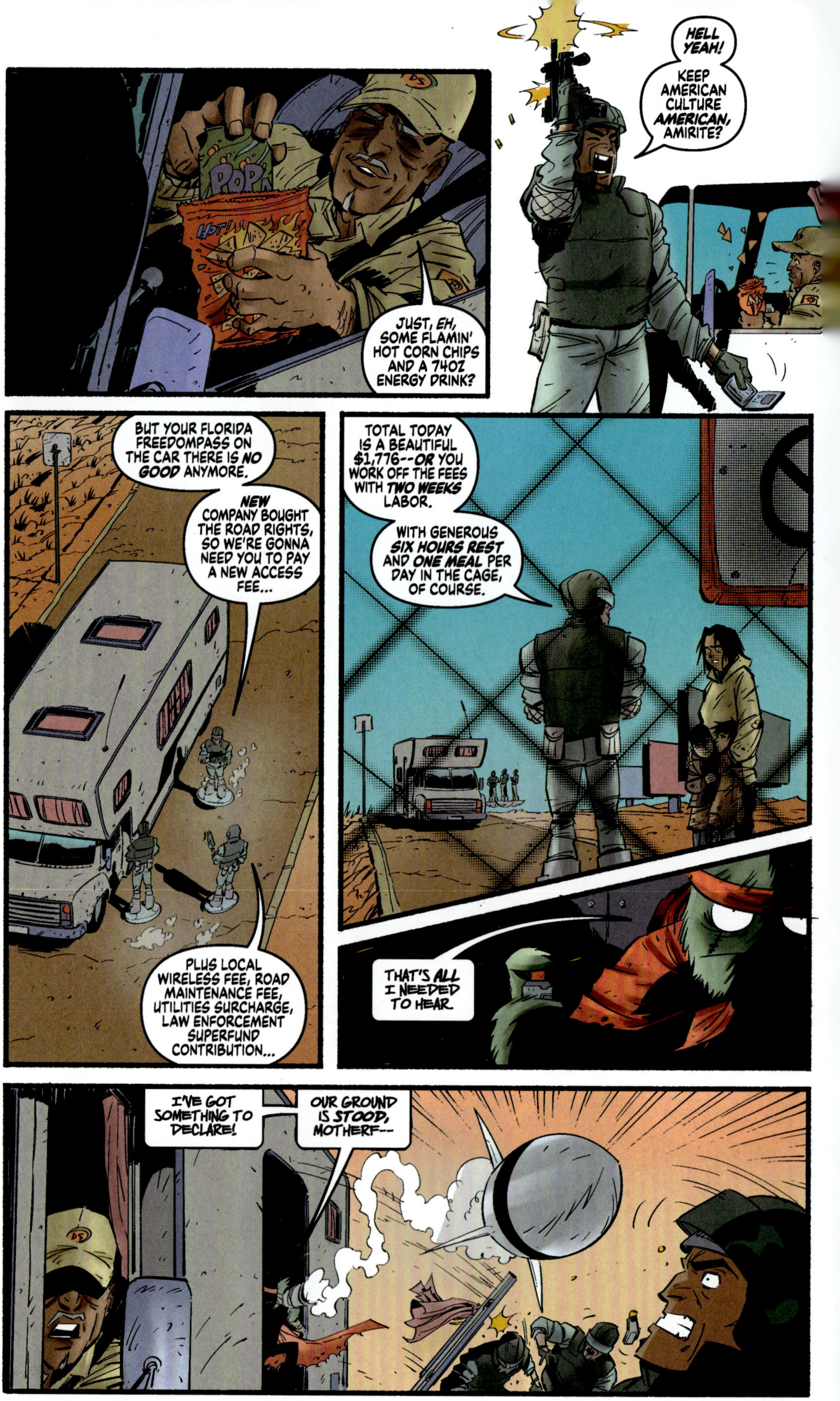
JUST, EH, SOME FLAMIN' HOT CORN CHIPS AND A 74OZ ENERGY DRINK?
HELL YEAH!
KEEP AMERICAN CULTURE AMERICAN, AMIRITE?
BUT YOUR FLORIDA FREEDOMPASS ON THE CAR THERE IS NO GOOD ANYMORE.
NEW COMPANY BOUGHT THE ROAD RIGHTS, SO WE'RE GONNA NEED YOU TO PAY A NEW ACCESS FEE...
PLUS LOCAL WIRELESS FEE, ROAD MAINTENANCE FEE, UTILITIES SURCHARGE, LAW ENFORCEMENT SUPERFUND CONTRIBUTION...
TOTAL TODAY IS A BEAUTIFUL $1,776--OR YOU WORK OFF THE FEES WITH TWO WEEKS LABOR.
WITH GENEROUS SIX HOURS REST AND ONE MEAL PER DAY IN THE CAGE, OF COURSE.
THAT'S ALL I NEEDED TO HEAR.
I'VE GOT SOMETHING TO DECLARE!
OUR GROUND IS STOOD, MOTHERF--

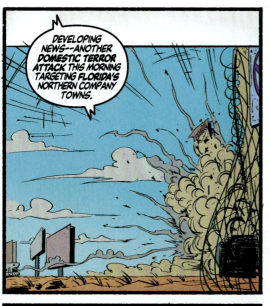

DEVELOPING NEWS--ANOTHER DOMESTIC TERROR ATTACK THIS MORNING TARGETING FLORIDA'S NORTHERN COMPANY TOWNS.

ANOTHER ACT OF *VIOLENCE* FROM PUPPET EXTREMISTS.

SOME SAY THE DEATH TOLL MIGHT HAVE EVEN BEEN IN THE *DOZENS!* AND THAT THE ATTACK WAS SPECIFICALLY TARGETED...AT CHILDREN.

COMING TO YOUR STREET?

IRMA!

ONCE AGAIN THESE... *MONSTERS* ARE PROVING AMERICA NEVER SHOULD HAVE ALLOWED THEM TO MASS-MIGRATE INTO THIS COUNTRY--LET ALONE OUR HOMES!

FOR DECADES, THESE *PUPPETS*-- AND I KNOW SOME DON'T LIKE THAT TERM, BUT I'M A FELT-AMERICAN MYSELF, AND IN THIS CASE, THERE'S JUST NO OTHER WORD!

PARTING SHOTS

FOR *DECADES,* AMERICA GENEROUSLY GAVE SO MANY WORK--EVEN *FAME,* AND UNDUE *INFLUENCE* OVER THIS COUNTRY'S YOUNG MINDS!

BUT CLEARLY, SOME *EXTREMISTS* ARE HELL-BENT ON ESCALATING FROM "CODDLE-CULTURE" TO FULL-BLOWN "FAUX-EQUALITY COMMUNISM"!

PARTING SHOTS

BUT I IMAGINE WE'LL HEAR MORE ON THIS FROM MY COLLEAGUES BOB AND ROB, COMING UP NEXT!

YOU BET, IRMA! PLUS-- THE PRESIDENT WILL BE APPEARING BEFORE THE FORTUNE 500 FOR HIS ANNUAL EMPLOYEE REVIEW!

STARTING NOW: LEFT VS. RIGHT

SSSNNFFFFFF!

BUT *COMING UP* AFTER THE BREAK-- A GLIMPSE AT THE GLAMOROUS EVENT THE FIRST SON WILL BE HOSTING TONIGHT IN *FLORIDA* AT THEIR--

SIR? THEY'RE READY FOR YOU.

PLEASE--

--CALL ME "MR. PRESIDENT. JUNIOR."

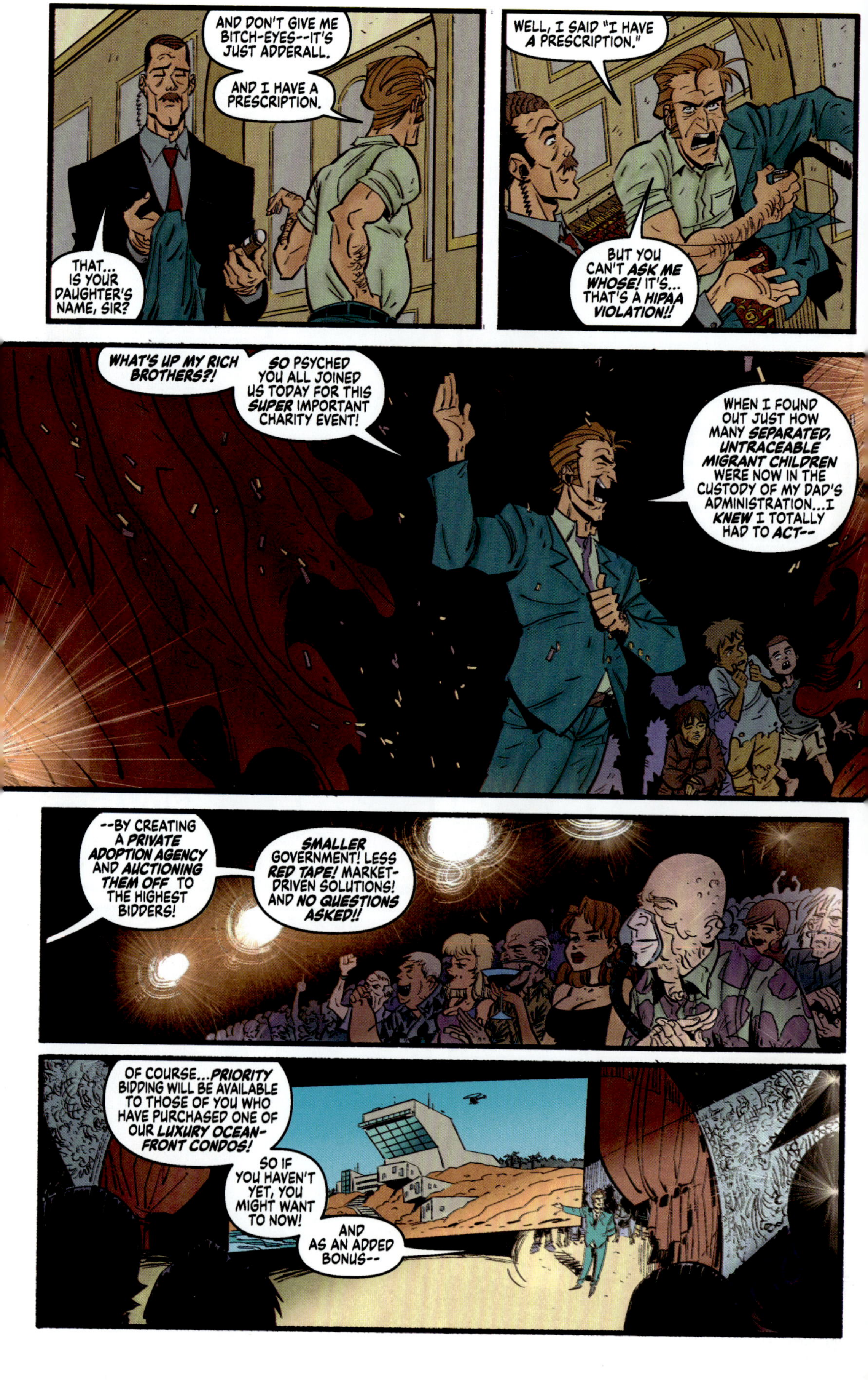
AND DON'T GIVE ME BITCH-EYES--IT'S JUST ADDERALL.
AND I HAVE A PRESCRIPTION.
THAT... IS YOUR DAUGHTER'S NAME, SIR?
WELL, I SAID "I HAVE A PRESCRIPTION."
BUT YOU CAN'T ASK ME WHOSE! IT'S... THAT'S A HIPAA VIOLATION!!
WHAT'S UP MY RICH BROTHERS?!
SO PSYCHED YOU ALL JOINED US TODAY FOR THIS SUPER IMPORTANT CHARITY EVENT!
WHEN I FOUND OUT JUST HOW MANY SEPARATED, UNTRACEABLE MIGRANT CHILDREN WERE NOW IN THE CUSTODY OF MY DAD'S ADMINISTRATION...I KNEW I TOTALLY HAD TO ACT--
--BY CREATING A PRIVATE ADOPTION AGENCY AND AUCTIONING THEM OFF TO THE HIGHEST BIDDERS!
SMALLER GOVERNMENT! LESS RED TAPE! MARKET-DRIVEN SOLUTIONS! AND NO QUESTIONS ASKED!!
OF COURSE...PRIORITY BIDDING WILL BE AVAILABLE TO THOSE OF YOU WHO HAVE PURCHASED ONE OF OUR LUXURY OCEAN-FRONT CONDOS!
SO IF YOU HAVEN'T YET, YOU MIGHT WANT TO NOW!
AND AS AN ADDED BONUS--

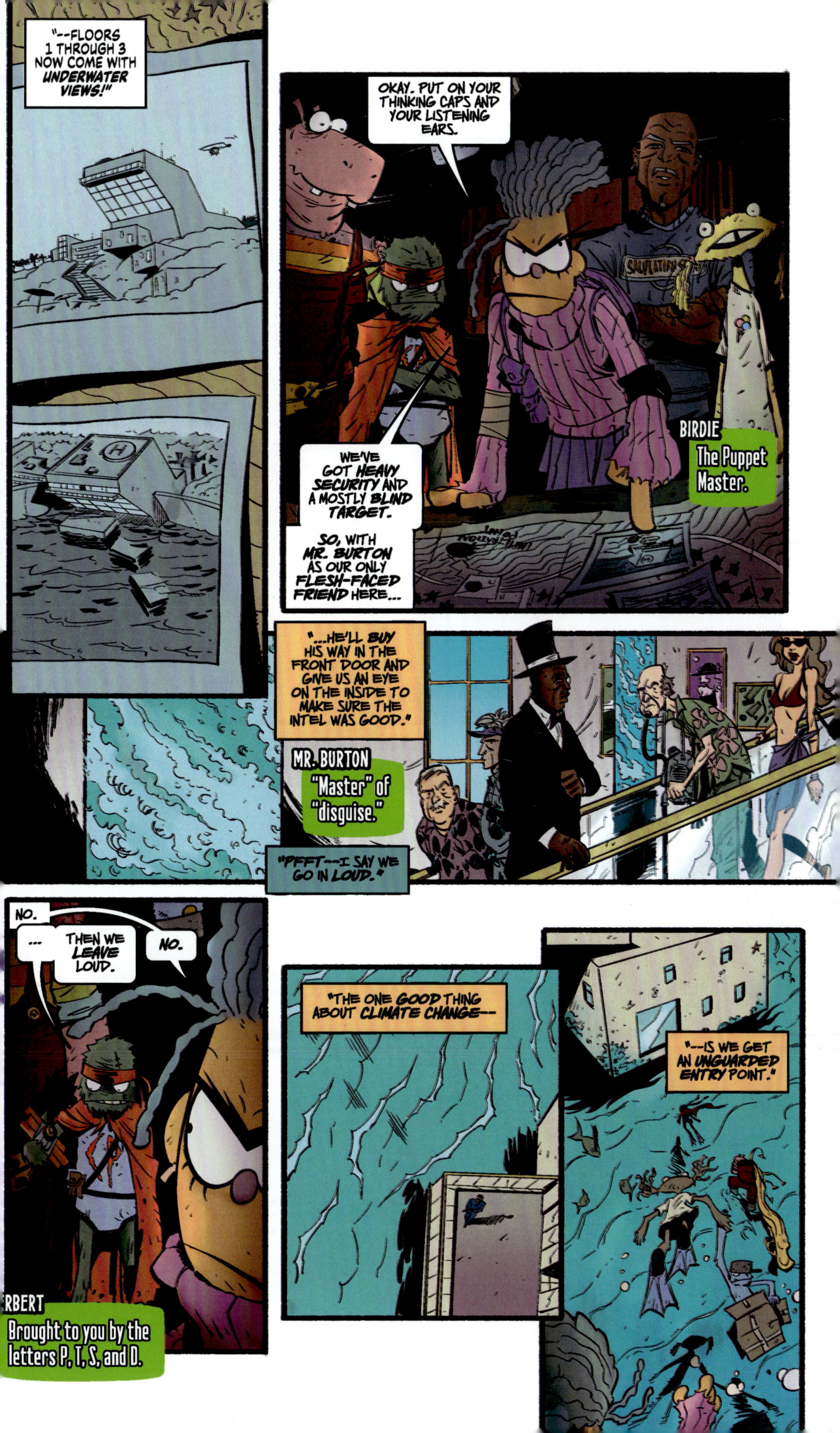
"--FLOORS 1 THROUGH 3 NOW COME WITH UNDERWATER VIEWS!"
OKAY. PUT ON YOUR THINKING CAPS AND YOUR LISTENING EARS.
SALVATION
BIRDIE
The Puppet Master.
WE'VE GOT HEAVY SECURITY AND A MOSTLY BLIND TARGET.
SO, WITH MR. BURTON AS OUR ONLY FLESH-FACED FRIEND HERE...
"...HE'LL BUY HIS WAY IN THE FRONT DOOR AND GIVE US AN EYE ON THE INSIDE TO MAKE SURE THE INTEL WAS GOOD."
MR. BURTON
"Master" of "disguise."
"PFFT--I SAY WE GO IN LOUD."
NO.
...
THEN WE LEAVE LOUD.
NO.
RBERT
Brought to you by the letters P, T, S, and D.
"THE ONE GOOD THING ABOUT CLIMATE CHANGE--
"--IS WE GET AN UNGUARDED ENTRY POINT."

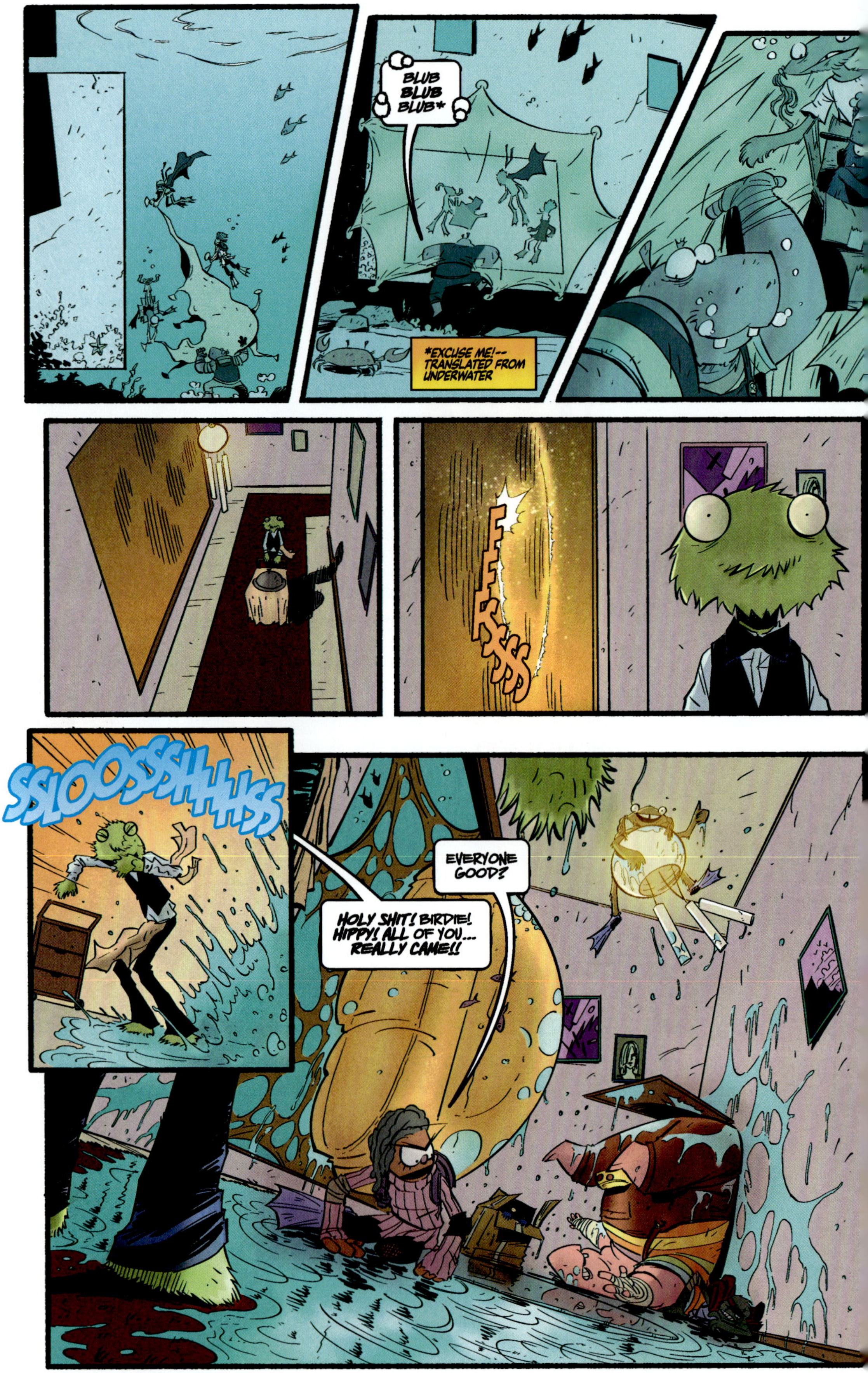
BLUB BLUB BLUB*
*EXCUSE ME!--TRANSLATED FROM UNDERWATER
FFFKSSS
SSLOOSSSHHHSS
HOLY SHIT! BIRDIE! HIPPY! ALL OF YOU... REALLY CAME!!
EVERYONE GOOD?

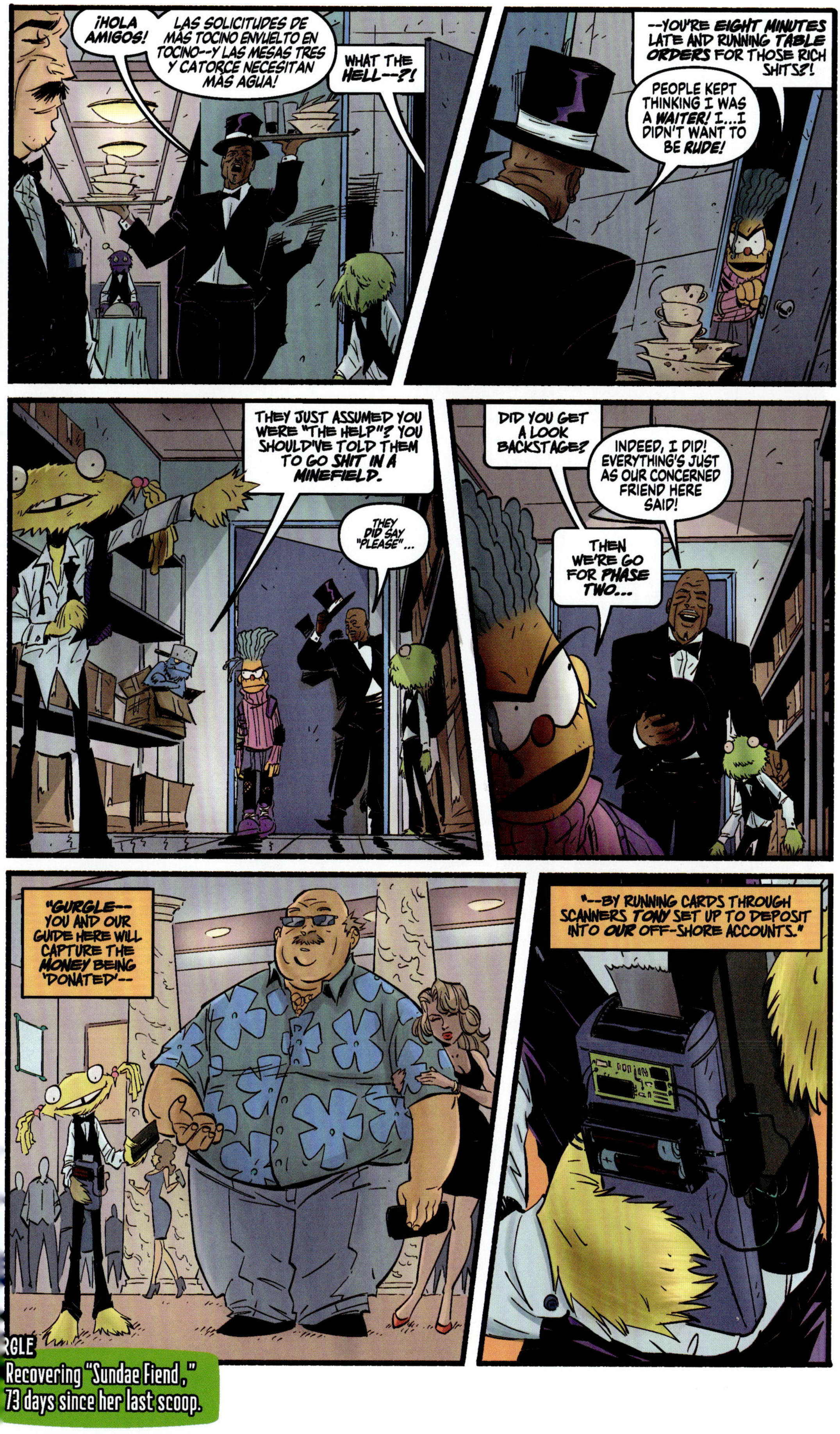
¡HOLA AMIGOS!
LAS SOLICITUDES DE MÁS TOCINO ENVUELTO EN TOCINO--Y LAS MESAS TRES Y CATORCE NECESITAN MÁS AGUA!
WHAT THE HELL--?!
--YOU'RE EIGHT MINUTES LATE AND RUNNING TABLE ORDERS FOR THOSE RICH SHITS?!
PEOPLE KEPT THINKING I WAS A WAITER! I...I DIDN'T WANT TO BE RUDE!
THEY JUST ASSUMED YOU WERE "THE HELP"? YOU SHOULD'VE TOLD THEM TO GO SHIT IN A MINEFIELD.
THEY DID SAY "PLEASE"...
DID YOU GET A LOOK BACKSTAGE?
INDEED, I DID! EVERYTHING'S JUST AS OUR CONCERNED FRIEND HERE SAID!
THEN WE'RE GO FOR PHASE TWO...
"GURGLE--YOU AND OUR GUIDE HERE WILL CAPTURE THE MONEY BEING 'DONATED'--
"--BY RUNNING CARDS THROUGH SCANNERS TONY SET UP TO DEPOSIT INTO OUR OFF-SHORE ACCOUNTS."
RGLE
Recovering "Sundae Fiend," 73 days since her last scoop.

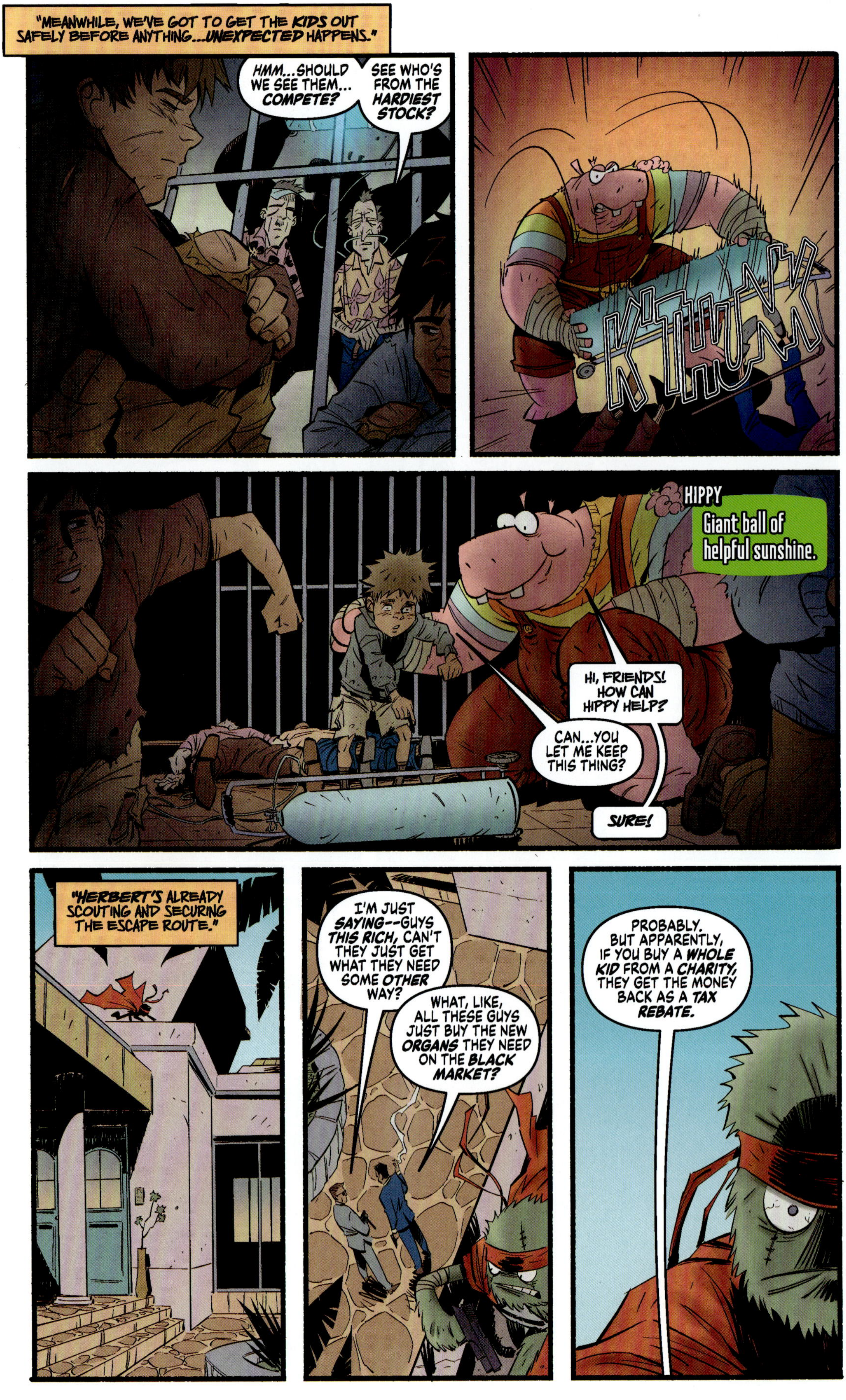

"MEANWHILE, WE'VE GOT TO GET THE KIDS OUT SAFELY BEFORE ANYTHING...UNEXPECTED HAPPENS."
HMM...SHOULD WE SEE THEM... COMPETE?
SEE WHO'S FROM THE HARDIEST STOCK?
K'THUNK
HIPPY
Giant ball of helpful sunshine.
HI, FRIENDS! HOW CAN HIPPY HELP?
CAN...YOU LET ME KEEP THIS THING?
SURE!
"HERBERT'S ALREADY SCOUTING AND SECURING THE ESCAPE ROUTE."
I'M JUST SAYING--GUYS THIS RICH, CAN'T THEY JUST GET WHAT THEY NEED SOME OTHER WAY?
WHAT, LIKE, ALL THESE GUYS JUST BUY THE NEW ORGANS THEY NEED ON THE BLACK MARKET?
PROBABLY. BUT APPARENTLY, IF YOU BUY A WHOLE KID FROM A CHARITY, THEY GET THE MONEY BACK AS A TAX REBATE.

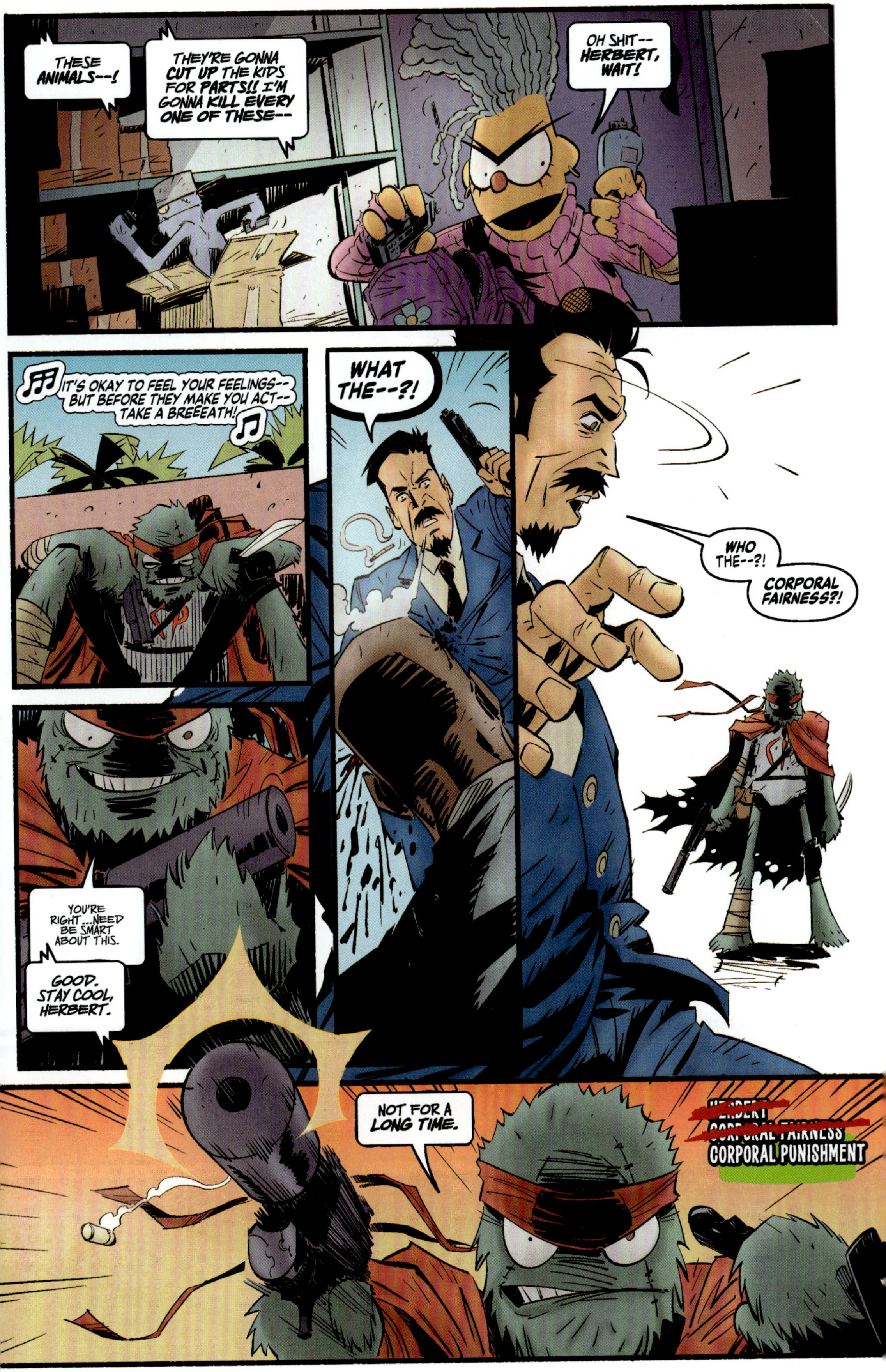
THESE ANIMALS--!
THEY'RE GONNA CUT UP THE KIDS FOR PARTS!! I'M GONNA KILL EVERY ONE OF THESE--
OH SHIT-- HERBERT, WAIT!
IT'S OKAY TO FEEL YOUR FEELINGS-- BUT BEFORE THEY MAKE YOU ACT-- TAKE A BREEEATH!
WHAT THE--?!
WHO THE--?!
CORPORAL FAIRNESS?!
YOU'RE RIGHT...NEED BE SMART ABOUT THIS.
GOOD. STAY COOL, HERBERT.
NOT FOR A LONG TIME.
HERBERT
CORPORAL FAIRNESS
CORPORAL PUNISHMENT

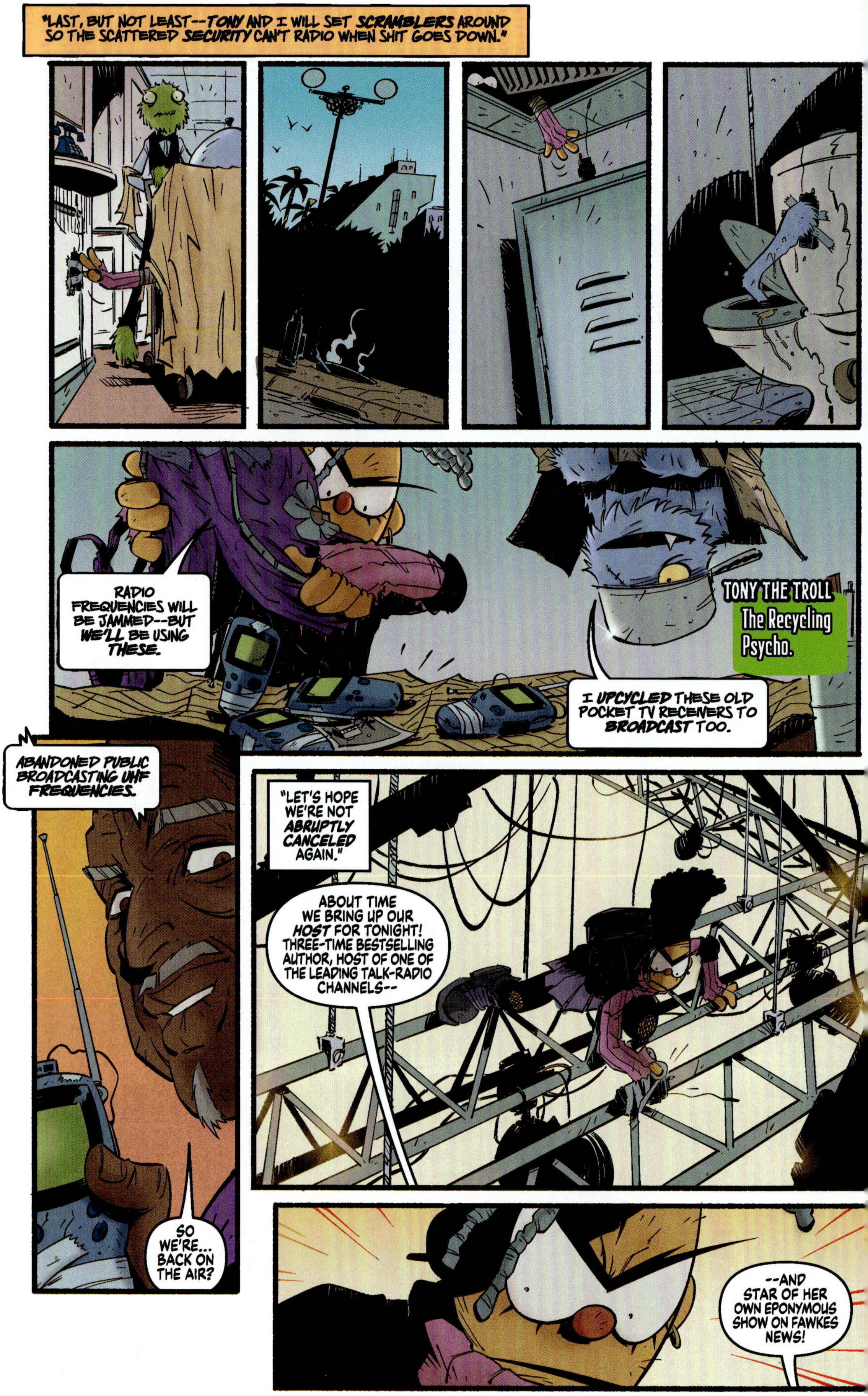
"LAST, BUT NOT LEAST--TONY AND I WILL SET SCRAMBLERS AROUND SO THE SCATTERED SECURITY CAN'T RADIO WHEN SHIT GOES DOWN."
RADIO FREQUENCIES WILL BE JAMMED--BUT WE'LL BE USING THESE.
TONY THE TROLL
The Recycling Psycho.
I UPCYCLED THESE OLD POCKET TV RECEIVERS TO BROADCAST TOO.
ABANDONED PUBLIC BROADCASTING UHF FREQUENCIES.
"LET'S HOPE WE'RE NOT ABRUPTLY CANCELED AGAIN."
ABOUT TIME WE BRING UP OUR HOST FOR TONIGHT! THREE-TIME BESTSELLING AUTHOR, HOST OF ONE OF THE LEADING TALK-RADIO CHANNELS--
SO WE'RE... BACK ON THE AIR?
--AND STAR OF HER OWN EPONYMOUS SHOW ON FAWKES NEWS!

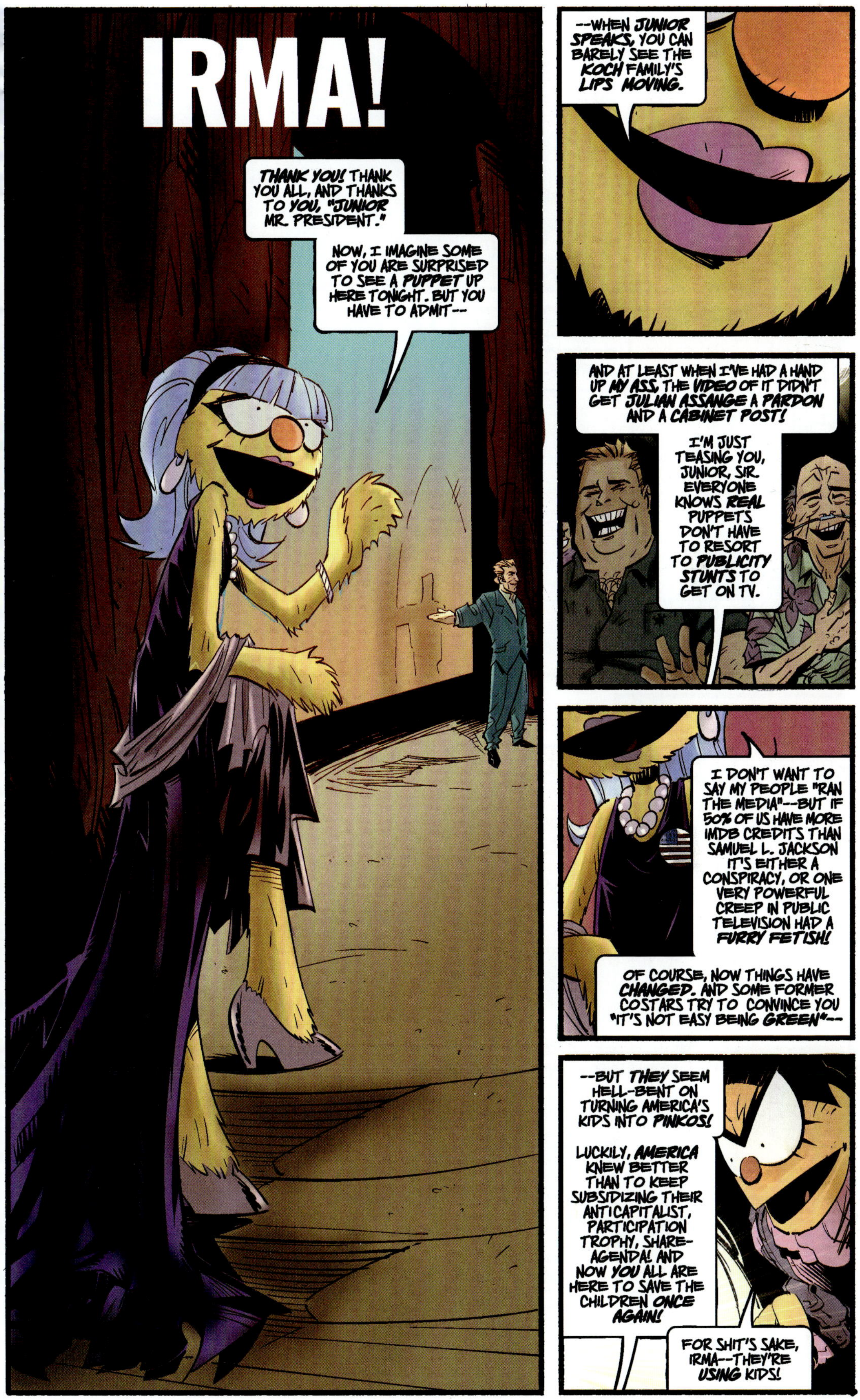
IRMA!
THANK YOU! THANK YOU ALL, AND THANKS TO YOU, "JUNIOR MR. PRESIDENT."
NOW, I IMAGINE SOME OF YOU ARE SURPRISED TO SEE A PUPPET UP HERE TONIGHT. BUT YOU HAVE TO ADMIT--
--WHEN JUNIOR SPEAKS, YOU CAN BARELY SEE THE KOCH FAMILY'S LIPS MOVING.
AND AT LEAST WHEN I'VE HAD A HAND UP MY ASS, THE VIDEO OF IT DIDN'T GET JULIAN ASSANGE A PARDON AND A CABINET POST!
I'M JUST TEASING YOU, JUNIOR, SIR. EVERYONE KNOWS REAL PUPPETS DON'T HAVE TO RESORT TO PUBLICITY STUNTS TO GET ON TV.
I DON'T WANT TO SAY MY PEOPLE "RAN THE MEDIA"--BUT IF 50% OF US HAVE MORE IMDB CREDITS THAN SAMUEL L. JACKSON IT'S EITHER A CONSPIRACY, OR ONE VERY POWERFUL CREEP IN PUBLIC TELEVISION HAD A FURRY FETISH!
OF COURSE, NOW THINGS HAVE CHANGED. AND SOME FORMER COSTARS TRY TO CONVINCE YOU "IT'S NOT EASY BEING GREEN"--
--BUT THEY SEEM HELL-BENT ON TURNING AMERICA'S KIDS INTO PINKOS!
LUCKILY, AMERICA KNEW BETTER THAN TO KEEP SUBSIDIZING THEIR ANTICAPITALIST, PARTICIPATION TROPHY, SHARE-AGENDA! AND NOW YOU ALL ARE HERE TO SAVE THE CHILDREN ONCE AGAIN!
FOR SHIT'S SAKE, IRMA--THEY'RE USING KIDS!

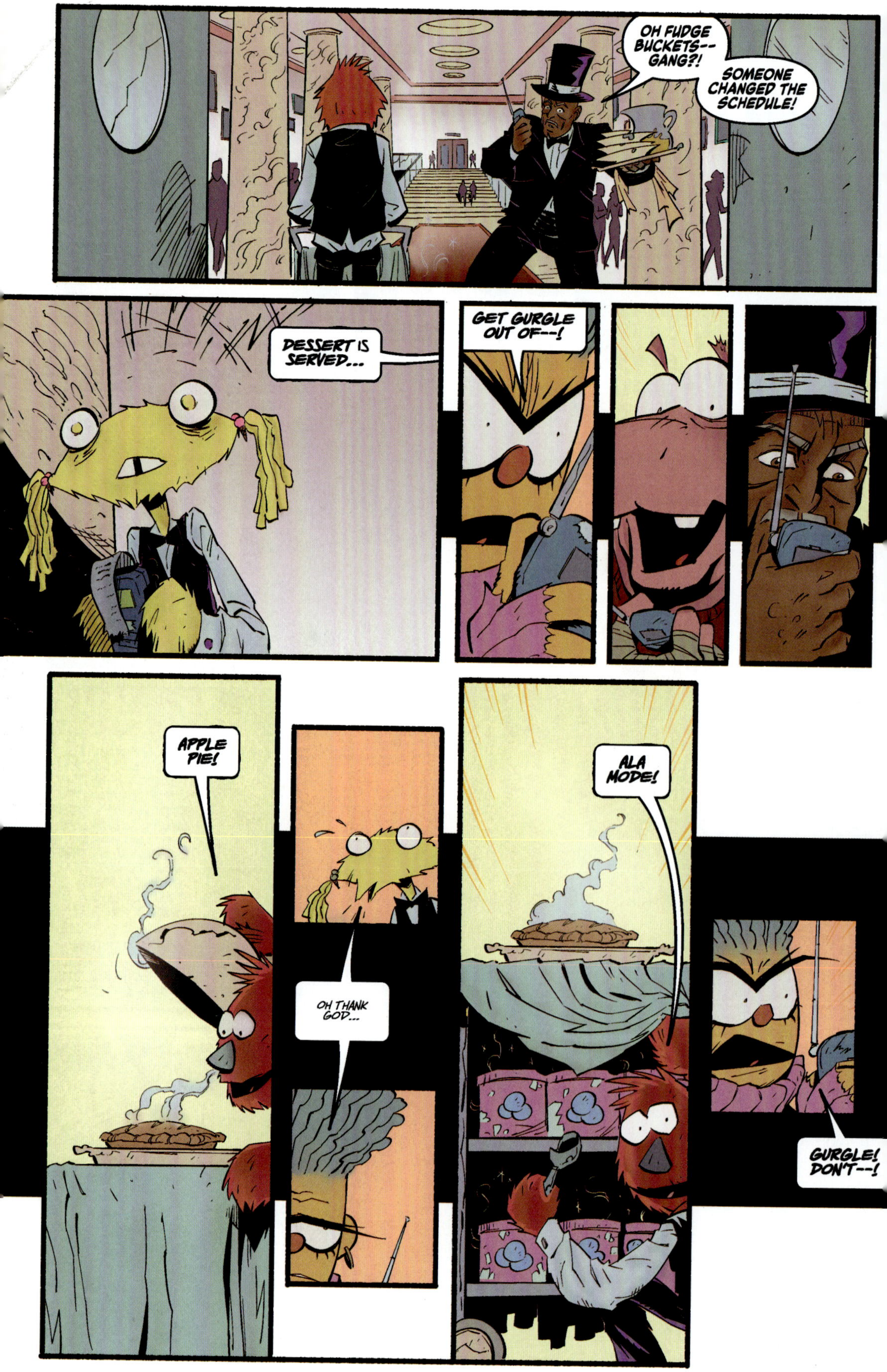
OH FUDGE BUCKETS-- GANG?!
SOMEONE CHANGED THE SCHEDULE!
DESSERT IS SERVED...
GET GURGLE OUT OF--!
APPLE PIE!
OH THANK GOD...
ALA MODE!
GURGLE! DON'T--!

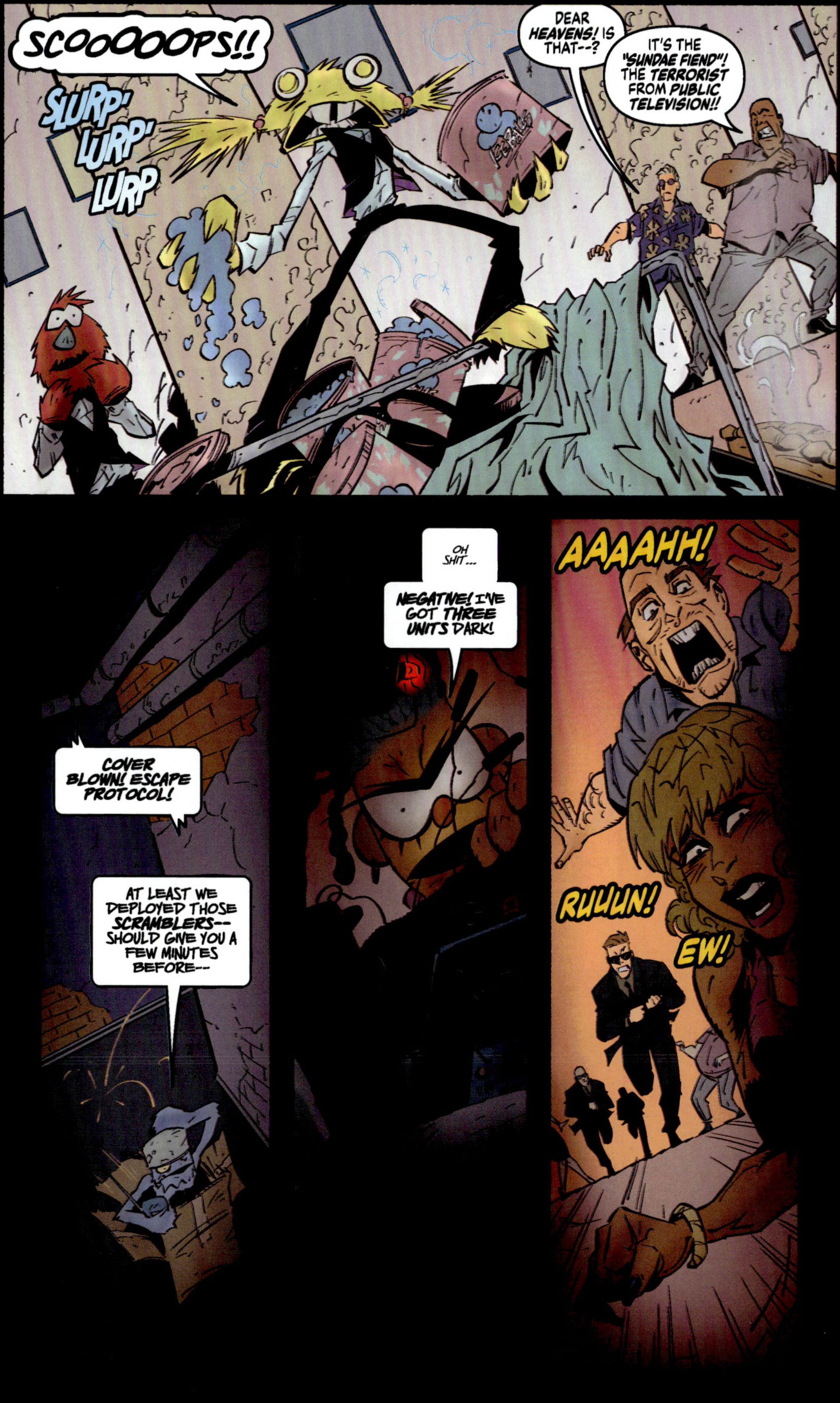
SCOOOOOOPS!!
SLURP' LURP' LURP
DEAR HEAVENS! IS THAT--?
IT'S THE "SUNDAE FIEND"! THE TERRORIST FROM PUBLIC TELEVISION!!
COVER BLOWN! ESCAPE PROTOCOL!
AT LEAST WE DEPLOYED THOSE SCRAMBLERS-- SHOULD GIVE YOU A FEW MINUTES BEFORE--
OH SHIT...
NEGATIVE! I'VE GOT THREE UNITS DARK!
AAAAHH!
RUUUN!
EW!

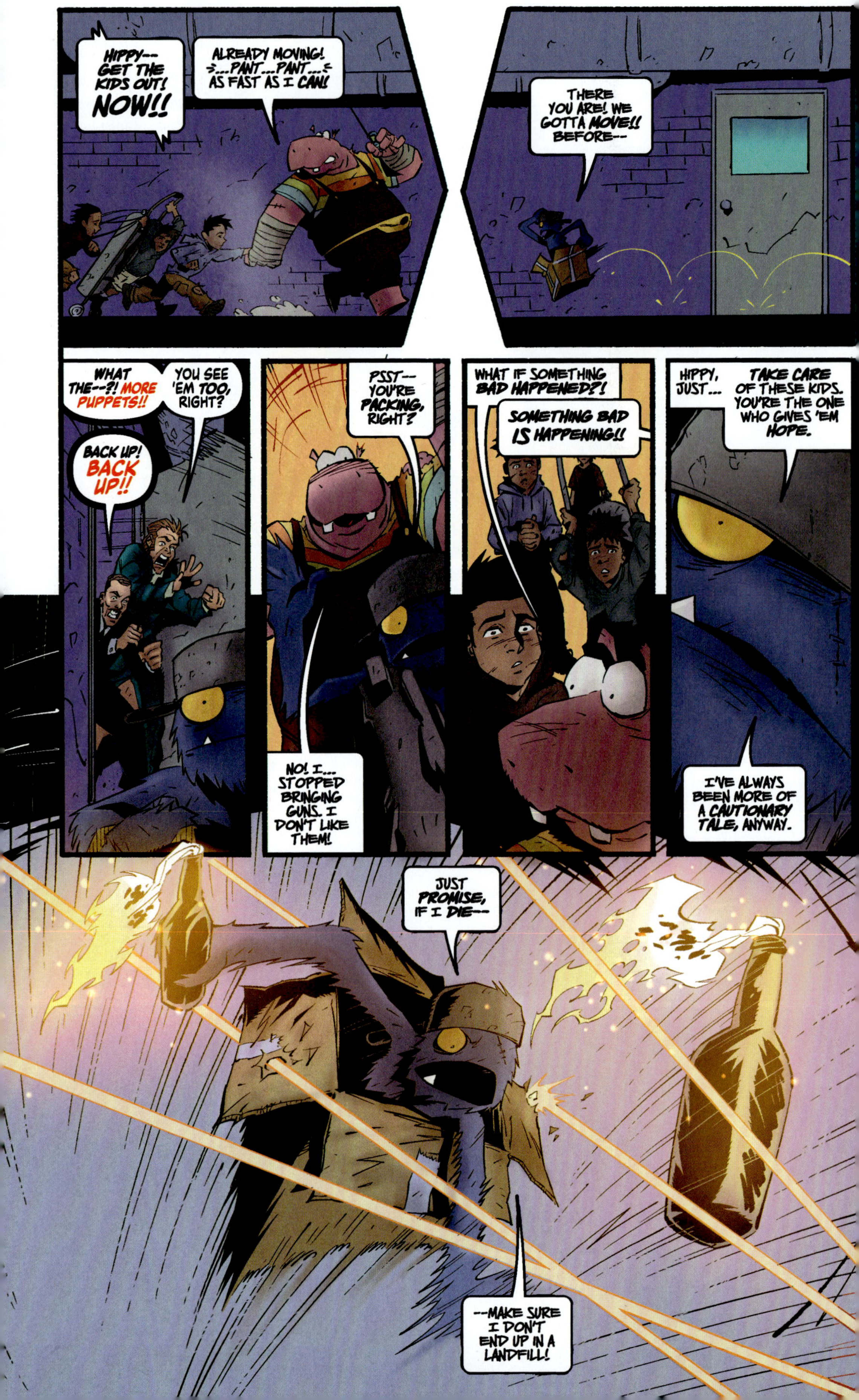
HIPPY-- GET THE KIDS OUT! NOW!!
ALREADY MOVING! ...PANT...PANT... AS FAST AS I CAN!
THERE YOU ARE! WE GOTTA MOVE!! BEFORE--
WHAT THE--?! MORE PUPPETS!!
YOU SEE 'EM TOO, RIGHT?
BACK UP! BACK UP!!
PSST-- YOU'RE PACKING, RIGHT?
NO! I... STOPPED BRINGING GUNS. I DON'T LIKE THEM!
WHAT IF SOMETHING BAD HAPPENED?!
SOMETHING BAD IS HAPPENING!!
HIPPY, JUST...
TAKE CARE OF THESE KIDS. YOU'RE THE ONE WHO GIVES 'EM HOPE.
I'VE ALWAYS BEEN MORE OF A CAUTIONARY TALE, ANYWAY.
JUST PROMISE, IF I DIE--
--MAKE SURE I DON'T END UP IN A LANDFILL!

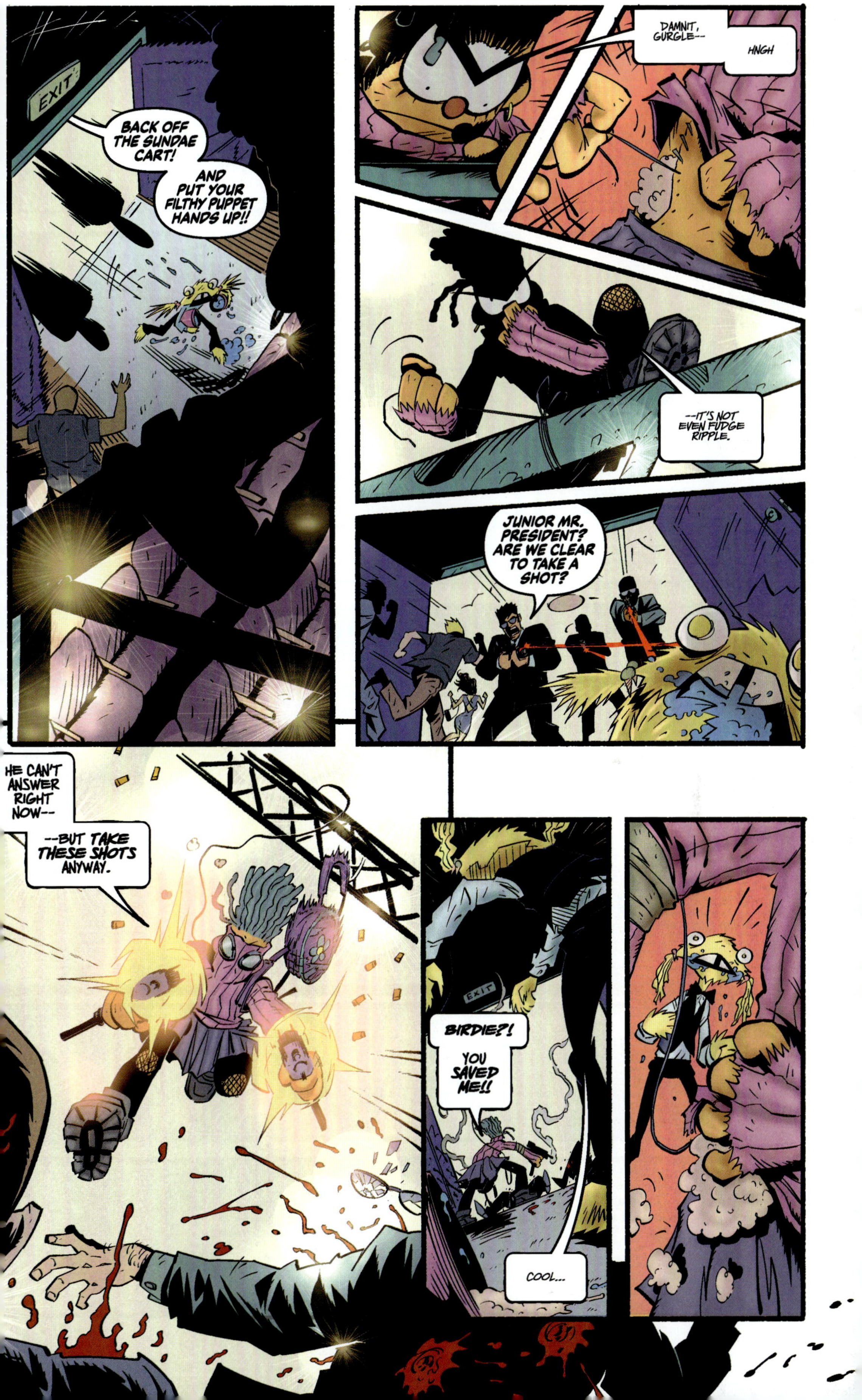
BACK OFF THE SUNDAE CART!
AND PUT YOUR FILTHY PUPPET HANDS UP!!
EXIT
DAMNIT, GURGLE--
HNGH
--IT'S NOT EVEN FUDGE RIPPLE.
JUNIOR MR. PRESIDENT? ARE WE CLEAR TO TAKE A SHOT?
HE CAN'T ANSWER RIGHT NOW--
--BUT TAKE THESE SHOTS ANYWAY.
EXIT
BIRDIE?!
YOU SAVED ME!!
COOL...

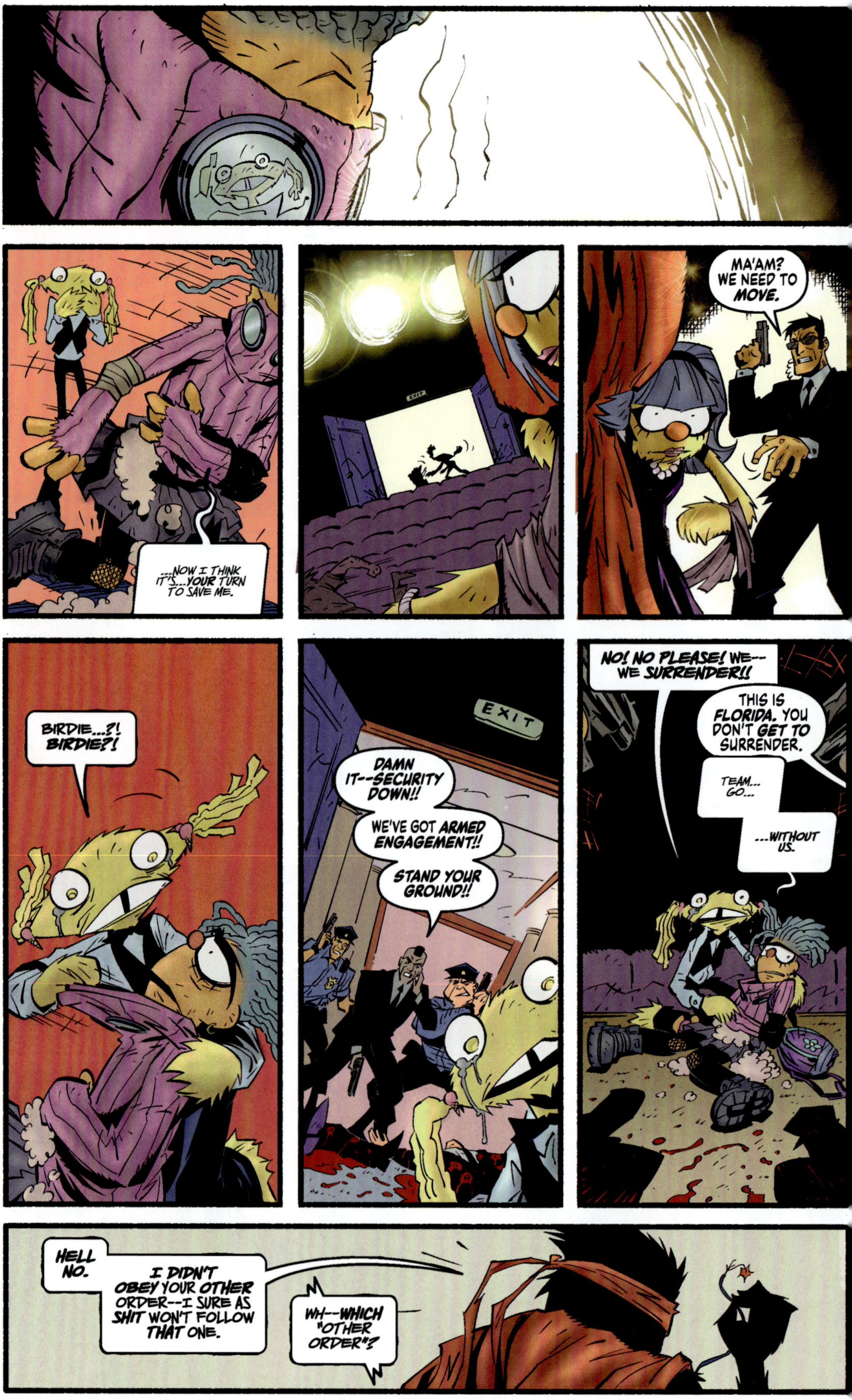
...NOW I THINK IT'S...YOUR TURN TO SAVE ME.
MA'AM? WE NEED TO MOVE.
BIRDIE...?! BIRDIE?!
EXIT
DAMN IT--SECURITY DOWN!!
WE'VE GOT ARMED ENGAGEMENT!!
STAND YOUR GROUND!!
NO! NO PLEASE! WE-- WE SURRENDER!!
THIS IS FLORIDA. YOU DON'T GET TO SURRENDER.
TEAM... GO...
...WITHOUT US.
HELL NO.
I DIDN'T OBEY YOUR OTHER ORDER--I SURE AS SHIT WON'T FOLLOW THAT ONE.
WH--WHICH "OTHER ORDER"?

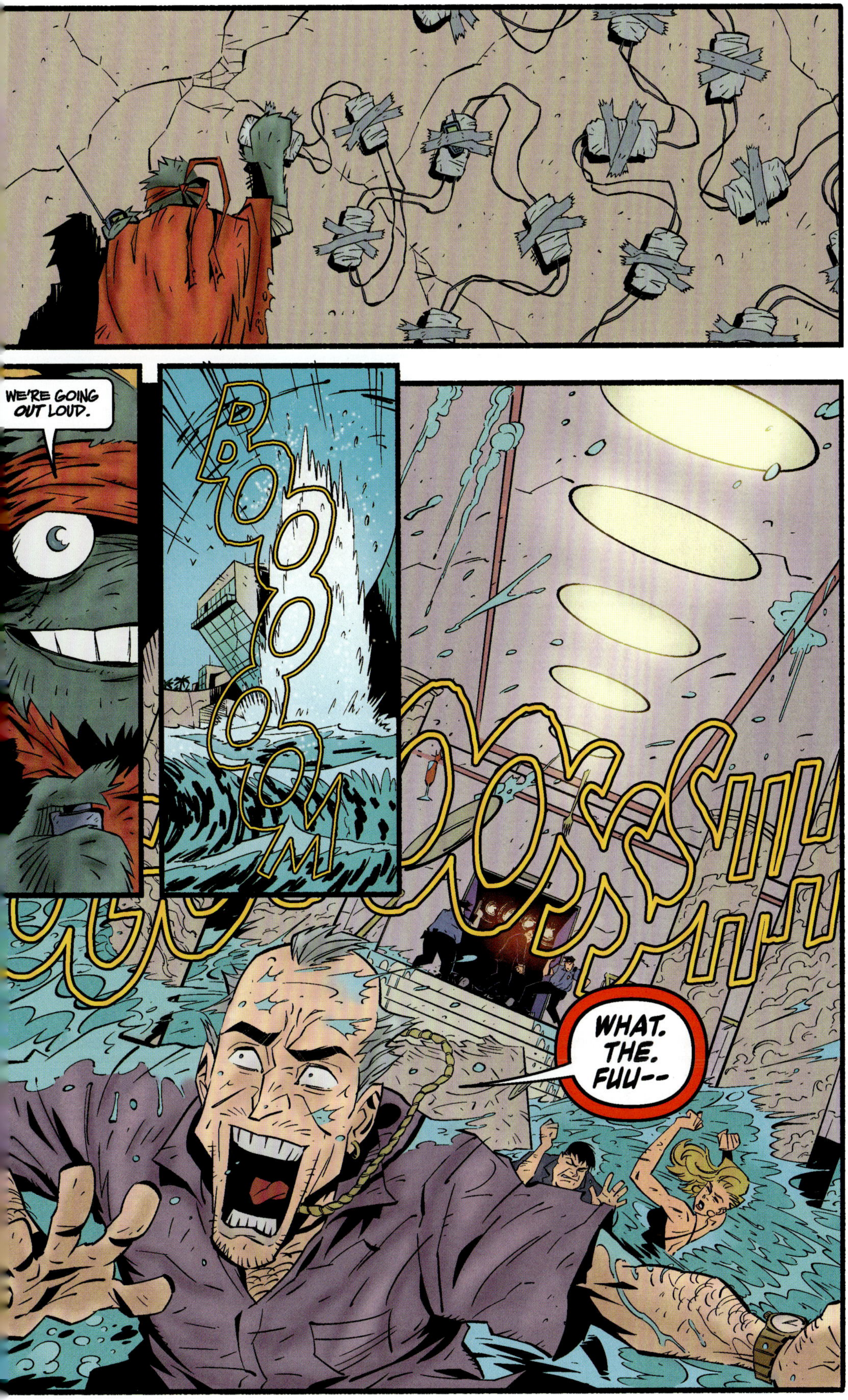
WE'RE GOING OUT LOUD.
WHAT. THE. FUU--

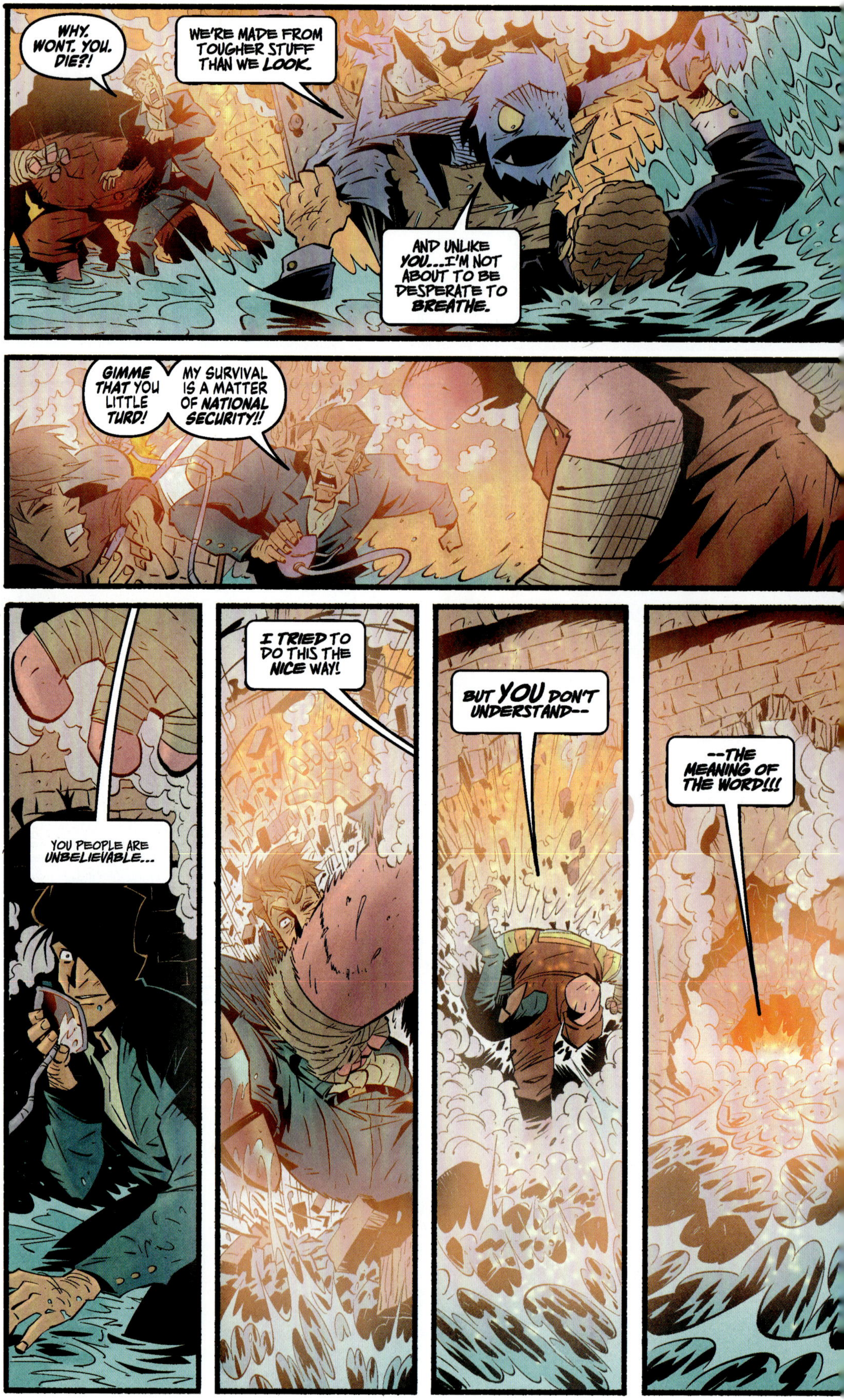
WHY. WONT. YOU. DIE?!
WE'RE MADE FROM TOUGHER STUFF THAN WE LOOK.
AND UNLIKE YOU...I'M NOT ABOUT TO BE DESPERATE TO BREATHE.
GIMME THAT YOU LITTLE TURD!
MY SURVIVAL IS A MATTER OF NATIONAL SECURITY!!
YOU PEOPLE ARE UNBELIEVABLE...
I TRIED TO DO THIS THE NICE WAY!
BUT YOU DON'T UNDERSTAND--
--THE MEANING OF THE WORD!!!

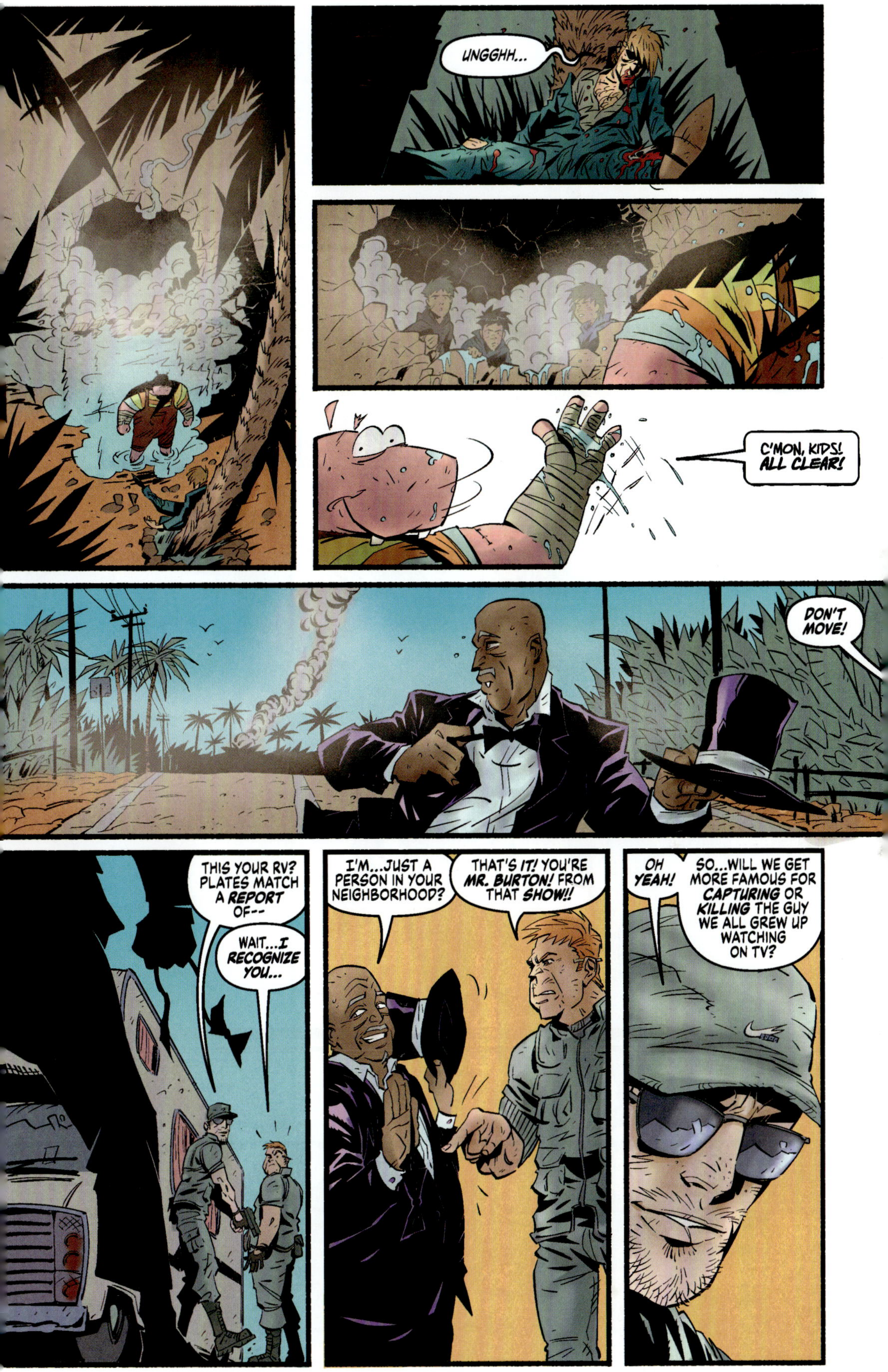
UNGGHH...
C'MON, KIDS! ALL CLEAR!
DON'T MOVE!
THIS YOUR RV? PLATES MATCH A REPORT OF--
WAIT...I RECOGNIZE YOU...
I'M...JUST A PERSON IN YOUR NEIGHBORHOOD?
THAT'S IT! YOU'RE MR. BURTON! FROM THAT SHOW!!
OH YEAH!
SO...WILL WE GET MORE FAMOUS FOR CAPTURING OR KILLING THE GUY WE ALL GREW UP WATCHING ON TV?

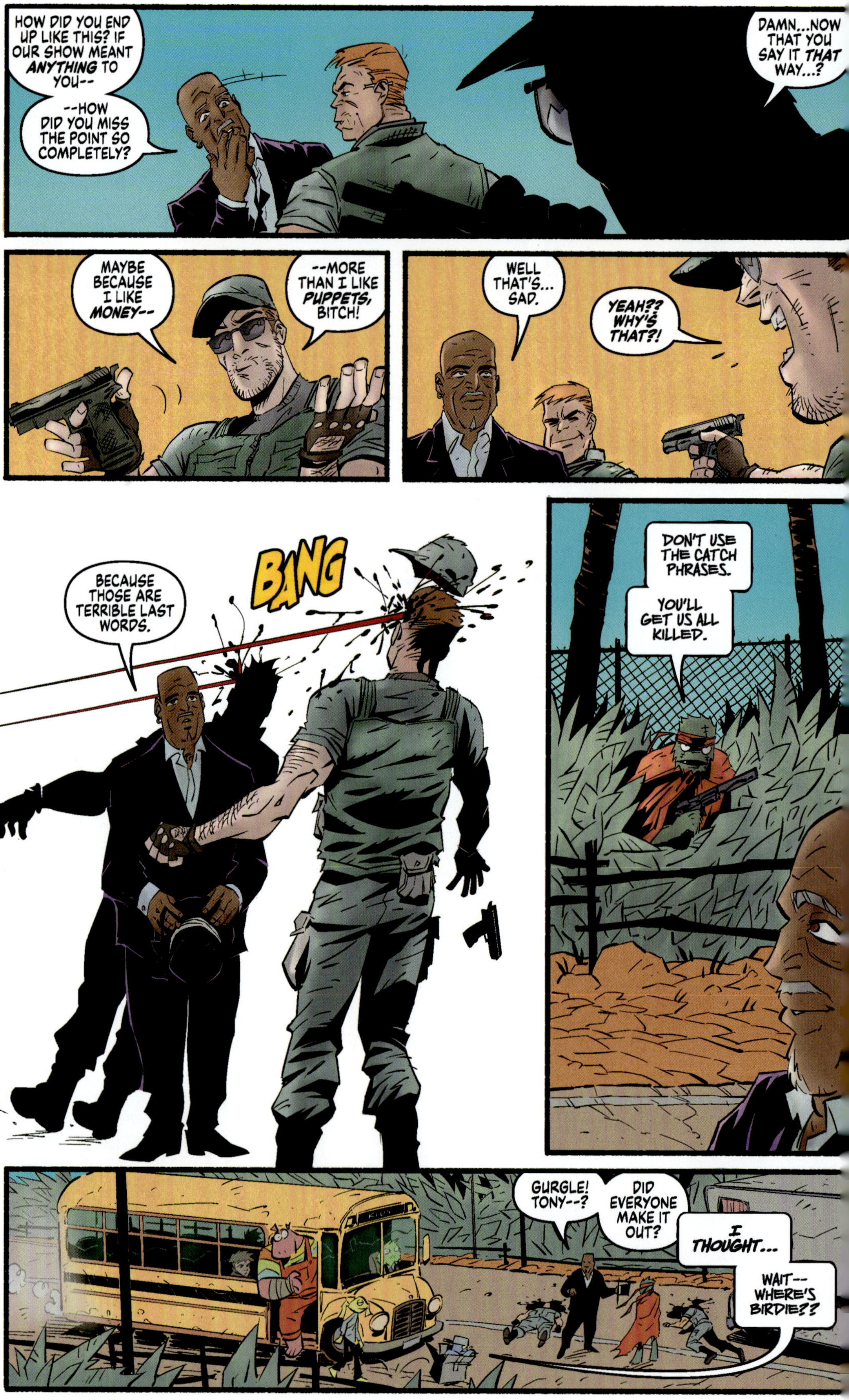

HOW DID YOU END UP LIKE THIS? IF OUR SHOW MEANT ANYTHING TO YOU--
--HOW DID YOU MISS THE POINT SO COMPLETELY?
DAMN...NOW THAT YOU SAY IT THAT WAY...?
MAYBE BECAUSE I LIKE MONEY--
--MORE THAN I LIKE PUPPETS, BITCH!
WELL THAT'S... SAD.
YEAH?? WHY'S THAT?!
BANG
BECAUSE THOSE ARE TERRIBLE LAST WORDS.
DON'T USE THE CATCH PHRASES.
YOU'LL GET US ALL KILLED.
GURGLE! TONY--?
DID EVERYONE MAKE IT OUT?
I THOUGHT...
WAIT-- WHERE'S BIRDIE??

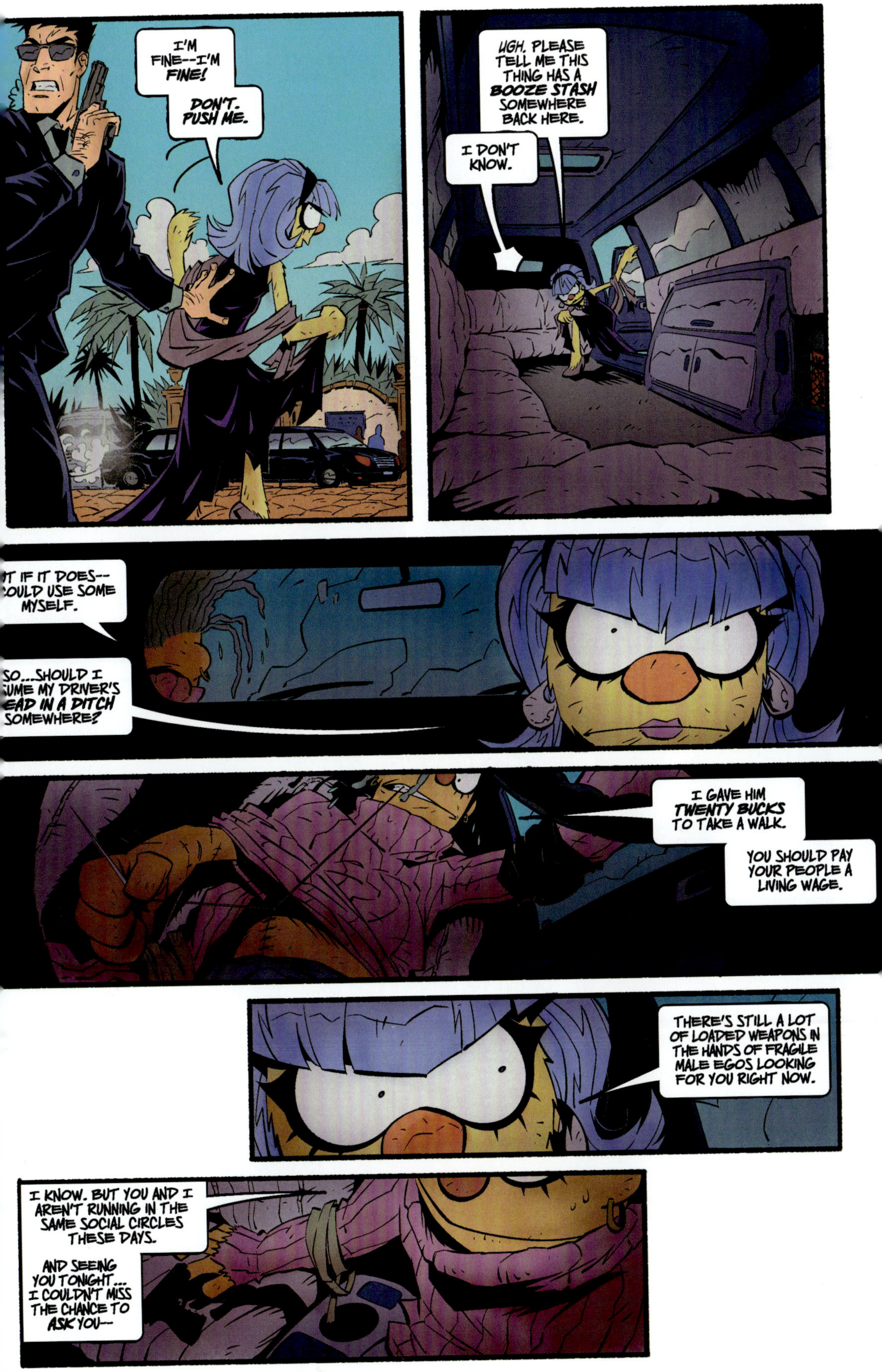

I'M FINE--I'M FINE!
DON'T. PUSH ME.
UGH. PLEASE TELL ME THIS THING HAS A BOOZE STASH SOMEWHERE BACK HERE.
I DON'T KNOW.
T IF IT DOES-- OULD USE SOME MYSELF.
SO...SHOULD I UME MY DRIVER'S EAD IN A DITCH SOMEWHERE?
I GAVE HIM TWENTY BUCKS TO TAKE A WALK.
YOU SHOULD PAY YOUR PEOPLE A LIVING WAGE.
THERE'S STILL A LOT OF LOADED WEAPONS IN THE HANDS OF FRAGILE MALE EGOS LOOKING FOR YOU RIGHT NOW.
I KNOW. BUT YOU AND I AREN'T RUNNING IN THE SAME SOCIAL CIRCLES THESE DAYS.
AND SEEING YOU TONIGHT... I COULDN'T MISS THE CHANCE TO ASK YOU--

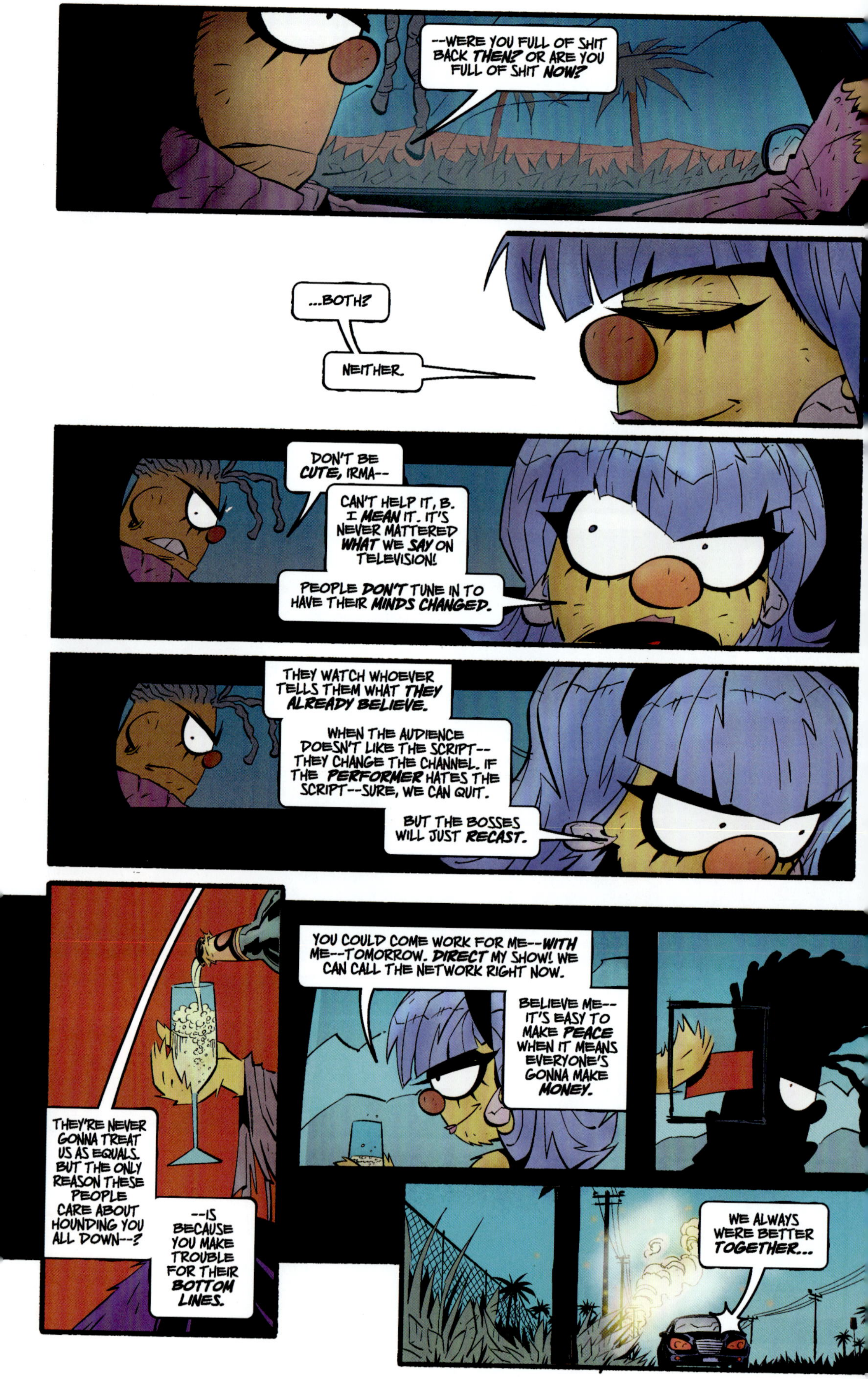
--WERE YOU FULL OF SHIT BACK THEN? OR ARE YOU FULL OF SHIT NOW?
...BOTH?
NEITHER.
DON'T BE CUTE, IRMA--
CAN'T HELP IT, B. I MEAN IT. IT'S NEVER MATTERED WHAT WE SAY ON TELEVISION!
PEOPLE DON'T TUNE IN TO HAVE THEIR MINDS CHANGED.
THEY WATCH WHOEVER TELLS THEM WHAT THEY ALREADY BELIEVE.
WHEN THE AUDIENCE DOESN'T LIKE THE SCRIPT-- THEY CHANGE THE CHANNEL. IF THE PERFORMER HATES THE SCRIPT--SURE, WE CAN QUIT.
BUT THE BOSSES WILL JUST RECAST.
THEY'RE NEVER GONNA TREAT US AS EQUALS. BUT THE ONLY REASON THESE PEOPLE CARE ABOUT HOUNDING YOU ALL DOWN--?
--IS BECAUSE YOU MAKE TROUBLE FOR THEIR BOTTOM LINES.
YOU COULD COME WORK FOR ME--WITH ME--TOMORROW. DIRECT MY SHOW! WE CAN CALL THE NETWORK RIGHT NOW.
BELIEVE ME-- IT'S EASY TO MAKE PEACE WHEN IT MEANS EVERYONE'S GONNA MAKE MONEY.
WE ALWAYS WERE BETTER TOGETHER...

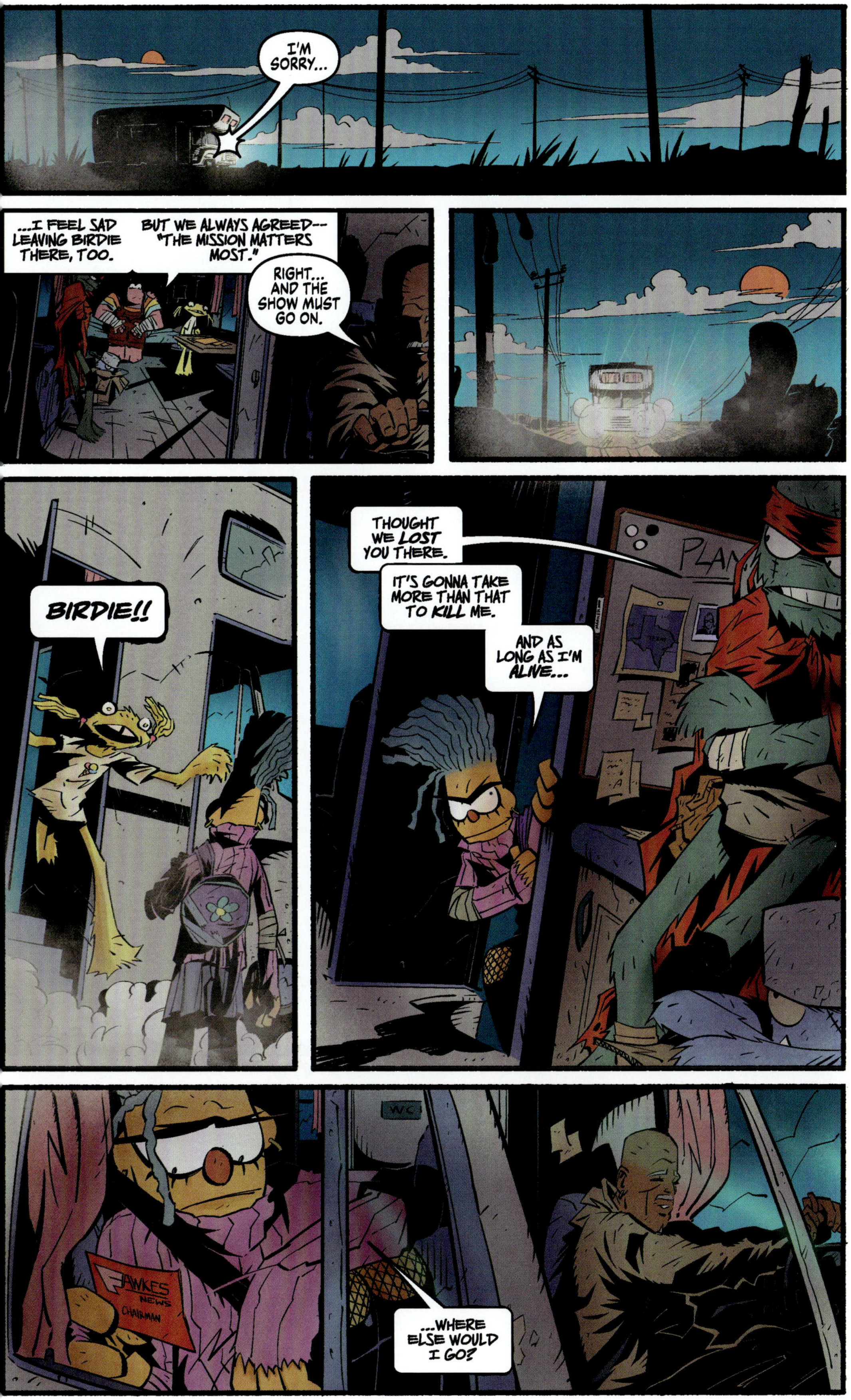
I'M SORRY...
...I FEEL SAD LEAVING BIRDIE THERE, TOO.
BUT WE ALWAYS AGREED-- "THE MISSION MATTERS MOST."
RIGHT... AND THE SHOW MUST GO ON.
BIRDIE!!
THOUGHT WE LOST YOU THERE.
IT'S GONNA TAKE MORE THAN THAT TO KILL ME.
AND AS LONG AS I'M ALIVE...
...WHERE ELSE WOULD I GO?

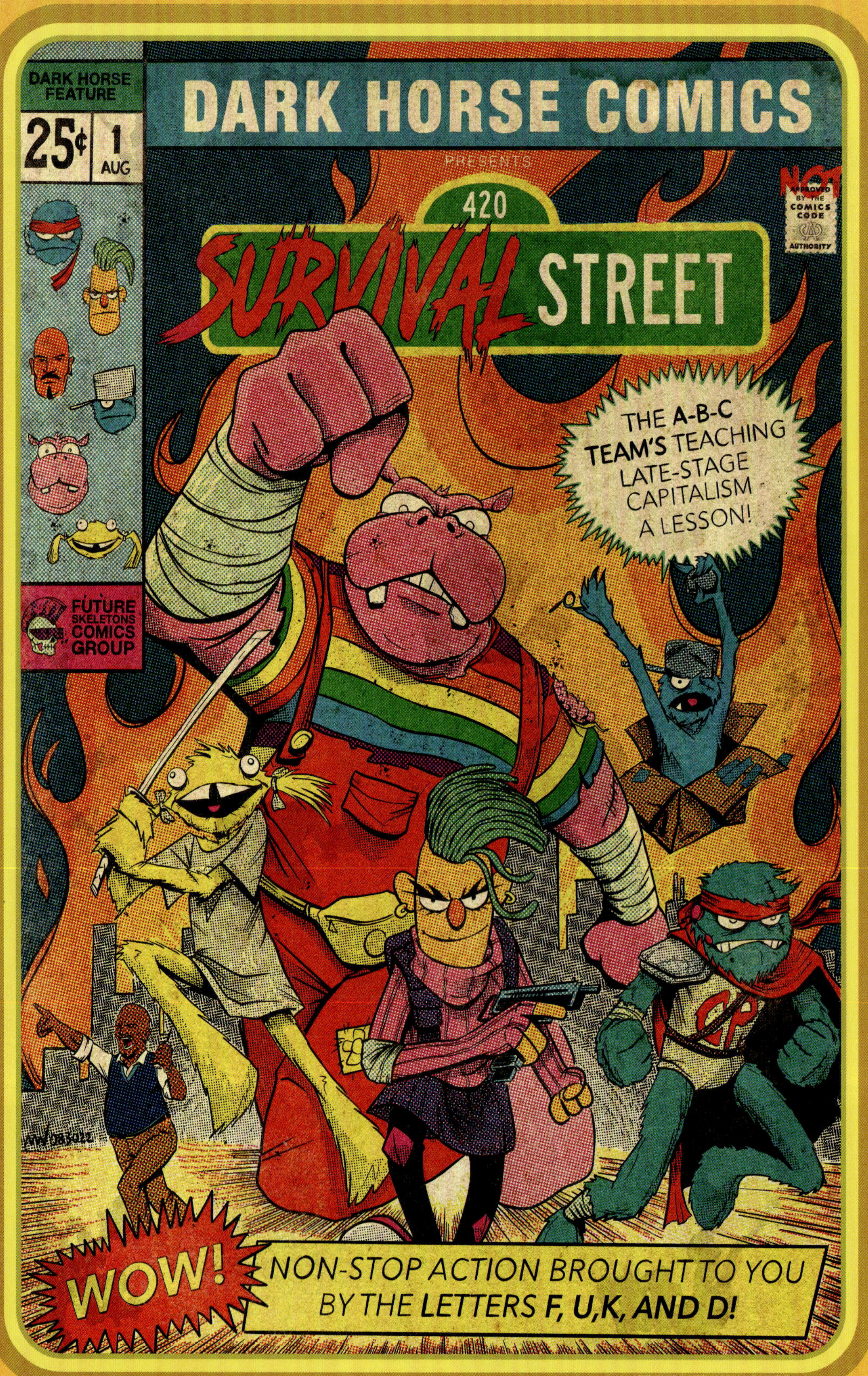
DARK HORSE FEATURE
25¢
1 AUG
DARK HORSE COMICS
PRESENTS
420
SURVIVAL STREET
NOT APPROVED BY THE COMICS CODE AUTHORITY
THE A-B-C TEAM'S TEACHING LATE-STAGE CAPITALISM A LESSON!
FUTURE SKELETONS COMICS GROUP
WOW!
NON-STOP ACTION BROUGHT TO YOU BY THE LETTERS F, U,K, AND D!

ART BY **MATT WAHLQUIST**

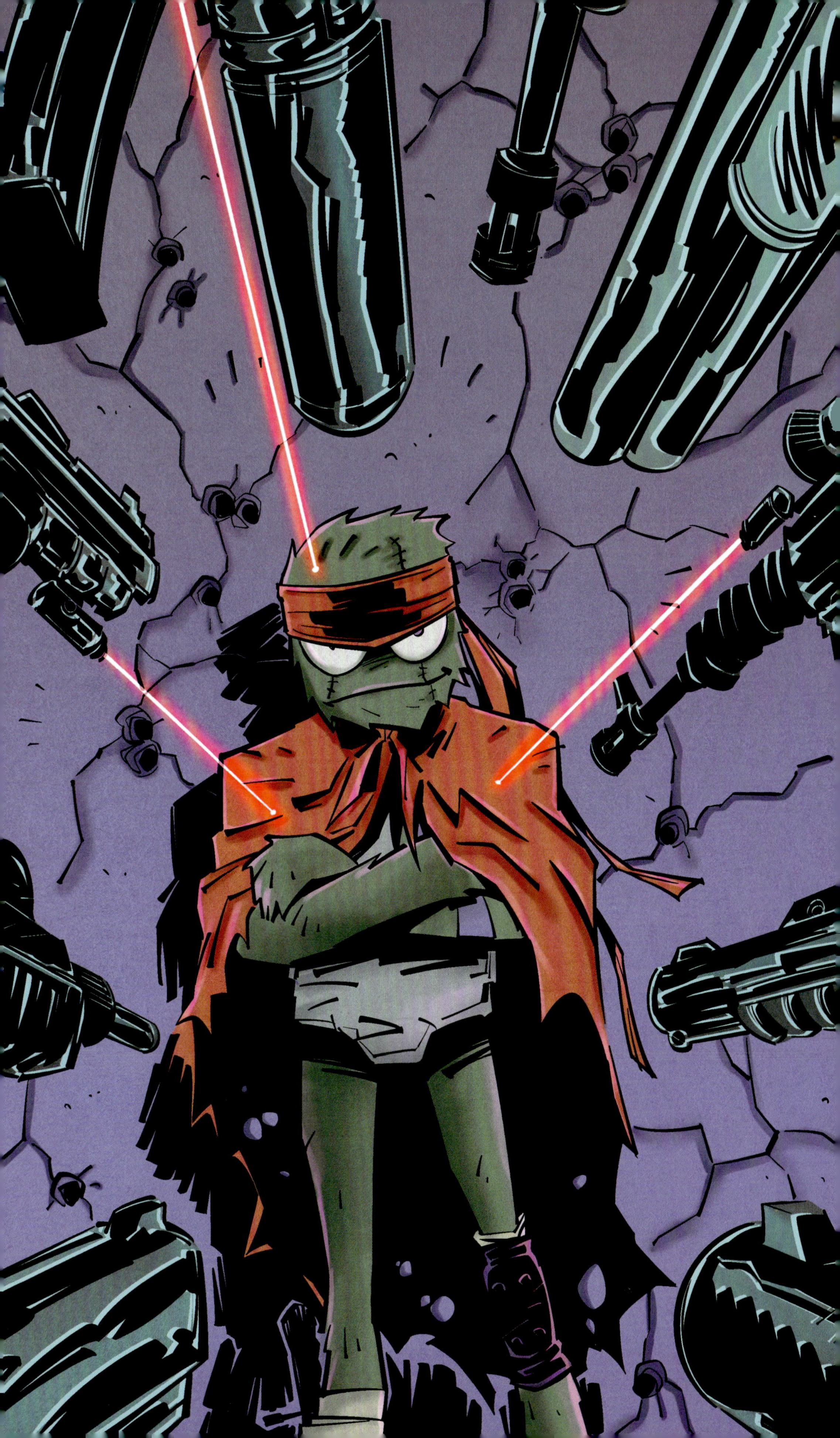

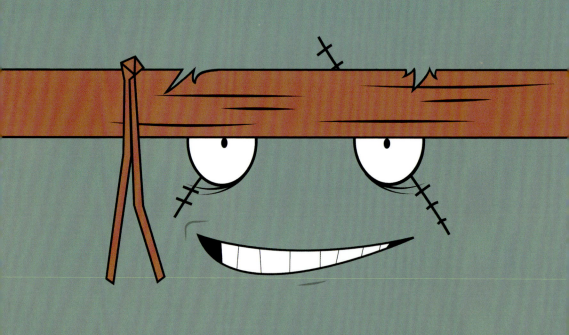

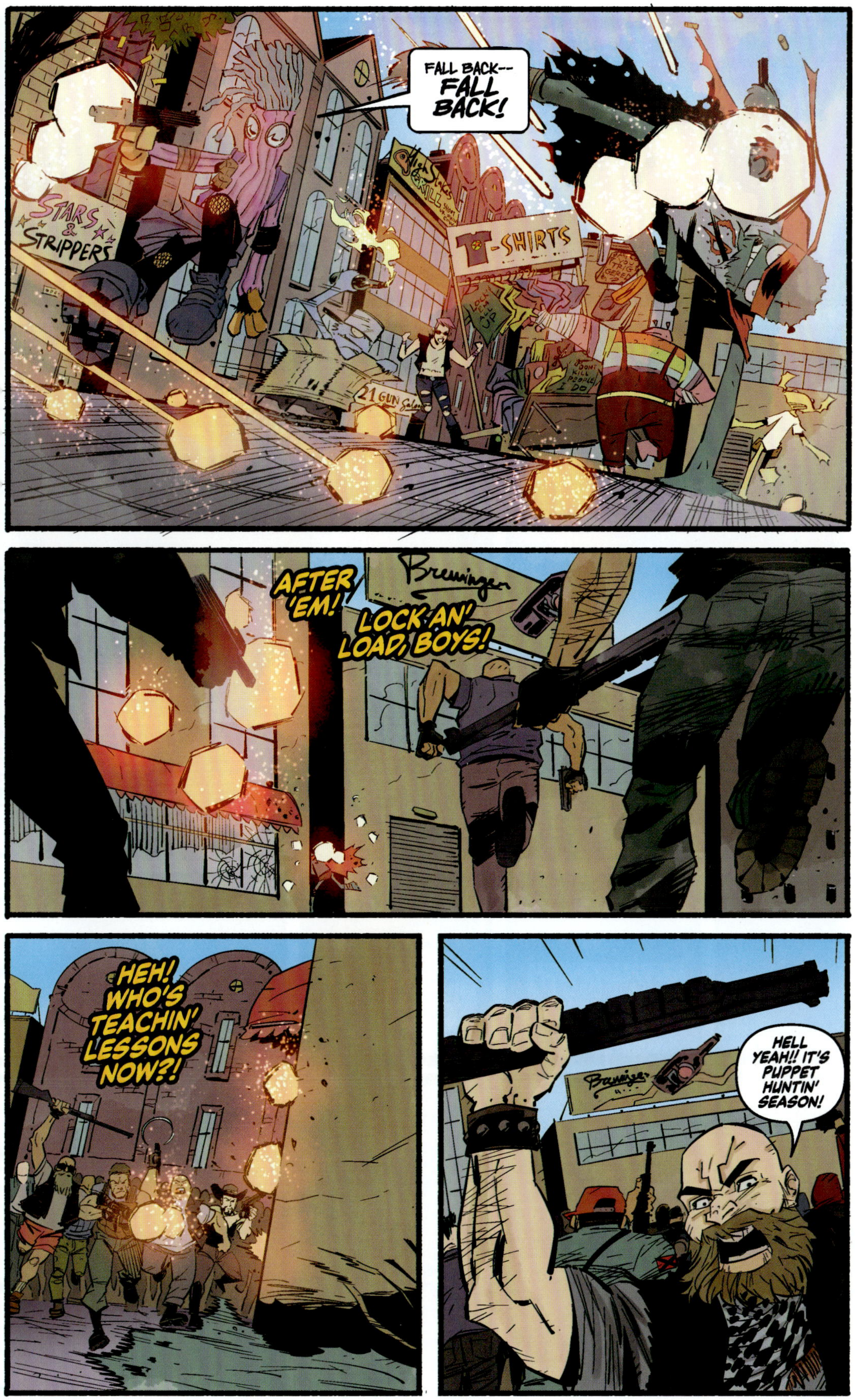
STARS & STRIPPERS
T-SHIRTS
FALL BACK-- FALL BACK!
21 GUN
Breuninger
AFTER 'EM!
LOCK AN' LOAD, BOYS!
HEH! WHO'S TEACHIN' LESSONS NOW?!
HELL YEAH!! IT'S PUPPET HUNTIN' SEASON!

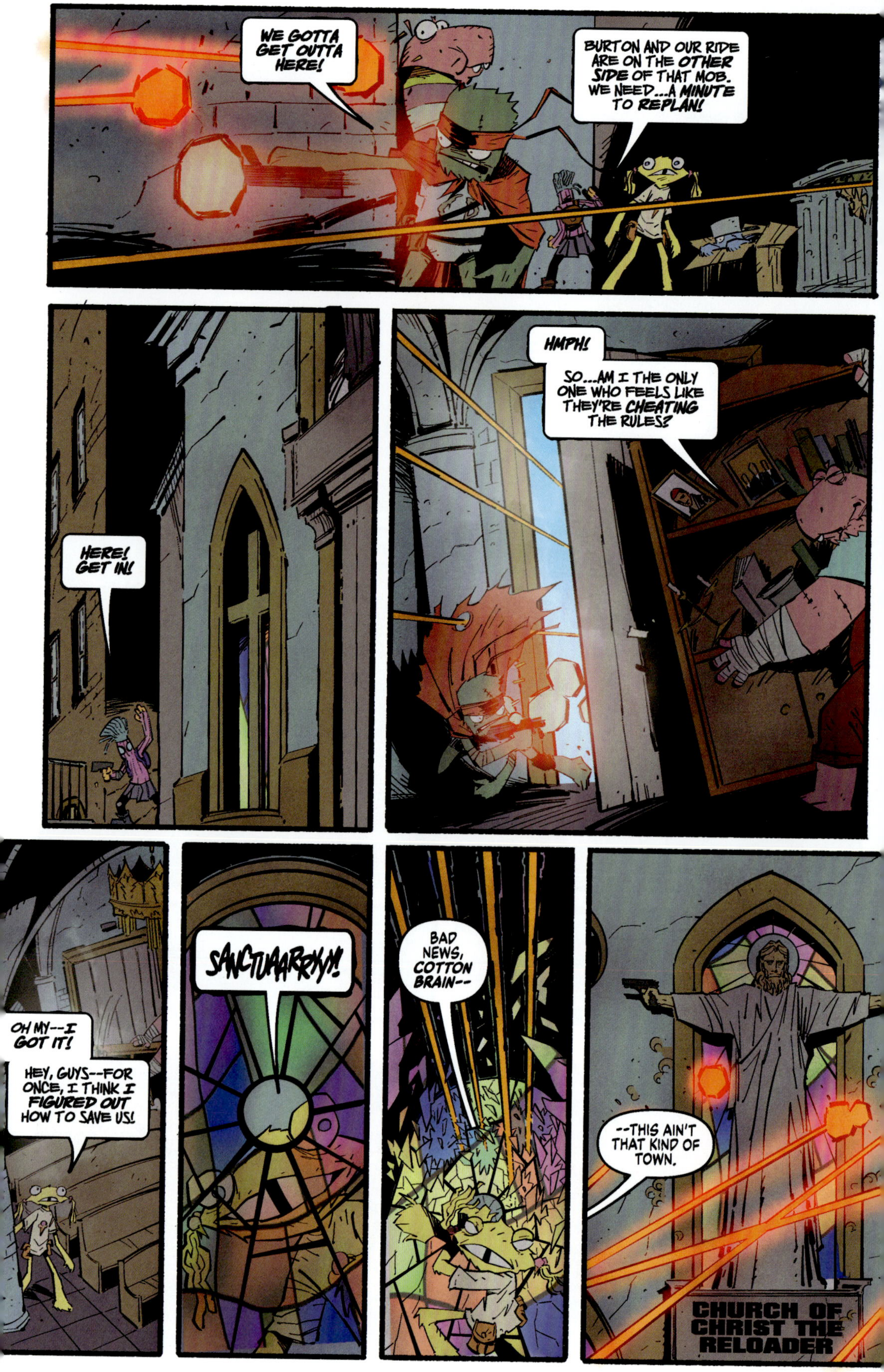
WE GOTTA GET OUTTA HERE!
BURTON AND OUR RIDE ARE ON THE OTHER SIDE OF THAT MOB. WE NEED...A MINUTE TO REPLAN!
HERE! GET IN!
HMPH!
SO...AM I THE ONLY ONE WHO FEELS LIKE THEY'RE CHEATING THE RULES?
OH MY--I GOT IT!
HEY, GUYS--FOR ONCE, I THINK I FIGURED OUT HOW TO SAVE US!
SANCTUAARRYY!
BAD NEWS, COTTON BRAIN--
--THIS AIN'T THAT KIND OF TOWN.
CHURCH OF CHRIST THE RELOADER

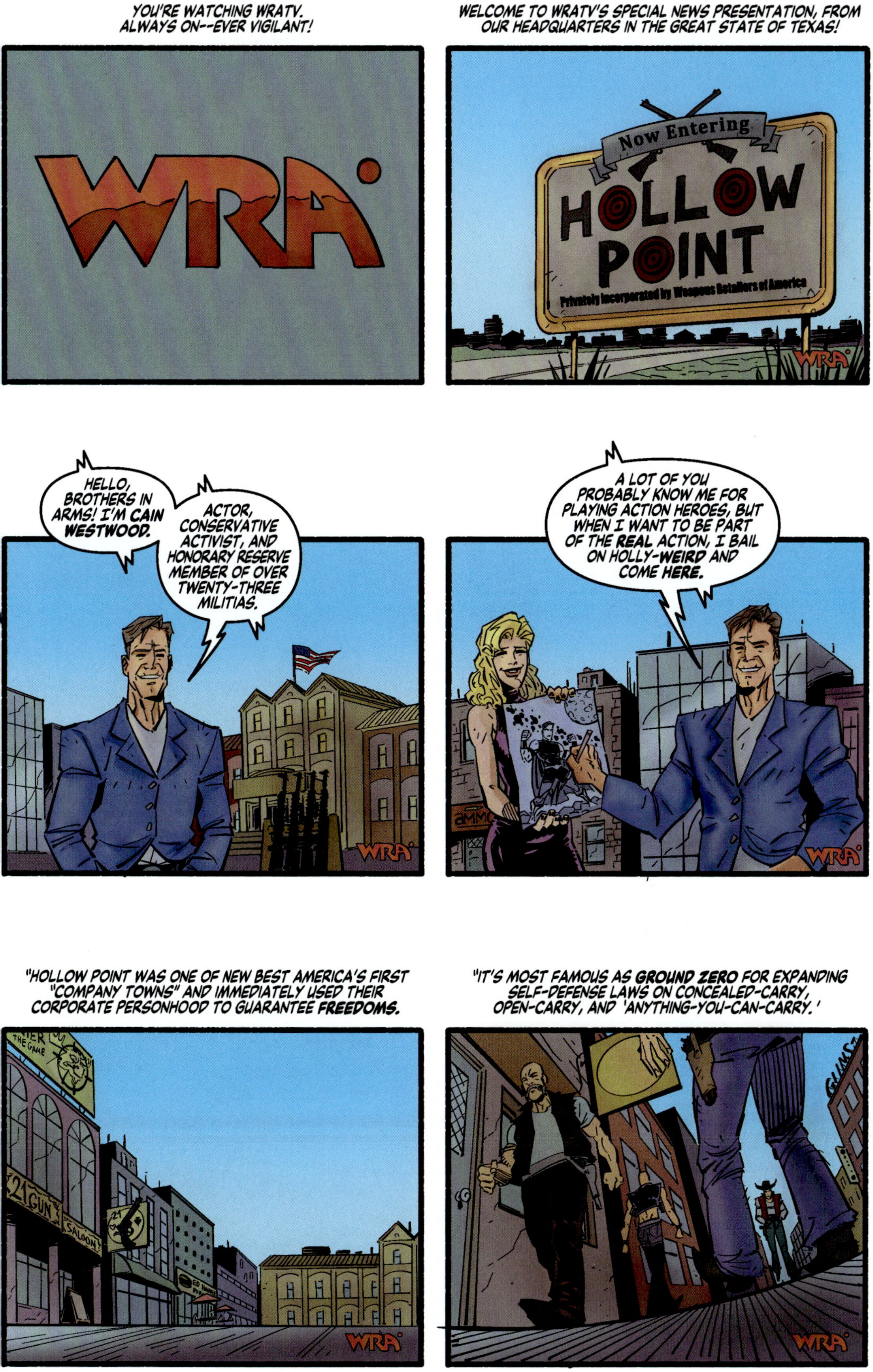
YOU'RE WATCHING WRATV. ALWAYS ON--EVER VIGILANT!
WRA
WELCOME TO WRATV'S SPECIAL NEWS PRESENTATION, FROM OUR HEADQUARTERS IN THE GREAT STATE OF TEXAS!
Now Entering
HOLLOW POINT
Privately Incorporated by Weapons Retailers of America
HELLO, BROTHERS IN ARMS! I'M CAIN WESTWOOD.
ACTOR, CONSERVATIVE ACTIVIST, AND HONORARY RESERVE MEMBER OF OVER TWENTY-THREE MILITIAS.
A LOT OF YOU PROBABLY KNOW ME FOR PLAYING ACTION HEROES, BUT WHEN I WANT TO BE PART OF THE REAL ACTION, I BAIL ON HOLLY-WEIRD AND COME HERE.
"HOLLOW POINT WAS ONE OF NEW BEST AMERICA'S FIRST "COMPANY TOWNS" AND IMMEDIATELY USED THEIR CORPORATE PERSONHOOD TO GUARANTEE FREEDOMS.
21 GUN SALOON
"IT'S MOST FAMOUS AS GROUND ZERO FOR EXPANDING SELF-DEFENSE LAWS ON CONCEALED-CARRY, OPEN-CARRY, AND 'ANYTHING-YOU-CAN-CARRY.'

"BUT IT'S ALSO BEEN AT THE FOREFRONT OF GETTING GOVERNMENT **OUT** OF OUR PRIVATE BUSINESS AND RETURNING AMERICA TO ITS **ORIGINAL** VALUES--

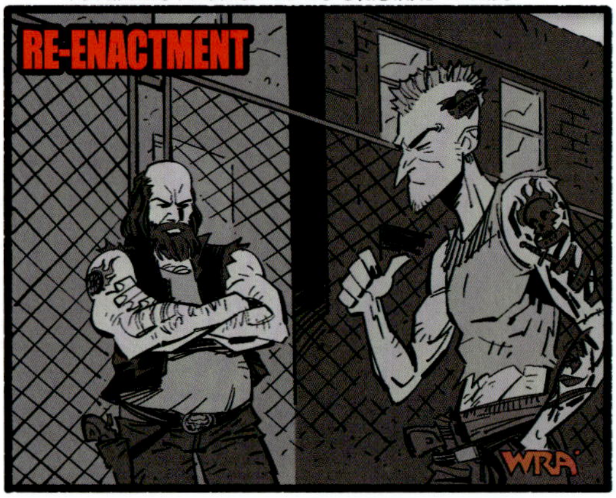
RE-ENACTMENT
WRA

"--BY ALLOWING PRIVATE CITIZENS TO SETTLE PRIVATE DISPUTES THROUGH **DUELS**, WITH THE RESULT ACTING AS THE **LEGALLY BINDING DECISION** IN THE CONFLICT.

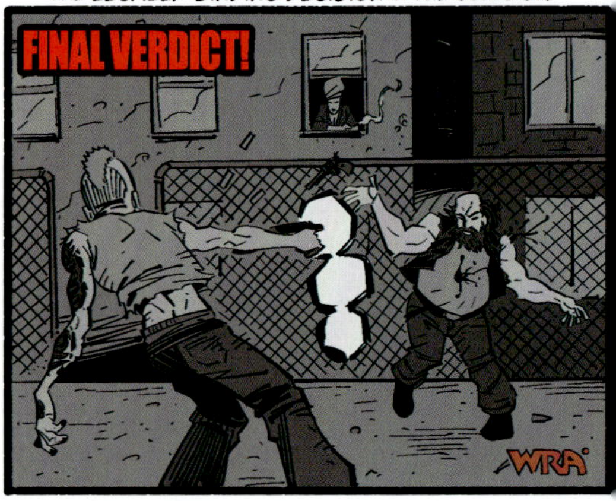
FINAL VERDICT!
WRA

"IT'S SETTLED ARGUMENTS FROM PROPERTY LINES, OR WHO GETS **EVERYTHING** IN THE DIVORCE, TO WHICH IS THE BEST BURGER IN HOLLOW POINT!

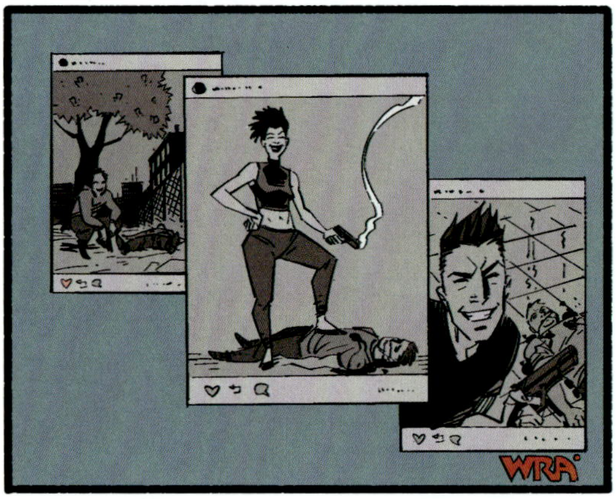
WRA

"LIBERALS WRING THEIR HANDS AND WHINE THAT THIS IS 'GUNTOPIA' **'MAIM** STREET, **U-S-A**,' AND 'BASICALLY WESTWORLD **WITHOUT ROBOTS**'.

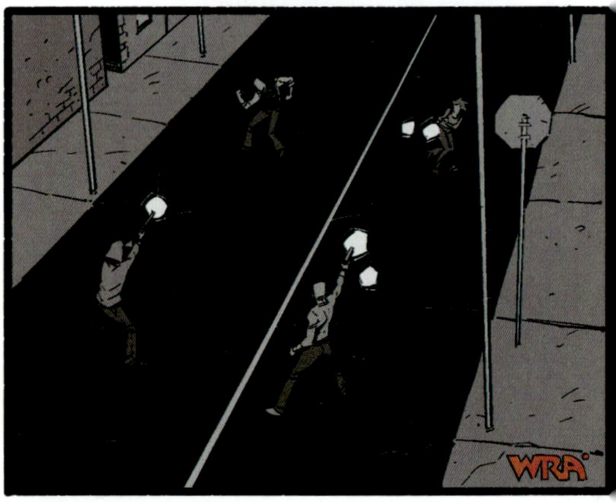
WRA

"BUT SHOWS WHAT THEY KNOW! WE **HAVE** A ROBOT--

"--A TRIBUTE TO THE LATE, GREAT **CHARLTON HESTON**."

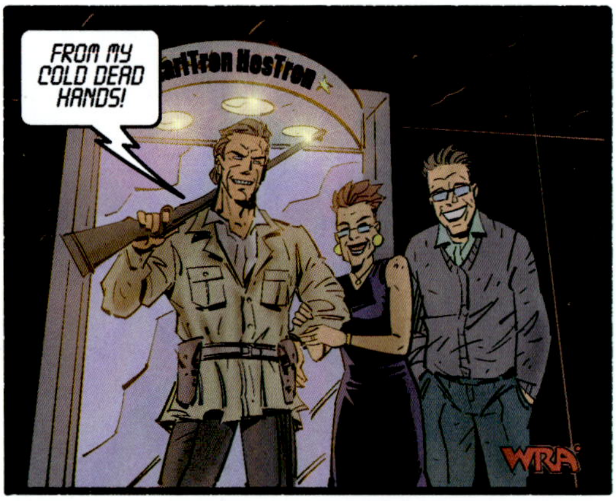
FROM MY COLD DEAD HANDS!
WRA

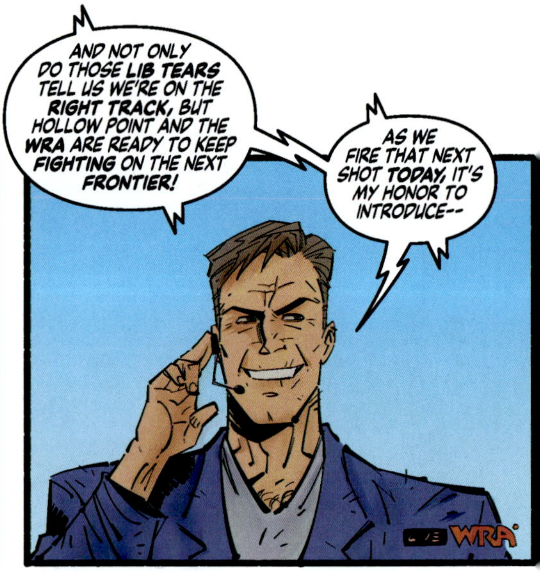
AND NOT ONLY DO THOSE **LIB TEARS** TELL US WE'RE ON THE **RIGHT TRACK**, BUT HOLLOW POINT AND THE **WRA** ARE READY TO KEEP **FIGHTING** ON THE NEXT **FRONTIER**!
AS WE FIRE THAT NEXT SHOT **TODAY**, IT'S MY HONOR TO INTRODUCE--
WRA

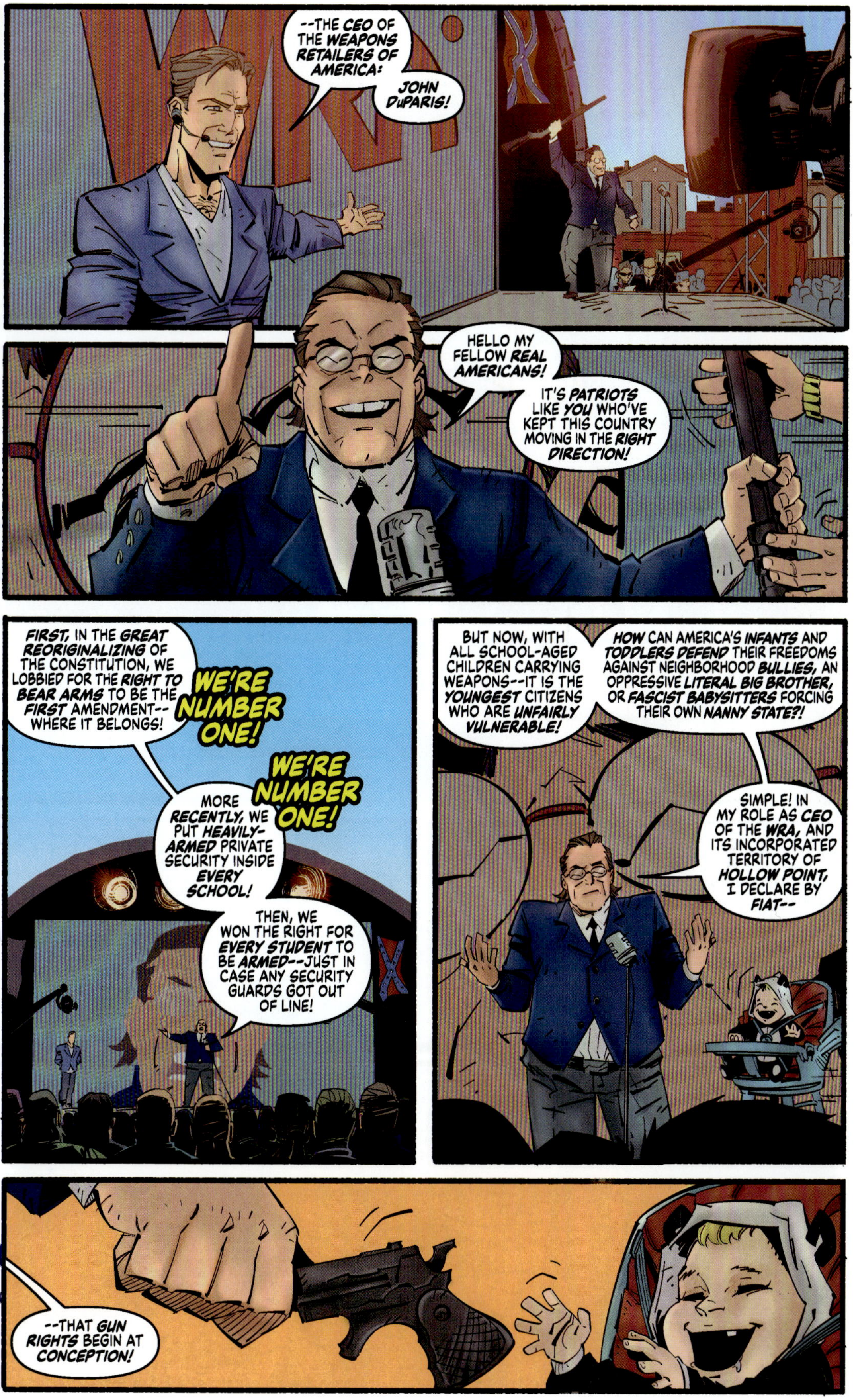
--THE CEO OF THE WEAPONS RETAILERS OF AMERICA:
JOHN DuPARIS!
HELLO MY FELLOW REAL AMERICANS!
IT'S PATRIOTS LIKE YOU WHO'VE KEPT THIS COUNTRY MOVING IN THE RIGHT DIRECTION!
FIRST, IN THE GREAT REORIGINALIZING OF THE CONSTITUTION, WE LOBBIED FOR THE RIGHT TO BEAR ARMS TO BE THE FIRST AMENDMENT--WHERE IT BELONGS!
WE'RE NUMBER ONE!
WE'RE NUMBER ONE!
MORE RECENTLY, WE PUT HEAVILY-ARMED PRIVATE SECURITY INSIDE EVERY SCHOOL!
THEN, WE WON THE RIGHT FOR EVERY STUDENT TO BE ARMED--JUST IN CASE ANY SECURITY GUARDS GOT OUT OF LINE!
BUT NOW, WITH ALL SCHOOL-AGED CHILDREN CARRYING WEAPONS--IT IS THE YOUNGEST CITIZENS WHO ARE UNFAIRLY VULNERABLE!
HOW CAN AMERICA'S INFANTS AND TODDLERS DEFEND THEIR FREEDOMS AGAINST NEIGHBORHOOD BULLIES, AN OPPRESSIVE LITERAL BIG BROTHER, OR FASCIST BABYSITTERS FORCING THEIR OWN NANNY STATE?!
SIMPLE! IN MY ROLE AS CEO OF THE WRA, AND ITS INCORPORATED TERRITORY OF HOLLOW POINT, I DECLARE BY FIAT--
--THAT GUN RIGHTS BEGIN AT CONCEPTION!

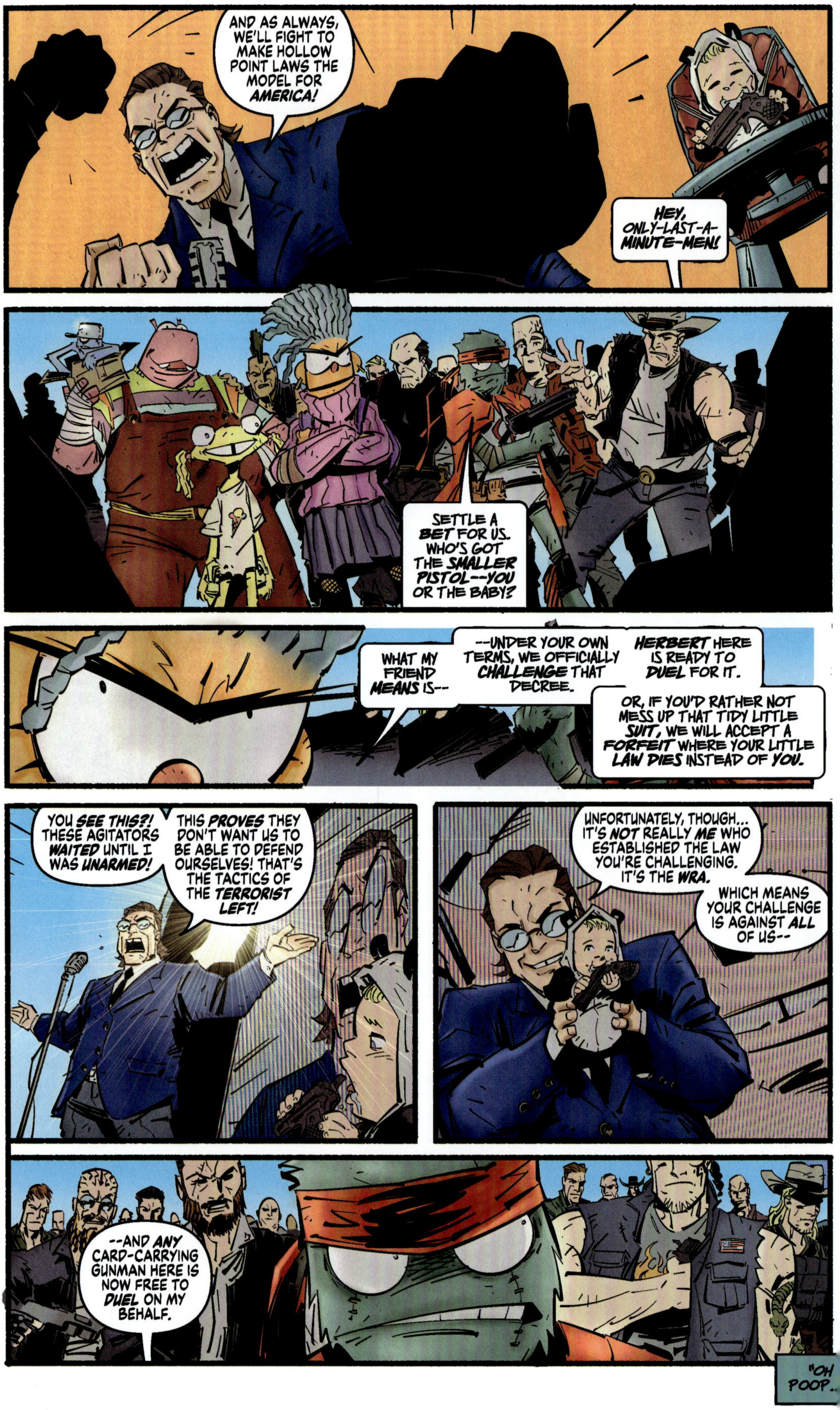
AND AS ALWAYS, WE'LL FIGHT TO MAKE HOLLOW POINT LAWS THE MODEL FOR AMERICA!
HEY, ONLY-LAST-A-MINUTE-MEN!
SETTLE A BET FOR US. WHO'S GOT THE SMALLER PISTOL--YOU OR THE BABY?
WHAT MY FRIEND MEANS IS--
--UNDER YOUR OWN TERMS, WE OFFICIALLY CHALLENGE THAT DECREE.
HERBERT HERE IS READY TO DUEL FOR IT.
OR, IF YOU'D RATHER NOT MESS UP THAT TIDY LITTLE SUIT, WE WILL ACCEPT A FORFEIT WHERE YOUR LITTLE LAW DIES INSTEAD OF YOU.
YOU SEE THIS?! THESE AGITATORS WAITED UNTIL I WAS UNARMED!
THIS PROVES THEY DON'T WANT US TO BE ABLE TO DEFEND OURSELVES! THAT'S THE TACTICS OF THE TERRORIST LEFT!
UNFORTUNATELY, THOUGH... IT'S NOT REALLY ME WHO ESTABLISHED THE LAW YOU'RE CHALLENGING. IT'S THE WRA.
WHICH MEANS YOUR CHALLENGE IS AGAINST ALL OF US--
--AND ANY CARD-CARRYING GUNMAN HERE IS NOW FREE TO DUEL ON MY BEHALF.
"OH POOP..

HERBERT!

WHAT?

THAT WASN'T ME SAYING IT, IT WAS THE DADDY SHEEP!

WELL, I WAS GOING TO ASK IF "YOU WERE BORN IN A BARN" TO TALK LIKE THAT, BUT--

AND DOES DADDY SHEEP WANT SOME MORE SUPPER? BECAUSE IT'S ALMOST TIME TO GO--

"--AND FIND OUT WHAT HAS THE VILLAGE SO *EXCITED!*"

M'na M'nam, ...nufalapagos Islands ...xty-three Years Ago.

ANY IDEA WHO THEY ARE?

WE SAW THEIR BOAT.

I JUST HOPE THIS ENDS IN A SPONTANEOUSLY UNIFIED SONG AND DANCE!

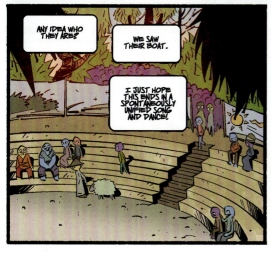

FRIENDS AND NEIGHBORS!

IT IS MY JOY AS YOUR ELECTED *GRAND POOH-BAH* OF THIS CYCLE TO SHARE *EXCITING NEWS* AND AN *INCREDIBLE OPPORTUNITY* FOR US ALL--

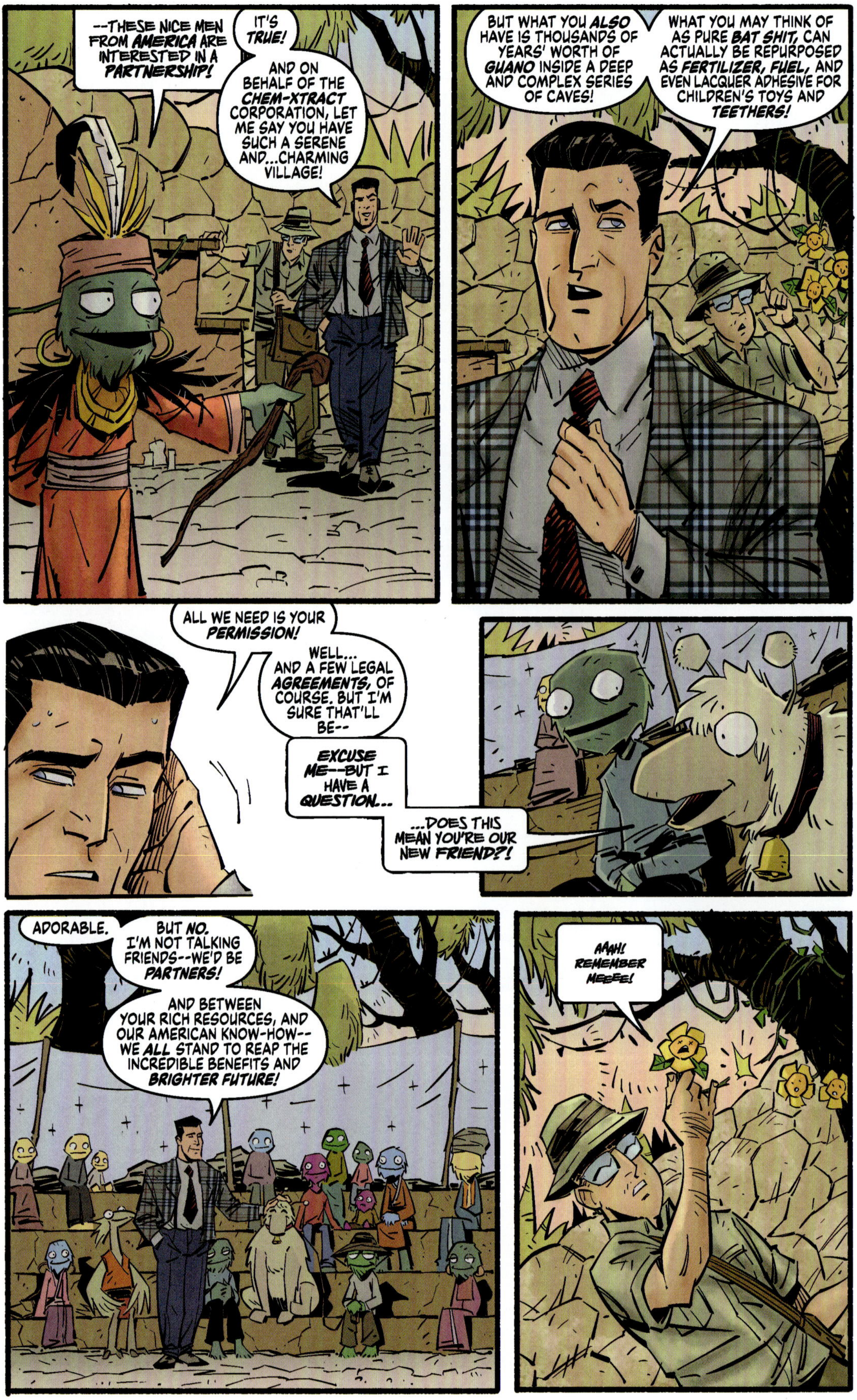
--THESE NICE MEN FROM AMERICA ARE INTERESTED IN A PARTNERSHIP!
IT'S TRUE!
AND ON BEHALF OF THE CHEM-XTRACT CORPORATION, LET ME SAY YOU HAVE SUCH A SERENE AND...CHARMING VILLAGE!
BUT WHAT YOU ALSO HAVE IS THOUSANDS OF YEARS' WORTH OF GUANO INSIDE A DEEP AND COMPLEX SERIES OF CAVES!
WHAT YOU MAY THINK OF AS PURE BAT SHIT, CAN ACTUALLY BE REPURPOSED AS FERTILIZER, FUEL, AND EVEN LACQUER ADHESIVE FOR CHILDREN'S TOYS AND TEETHERS!
ALL WE NEED IS YOUR PERMISSION!
WELL... AND A FEW LEGAL AGREEMENTS, OF COURSE. BUT I'M SURE THAT'LL BE--
EXCUSE ME--BUT I HAVE A QUESTION...
...DOES THIS MEAN YOU'RE OUR NEW FRIEND?!
ADORABLE.
BUT NO. I'M NOT TALKING FRIENDS--WE'D BE PARTNERS!
AND BETWEEN YOUR RICH RESOURCES, AND OUR AMERICAN KNOW-HOW--WE ALL STAND TO REAP THE INCREDIBLE BENEFITS AND BRIGHTER FUTURE!
AAAH! REMEMBER MEEEE!

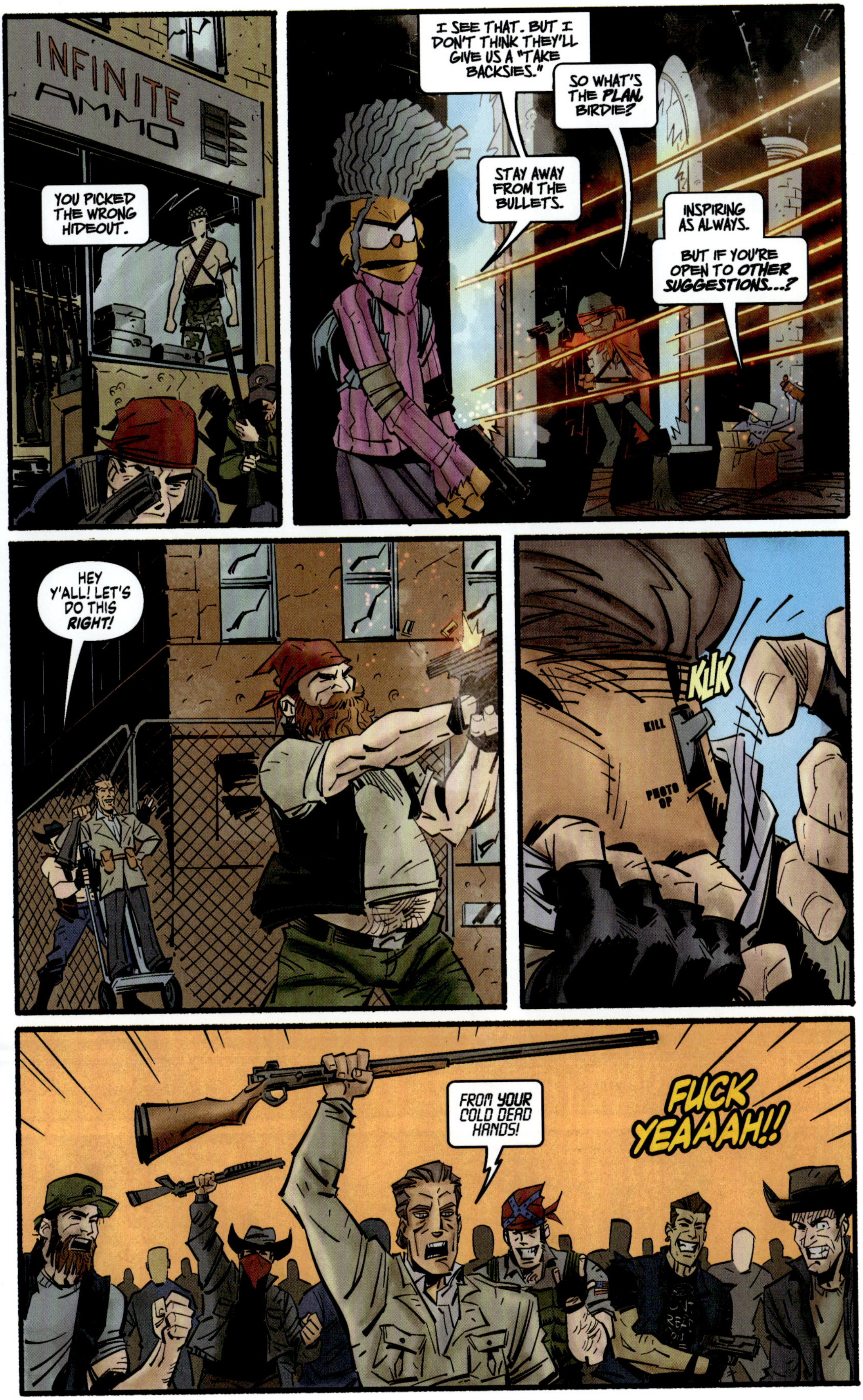
INFINITE AMMO
YOU PICKED THE WRONG HIDEOUT.
I SEE THAT. BUT I DON'T THINK THEY'LL GIVE US A "TAKE BACKSIES."
SO WHAT'S THE *PLAN*, BIRDIE?
STAY AWAY FROM THE BULLETS.
INSPIRING AS ALWAYS.
BUT IF YOU'RE OPEN TO *OTHER SUGGESTIONS*...?
HEY Y'ALL! LET'S DO THIS *RIGHT*!
KLIK
KILL
PHOTO OP
FROM *YOUR* COLD DEAD HANDS!
FUCK YEAAAH!!

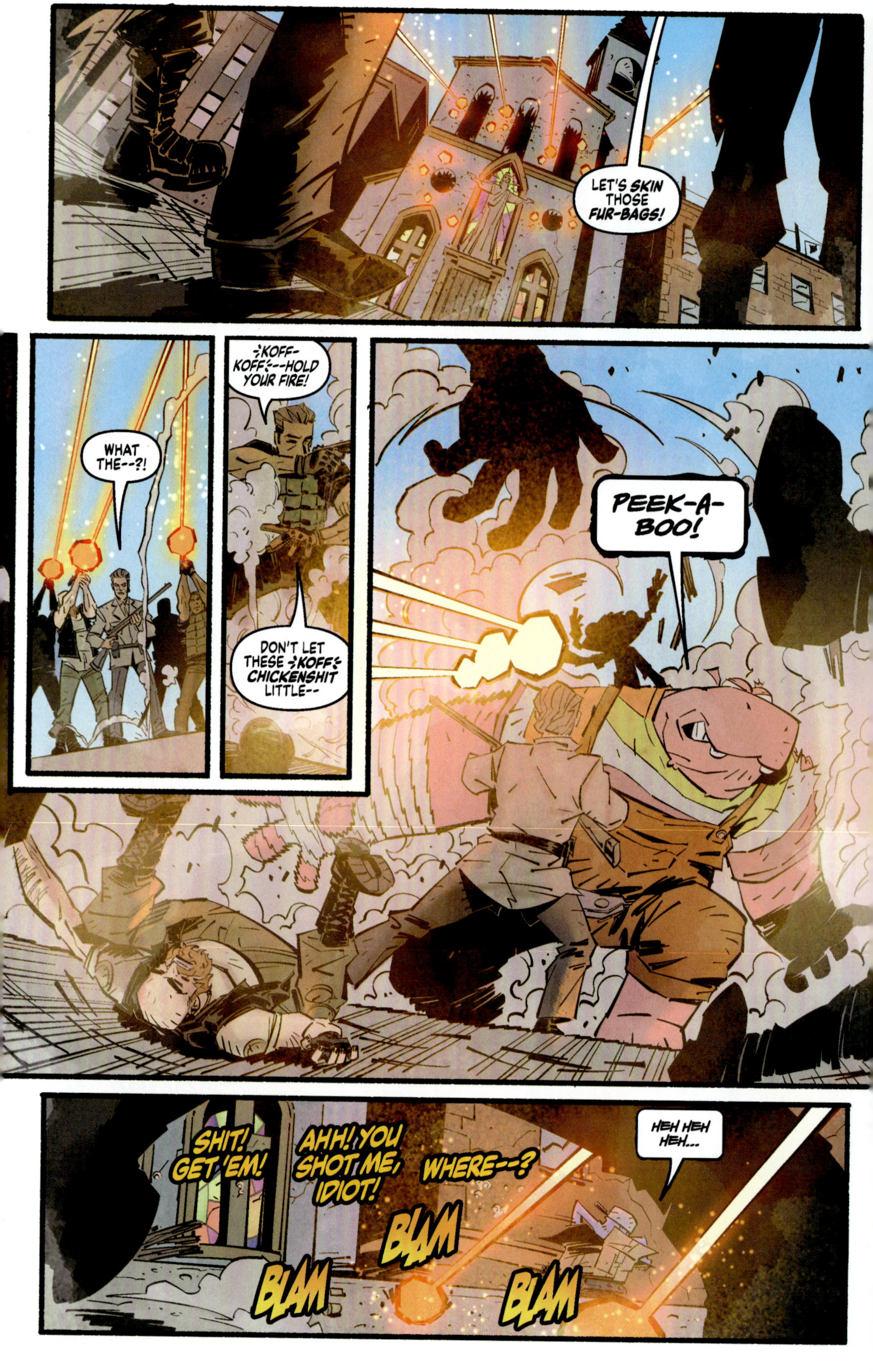
LET'S SKIN THOSE FUR-BAGS!
WHAT THE--?!
KOFF-KOFF--HOLD YOUR FIRE!
DON'T LET THESE *KOFF* CHICKENSHIT LITTLE--
PEEK-A-BOO!
SHIT! GET 'EM!
AHH! YOU SHOT ME, IDIOT!
WHERE--?
HEH HEH HEH...
BLAM
BLAM
BLAM

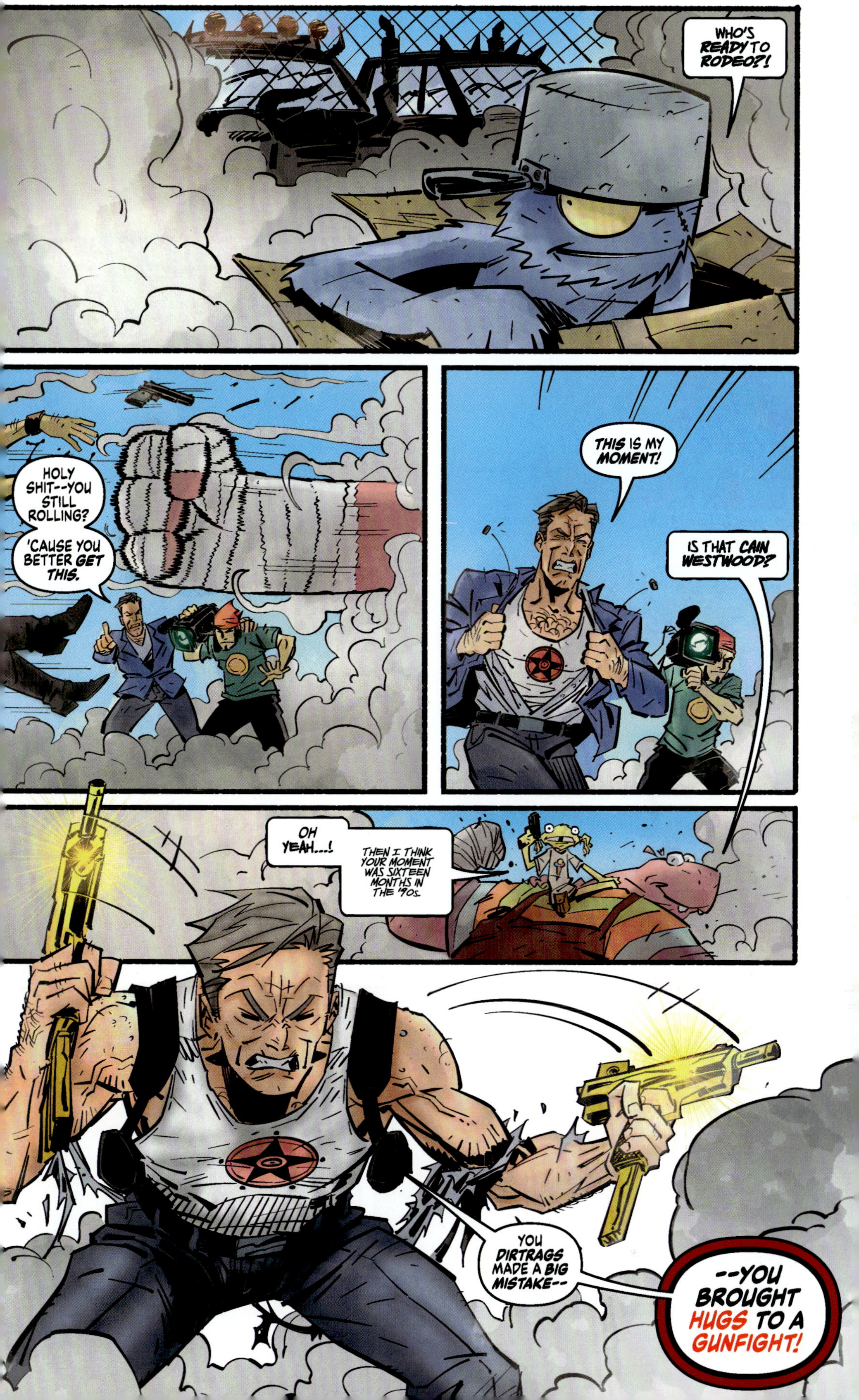
WHO'S READY TO RODEO?!
HOLY SHIT--YOU STILL ROLLING?
'CAUSE YOU BETTER GET THIS.
THIS IS MY MOMENT!
IS THAT CAIN WESTWOOD?
OH YEAH...!
THEN I THINK YOUR MOMENT WAS SIXTEEN MONTHS IN THE '90s.
YOU DIRTRAGS MADE A BIG MISTAKE--
--YOU BROUGHT HUGS TO A GUNFIGHT!

SHIT. THEY STOPPED TAKING THE BAIT!

SO?

SO WE'RE ABOUT TO BE SERIOUSLY OVERRUN, UNLESS--!

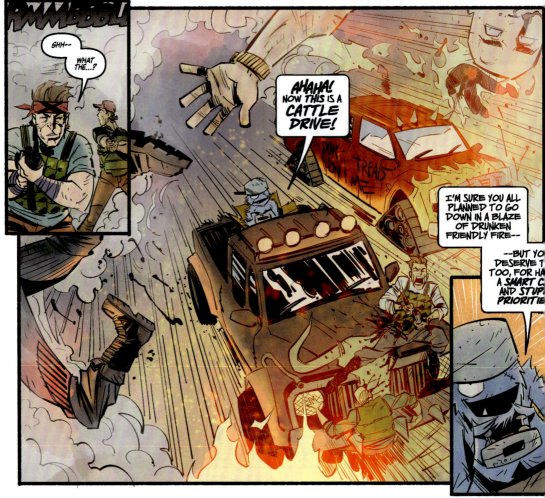

RMMBBBL

SHH--

WHAT THE...?

AHAHA! NOW THIS IS A CATTLE DRIVE!

I'M SURE YOU ALL PLANNED TO GO DOWN IN A BLAZE OF DRUNKEN FRIENDLY FIRE--

--BUT YO DESERVE T TOO, FOR HA A SMART C AND STUPI PRIORITIE

AAAAGGH!

*YOU SHOULDN'T B HERE, HERBERT.

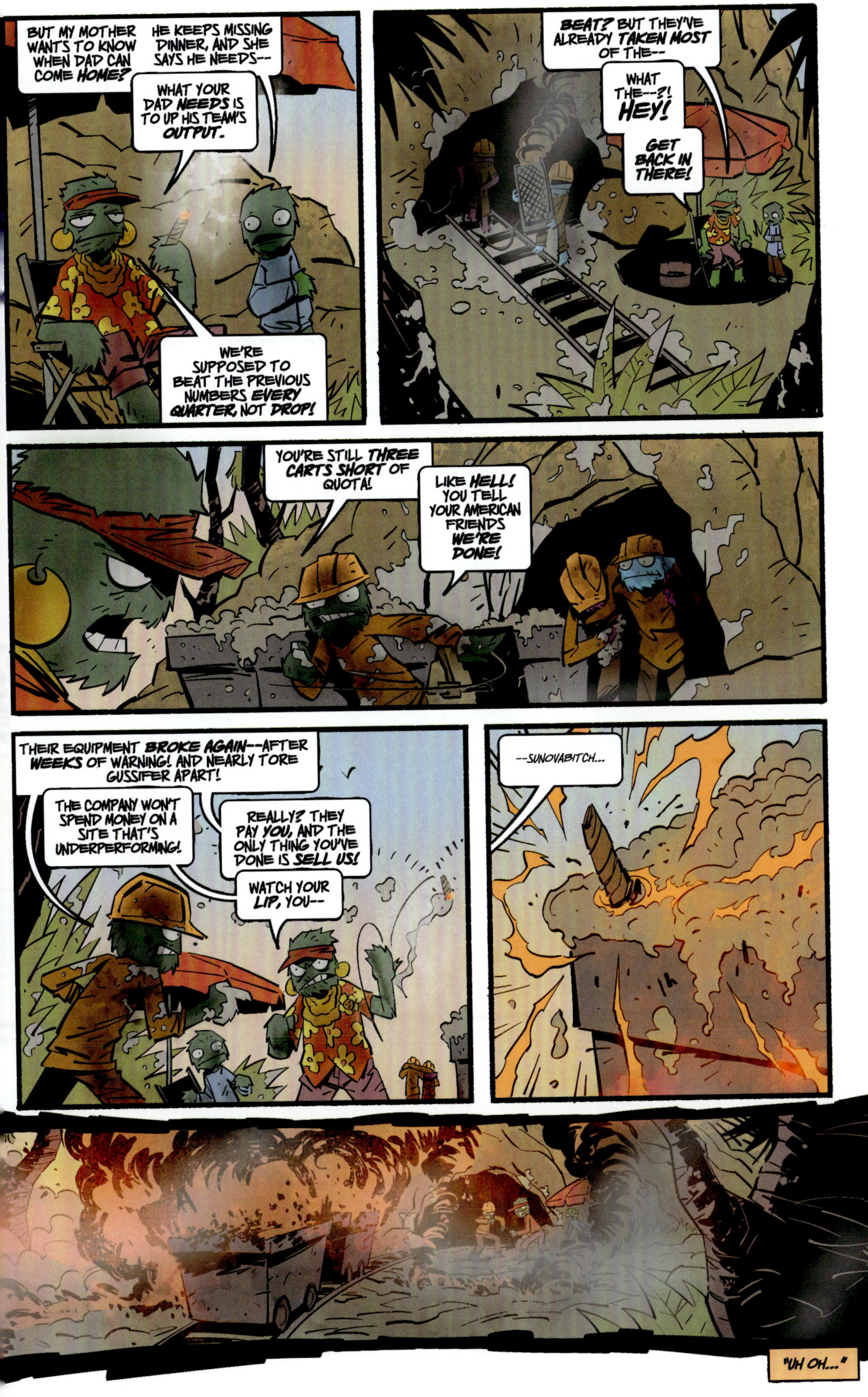

BUT MY MOTHER WANTS TO KNOW WHEN DAD CAN COME HOME?
HE KEEPS MISSING DINNER, AND SHE SAYS HE NEEDS--
WHAT YOUR DAD NEEDS IS TO UP HIS TEAM'S OUTPUT.
WE'RE SUPPOSED TO BEAT THE PREVIOUS NUMBERS EVERY QUARTER, NOT DROP!
BEAT? BUT THEY'VE ALREADY TAKEN MOST OF THE--
WHAT THE--?! HEY!
GET BACK IN THERE!
YOU'RE STILL THREE CARTS SHORT OF QUOTA!
LIKE HELL! YOU TELL YOUR AMERICAN FRIENDS WE'RE DONE!
THEIR EQUIPMENT BROKE AGAIN--AFTER WEEKS OF WARNING! AND NEARLY TORE GUSSIFER APART!
THE COMPANY WON'T SPEND MONEY ON A SITE THAT'S UNDERPERFORMING!
REALLY? THEY PAY YOU, AND THE ONLY THING YOU'VE DONE IS SELL US!
WATCH YOUR LIP, YOU--
--SUNOVABITCH...
"UH OH..."

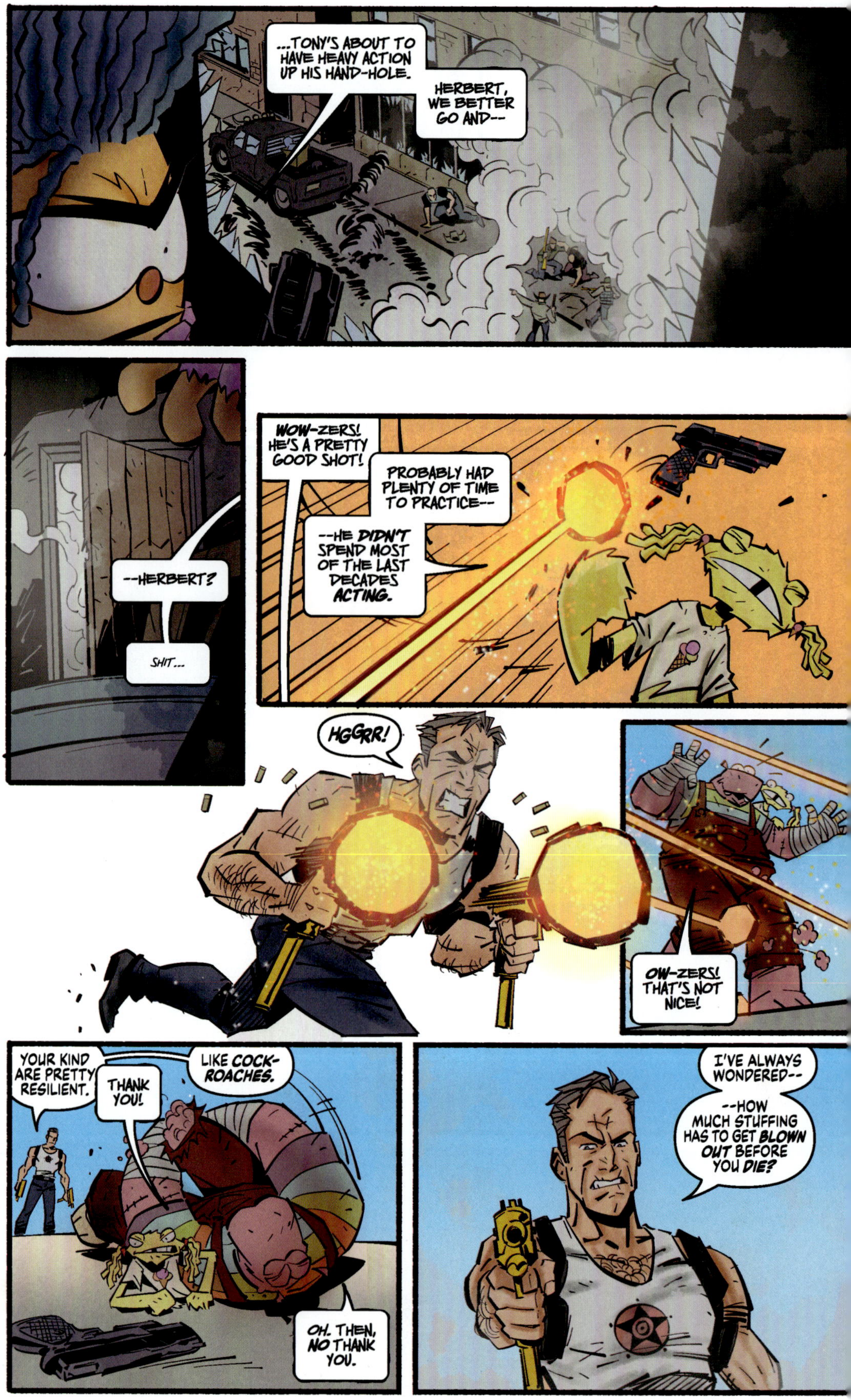
...TONY'S ABOUT TO HAVE HEAVY ACTION UP HIS HAND-HOLE.
HERBERT, WE BETTER GO AND--
--HERBERT?
SHIT...
WOW-ZERS! HE'S A PRETTY GOOD SHOT!
PROBABLY HAD PLENTY OF TIME TO PRACTICE--
--HE DIDN'T SPEND MOST OF THE LAST DECADES ACTING.
HGGRR!
OW-ZERS! THAT'S NOT NICE!
YOUR KIND ARE PRETTY RESILIENT.
THANK YOU!
LIKE COCK-ROACHES.
OH. THEN, NO THANK YOU.
I'VE ALWAYS WONDERED--
--HOW MUCH STUFFING HAS TO GET BLOWN OUT BEFORE YOU DIE?

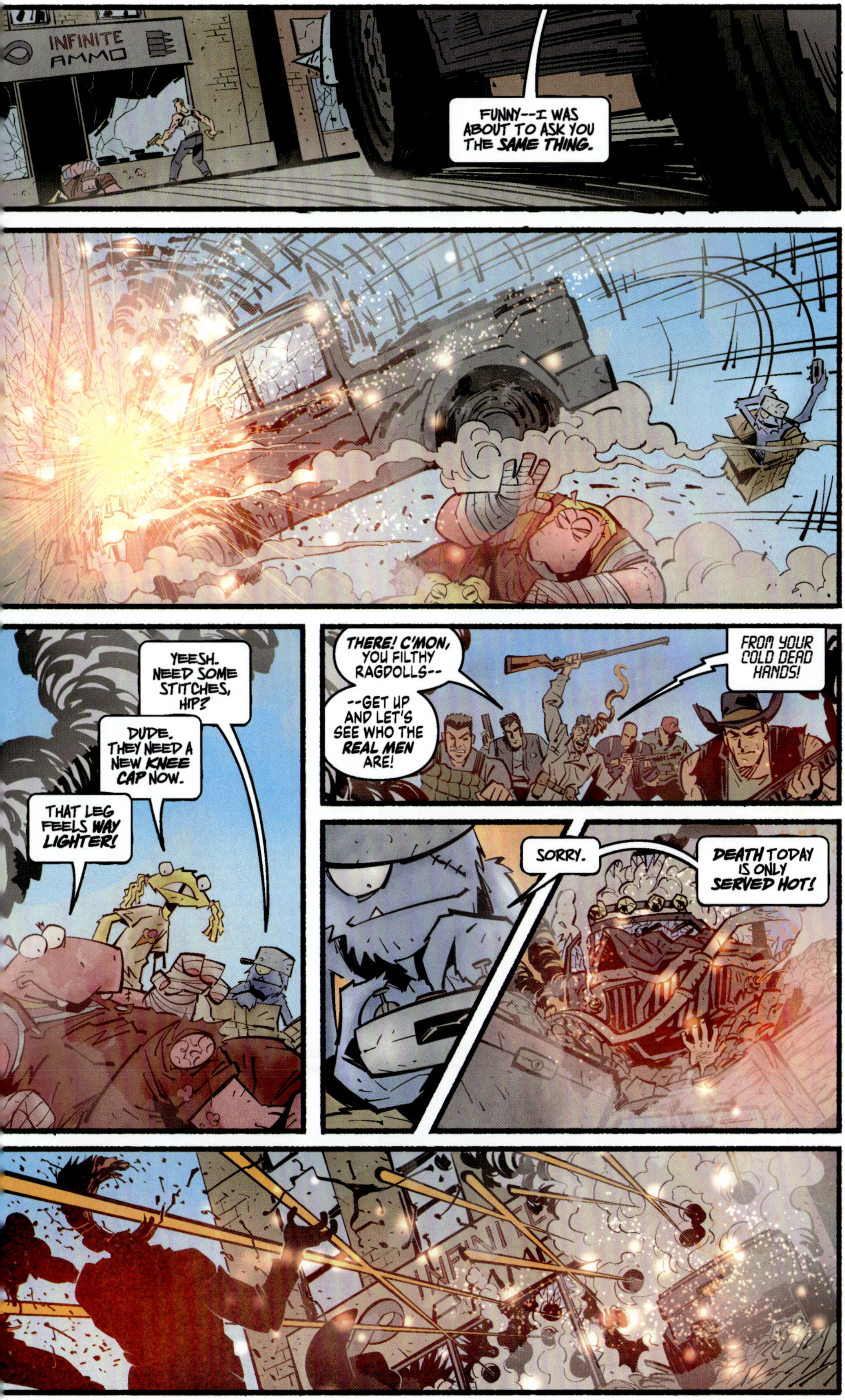
INFINITE AMMO
FUNNY--I WAS ABOUT TO ASK YOU THE SAME THING.
YEESH. NEED SOME STITCHES, HIP?
DUDE. THEY NEED A NEW KNEE CAP NOW.
THAT LEG FEELS WAY LIGHTER!
THERE! C'MON, YOU FILTHY RAGDOLLS--
--GET UP AND LET'S SEE WHO THE REAL MEN ARE!
FROM YOUR COLD DEAD HANDS!
SORRY.
DEATH TODAY IS ONLY SERVED HOT!

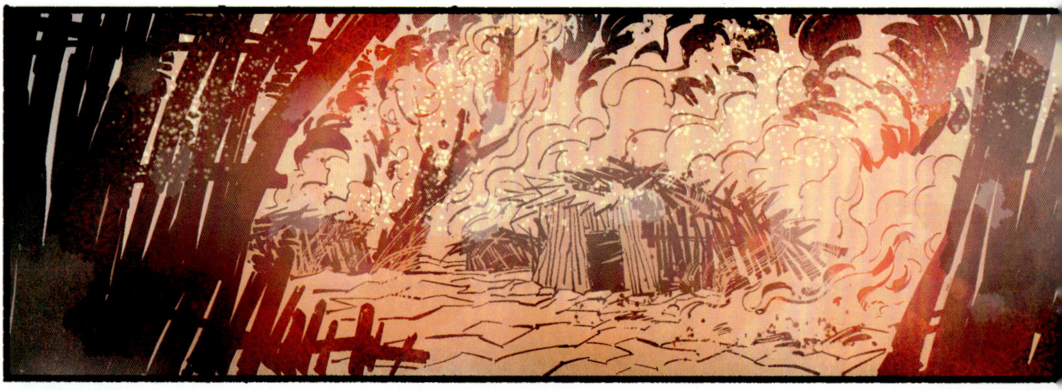

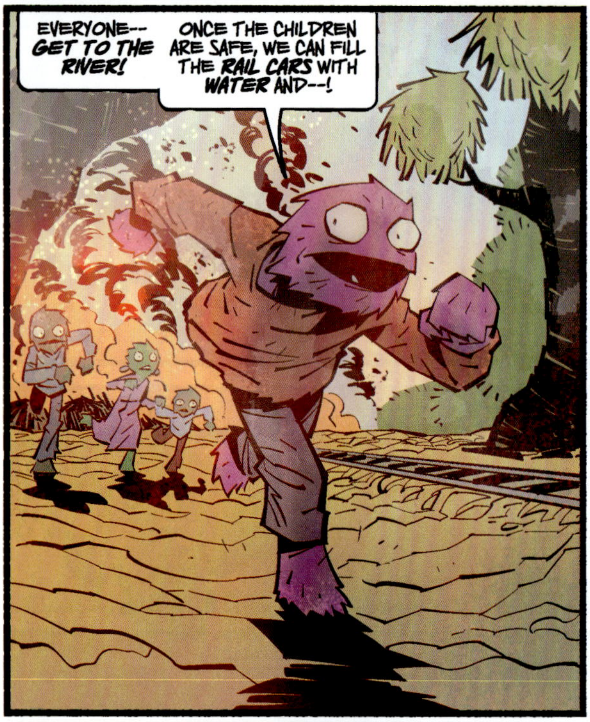
EVERYONE-- GET TO THE RIVER!
ONCE THE CHILDREN ARE SAFE, WE CAN FILL THE RAIL CARS WITH WATER AND--!

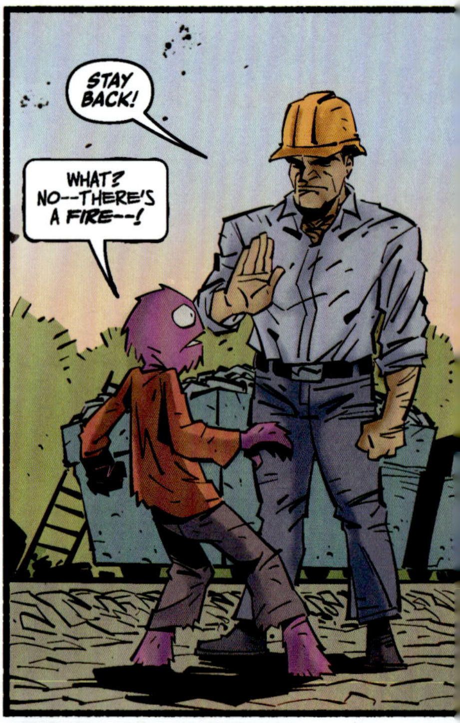
STAY BACK!
WHAT? NO--THERE'S A FIRE--!

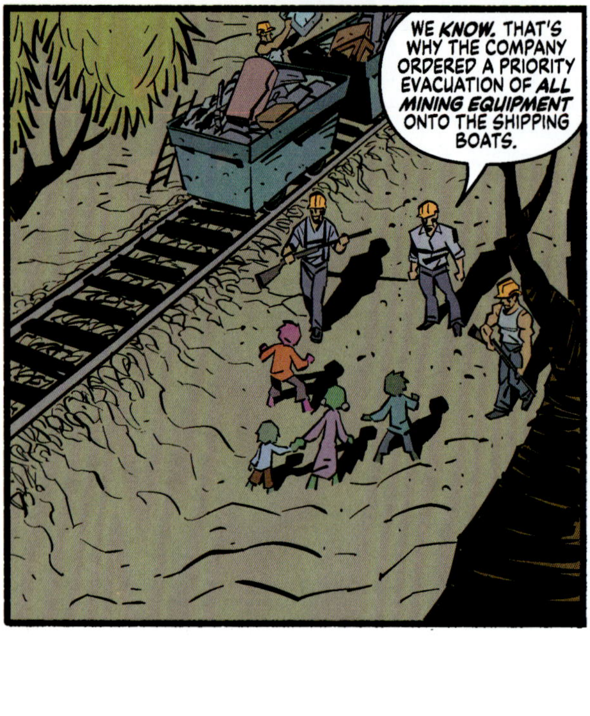
WE KNOW. THAT'S WHY THE COMPANY ORDERED A PRIORITY EVACUATION OF ALL MINING EQUIPMENT ONTO THE SHIPPING BOATS.

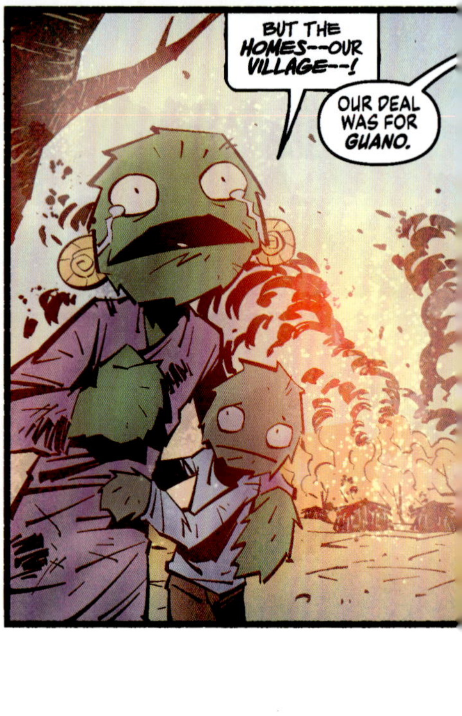
BUT THE HOMES--OUR VILLAGE--!
OUR DEAL WAS FOR GUANO.

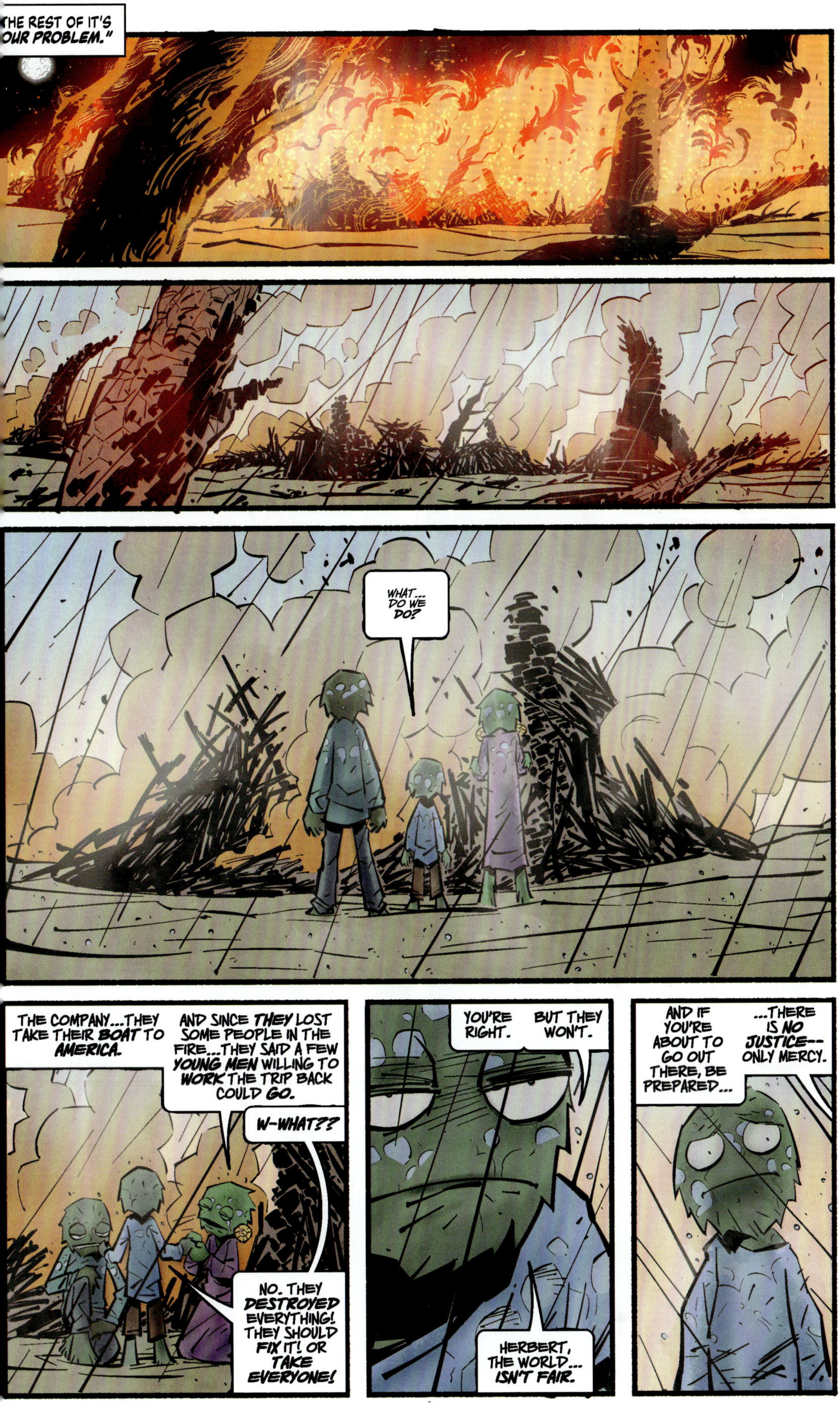
"THE REST OF IT'S OUR PROBLEM."
WHAT... DO WE DO?
THE COMPANY...THEY TAKE THEIR BOAT TO AMERICA.
AND SINCE THEY LOST SOME PEOPLE IN THE FIRE...THEY SAID A FEW YOUNG MEN WILLING TO WORK THE TRIP BACK COULD GO.
W-WHAT??
NO. THEY DESTROYED EVERYTHING! THEY SHOULD FIX IT! OR TAKE EVERYONE!
YOU'RE RIGHT.
BUT THEY WON'T.
HERBERT, THE WORLD... ISN'T FAIR.
AND IF YOU'RE ABOUT TO GO OUT THERE, BE PREPARED...
...THERE IS NO JUSTICE-- ONLY MERCY.

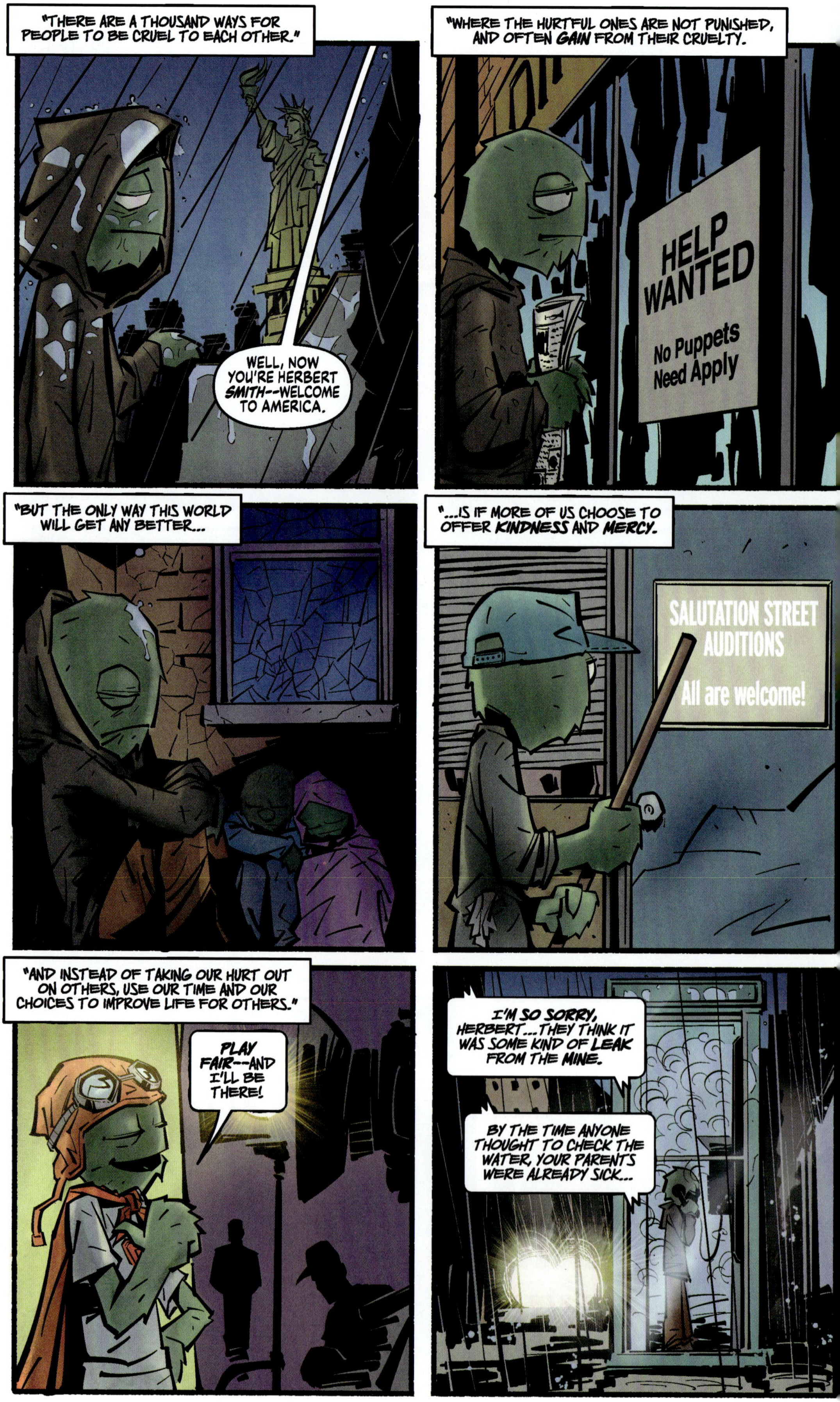
"THERE ARE A THOUSAND WAYS FOR PEOPLE TO BE CRUEL TO EACH OTHER."
WELL, NOW YOU'RE HERBERT SMITH--WELCOME TO AMERICA.
"WHERE THE HURTFUL ONES ARE NOT PUNISHED, AND OFTEN GAIN FROM THEIR CRUELTY.
HELP WANTED
No Puppets Need Apply
"BUT THE ONLY WAY THIS WORLD WILL GET ANY BETTER...
"...IS IF MORE OF US CHOOSE TO OFFER KINDNESS AND MERCY.
SALUTATION STREET AUDITIONS
All are welcome!
"AND INSTEAD OF TAKING OUR HURT OUT ON OTHERS, USE OUR TIME AND OUR CHOICES TO IMPROVE LIFE FOR OTHERS."
PLAY FAIR--AND I'LL BE THERE!
I'M SO SORRY, HERBERT...THEY THINK IT WAS SOME KIND OF LEAK FROM THE MINE.
BY THE TIME ANYONE THOUGHT TO CHECK THE WATER, YOUR PARENTS WERE ALREADY SICK...

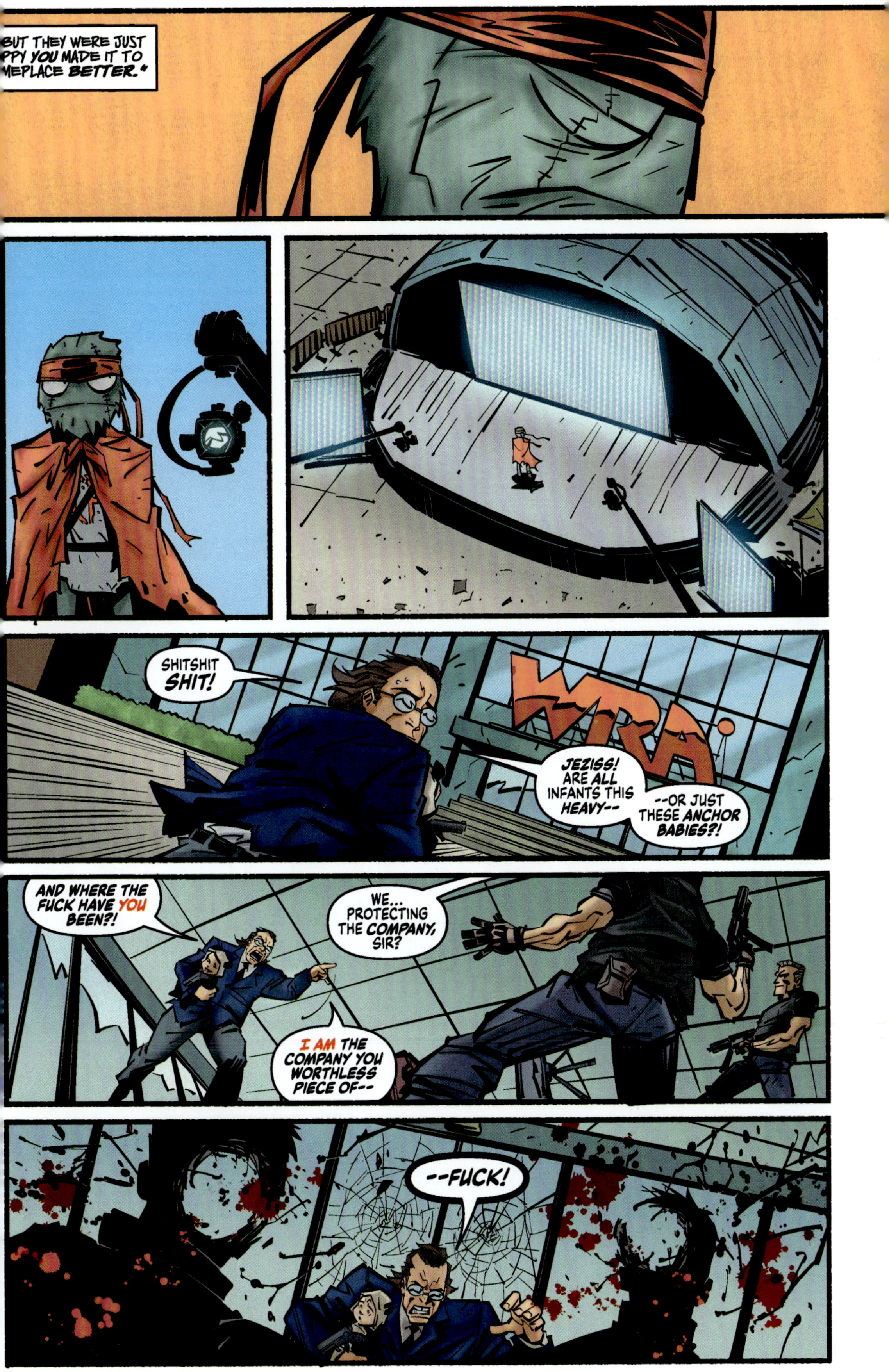
BUT THEY WERE JUST
PPY YOU MADE IT TO
MEPLACE BETTER."
SHITSHIT SHIT!
JEZISS! ARE ALL INFANTS THIS HEAVY--
--OR JUST THESE ANCHOR BABIES?!
AND WHERE THE FUCK HAVE YOU BEEN?!
WE... PROTECTING THE COMPANY, SIR?
I AM THE COMPANY YOU WORTHLESS PIECE OF--
--FUCK!

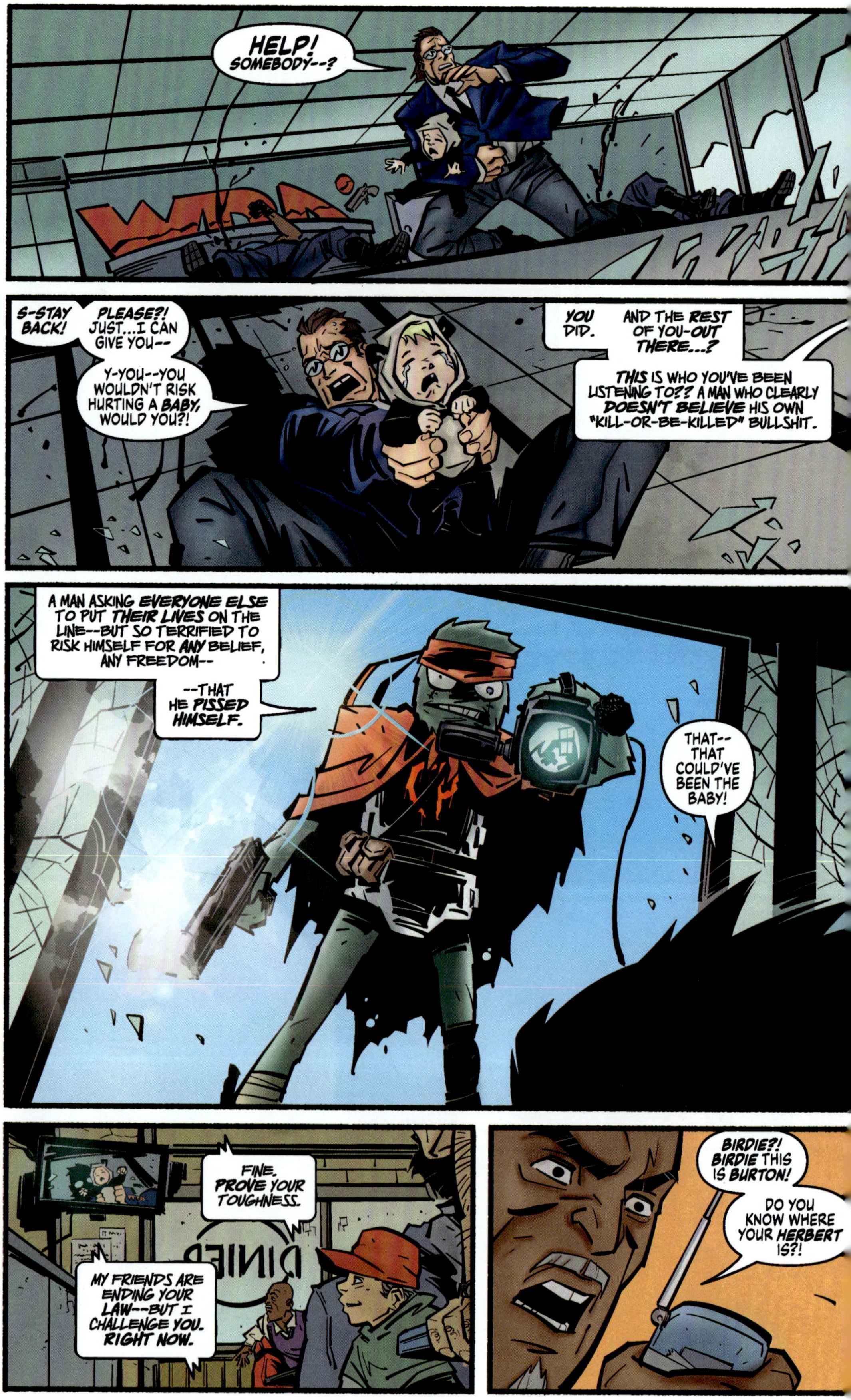
HELP! SOMEBODY--?
S-STAY BACK!
PLEASE?! JUST...I CAN GIVE YOU--
Y-YOU--YOU WOULDN'T RISK HURTING A BABY, WOULD YOU?!
YOU DID.
AND THE REST OF YOU-OUT THERE...?
THIS IS WHO YOU'VE BEEN LISTENING TO?? A MAN WHO CLEARLY DOESN'T BELIEVE HIS OWN "KILL-OR-BE-KILLED" BULLSHIT.
A MAN ASKING EVERYONE ELSE TO PUT THEIR LIVES ON THE LINE--BUT SO TERRIFIED TO RISK HIMSELF FOR ANY BELIEF, ANY FREEDOM--
--THAT HE PISSED HIMSELF.
THAT--THAT COULD'VE BEEN THE BABY!
FINE. PROVE YOUR TOUGHNESS.
MY FRIENDS ARE ENDING YOUR LAW--BUT I CHALLENGE YOU. RIGHT NOW.
DINER
BIRDIE?! BIRDIE THIS IS BURTON!
DO YOU KNOW WHERE YOUR HERBERT IS?!

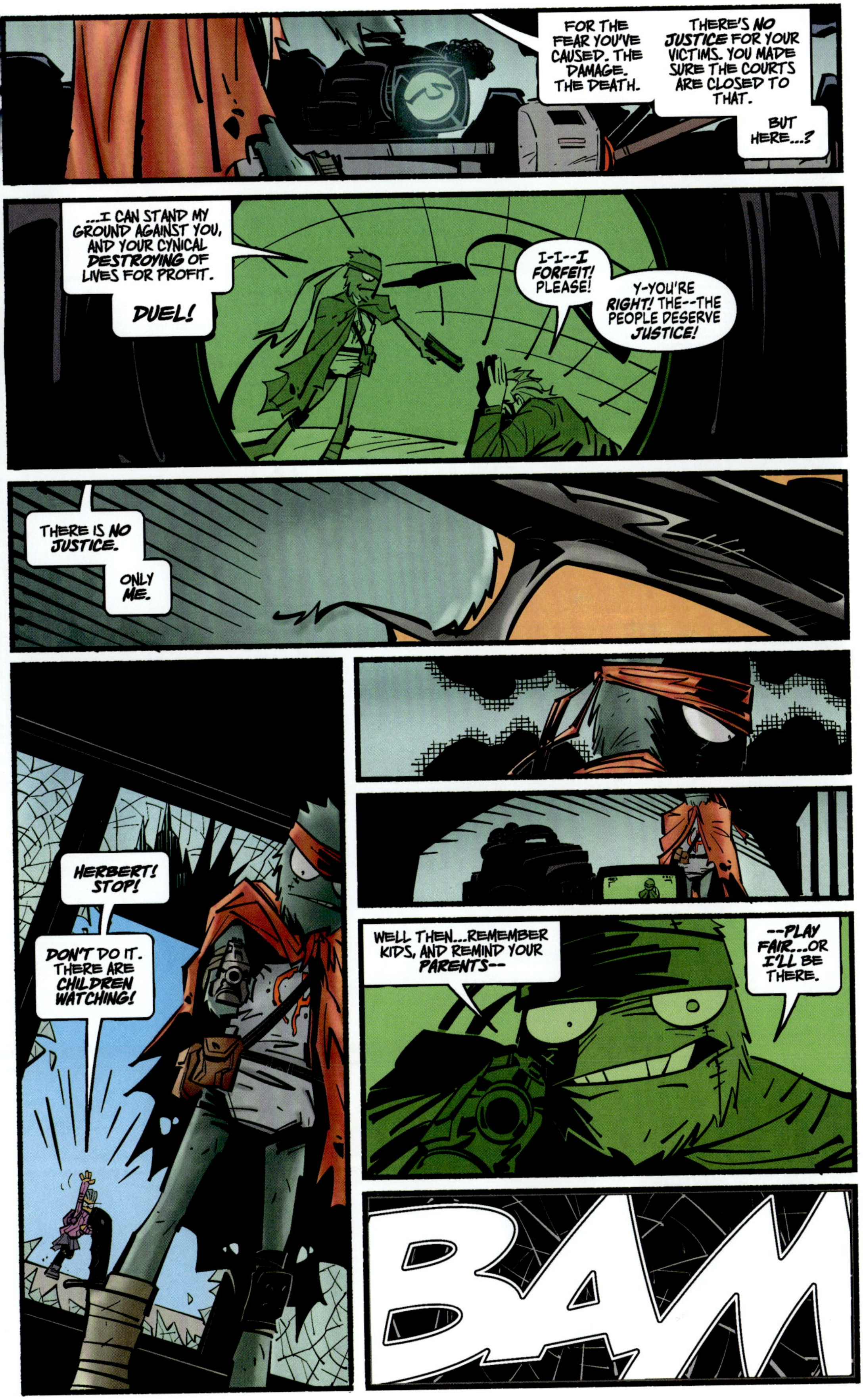
FOR THE FEAR YOU'VE CAUSED. THE DAMAGE. THE DEATH.
THERE'S NO JUSTICE FOR YOUR VICTIMS. YOU MADE SURE THE COURTS ARE CLOSED TO THAT.
BUT HERE...?
...I CAN STAND MY GROUND AGAINST YOU, AND YOUR CYNICAL DESTROYING OF LIVES FOR PROFIT.
DUEL!
I-I--I FORFEIT! PLEASE!
Y-YOU'RE RIGHT! THE--THE PEOPLE DESERVE JUSTICE!
THERE IS NO JUSTICE.
ONLY ME.
HERBERT! STOP!
DON'T DO IT. THERE ARE CHILDREN WATCHING!
WELL THEN...REMEMBER KIDS, AND REMIND YOUR PARENTS--
--PLAY FAIR...OR I'LL BE THERE.
BAM

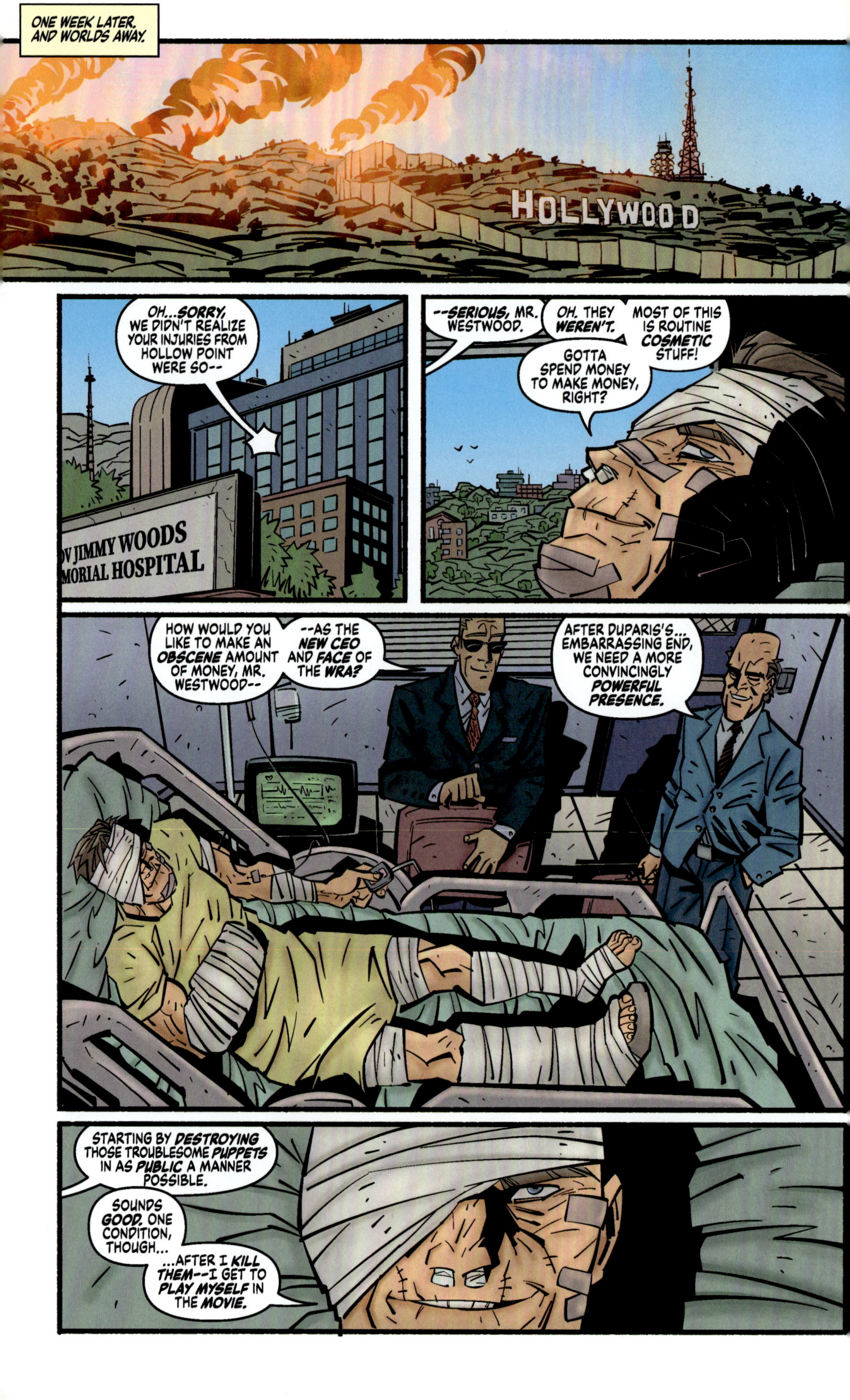
ONE WEEK LATER. AND WORLDS AWAY.
HOLLYWOOD
OH...SORRY, WE DIDN'T REALIZE YOUR INJURIES FROM HOLLOW POINT WERE SO--
JIMMY WOODS
MORIAL HOSPITAL
--SERIOUS, MR. WESTWOOD.
OH. THEY WEREN'T.
MOST OF THIS IS ROUTINE COSMETIC STUFF!
GOTTA SPEND MONEY TO MAKE MONEY, RIGHT?
HOW WOULD YOU LIKE TO MAKE AN OBSCENE AMOUNT OF MONEY, MR. WESTWOOD--
--AS THE NEW CEO AND FACE OF THE WRA?
AFTER DUPARIS'S... EMBARRASSING END, WE NEED A MORE CONVINCINGLY POWERFUL PRESENCE.
STARTING BY DESTROYING THOSE TROUBLESOME PUPPETS IN AS PUBLIC A MANNER POSSIBLE.
SOUNDS GOOD. ONE CONDITION, THOUGH...
...AFTER I KILL THEM--I GET TO PLAY MYSELF IN THE MOVIE.

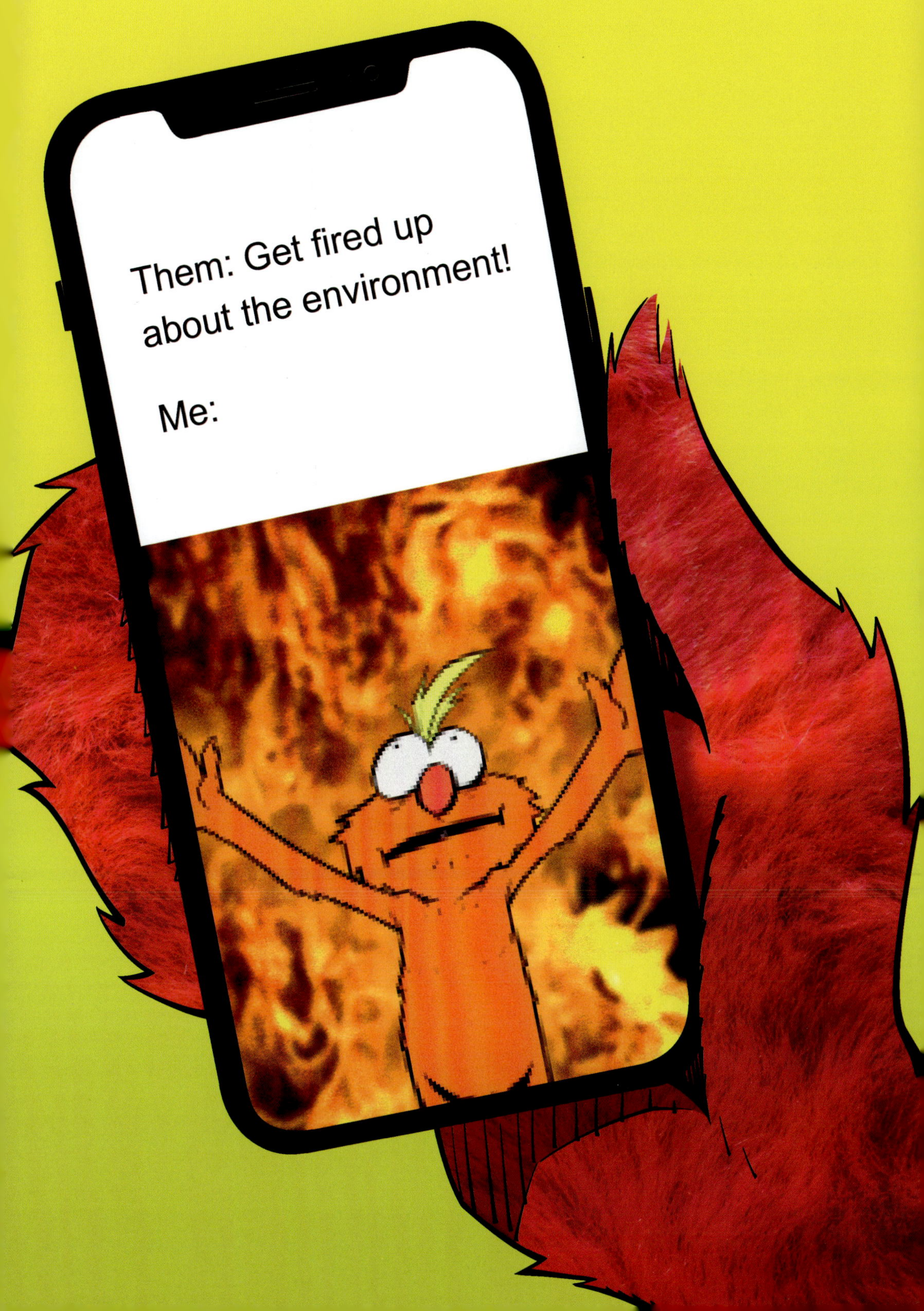
Them: Get fired up about the environment!
Me:

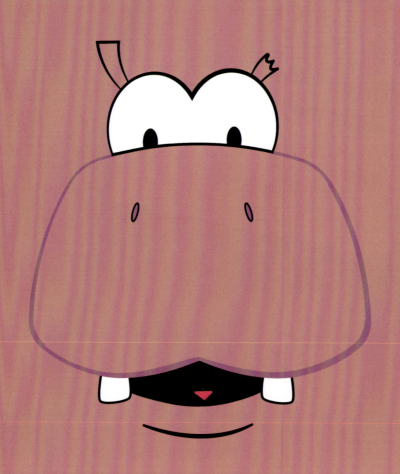

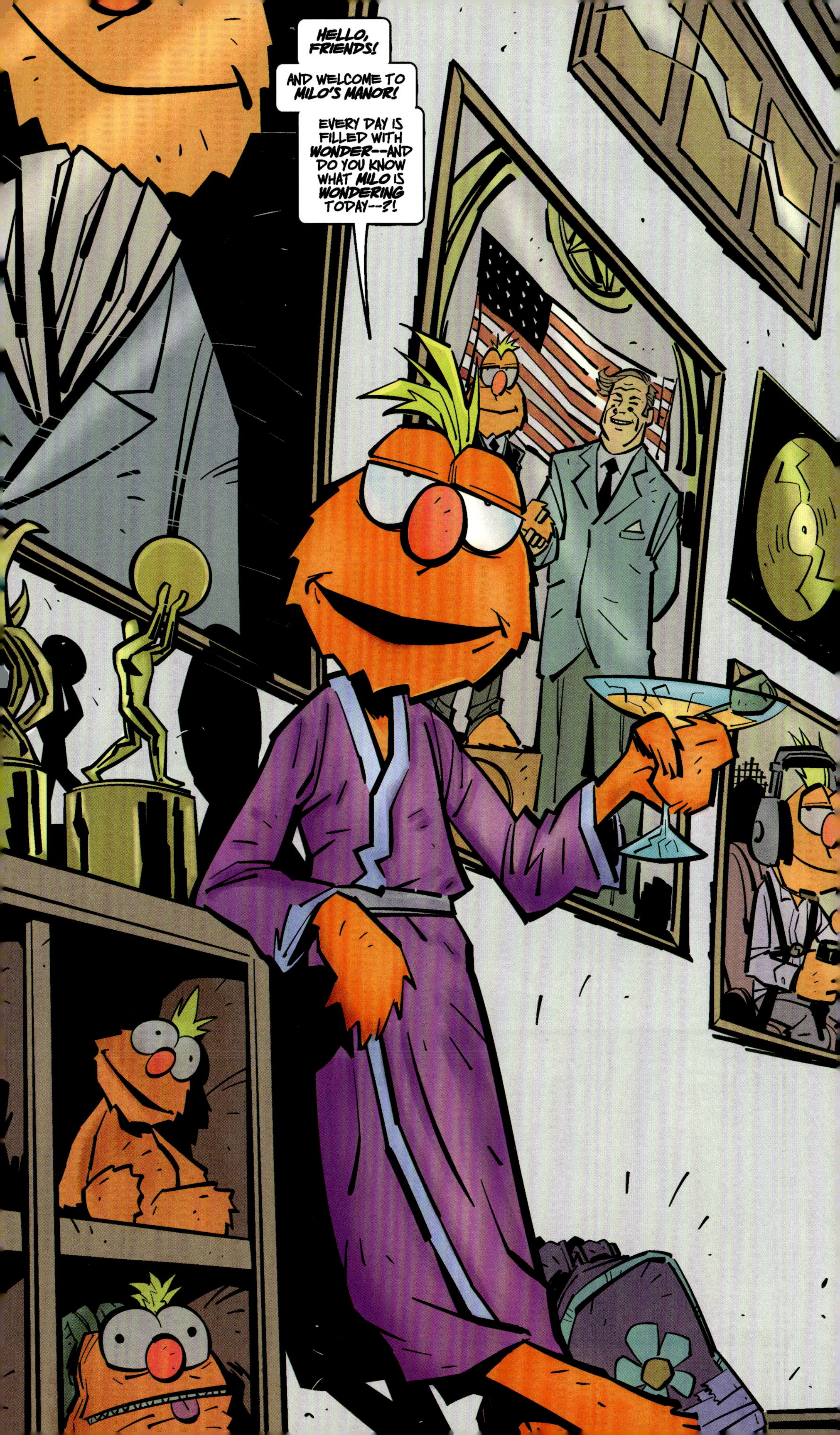
HELLO, FRIENDS!
AND WELCOME TO MILO'S MANOR!
EVERY DAY IS FILLED WITH WONDER--AND DO YOU KNOW WHAT MILO IS WONDERING TODAY--?!

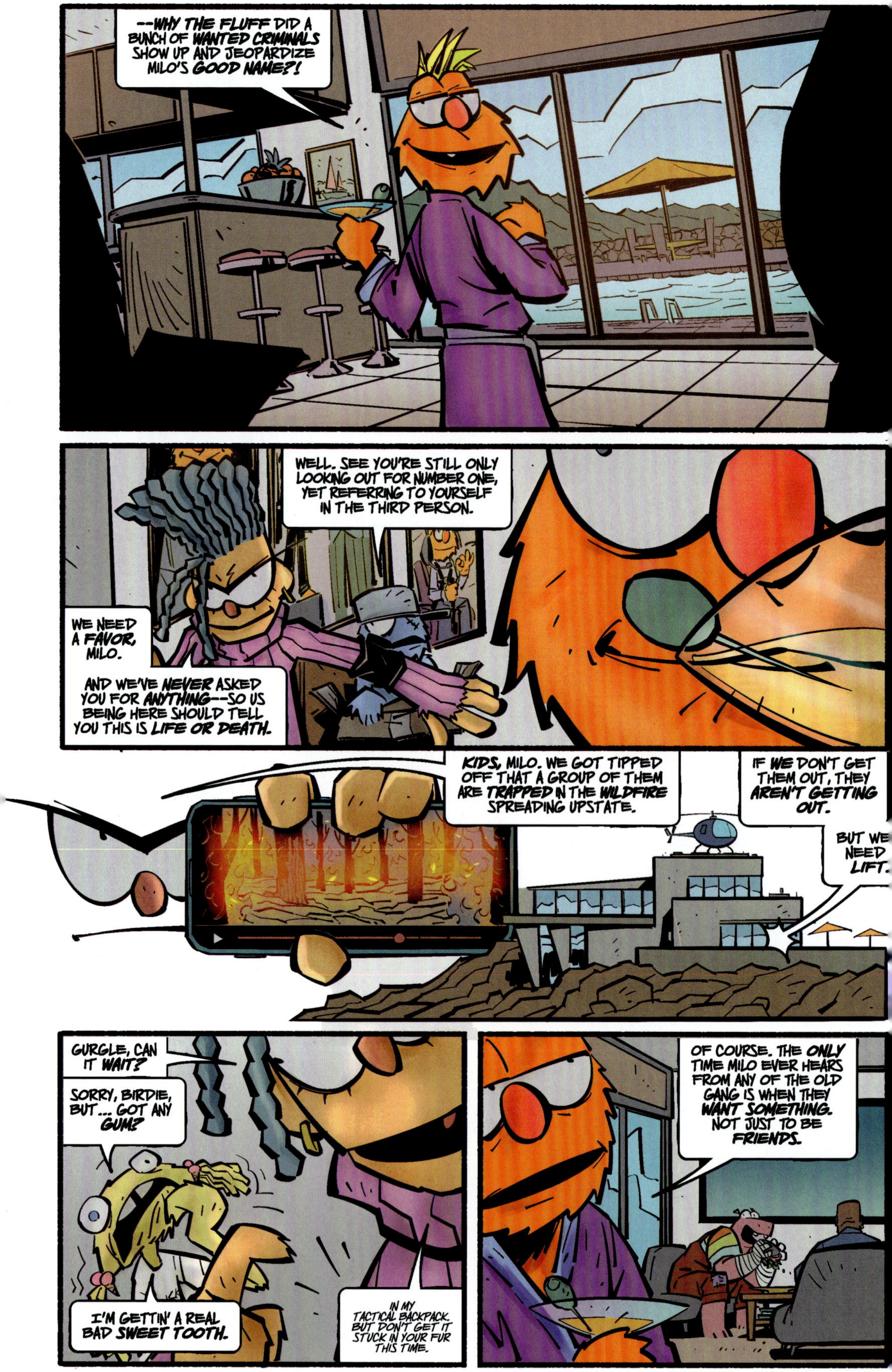
--WHY THE FLUFF DID A BUNCH OF WANTED CRIMINALS SHOW UP AND JEOPARDIZE MILO'S GOOD NAME?!
WELL. SEE YOU'RE STILL ONLY LOOKING OUT FOR NUMBER ONE, YET REFERRING TO YOURSELF IN THE THIRD PERSON.
WE NEED A FAVOR, MILO.
AND WE'VE NEVER ASKED YOU FOR ANYTHING--SO US BEING HERE SHOULD TELL YOU THIS IS LIFE OR DEATH.
KIDS, MILO. WE GOT TIPPED OFF THAT A GROUP OF THEM ARE TRAPPED IN THE WILDFIRE SPREADING UPSTATE.
IF WE DON'T GET THEM OUT, THEY AREN'T GETTING OUT.
BUT WE NEED LIFT.
GURGLE, CAN IT WAIT?
SORRY, BIRDIE, BUT... GOT ANY GUM?
I'M GETTIN' A REAL BAD SWEET TOOTH.
IN MY TACTICAL BACKPACK. BUT DON'T GET IT STUCK IN YOUR FUR THIS TIME.
OF COURSE. THE ONLY TIME MILO EVER HEARS FROM ANY OF THE OLD GANG IS WHEN THEY WANT SOMETHING. NOT JUST TO BE FRIENDS.

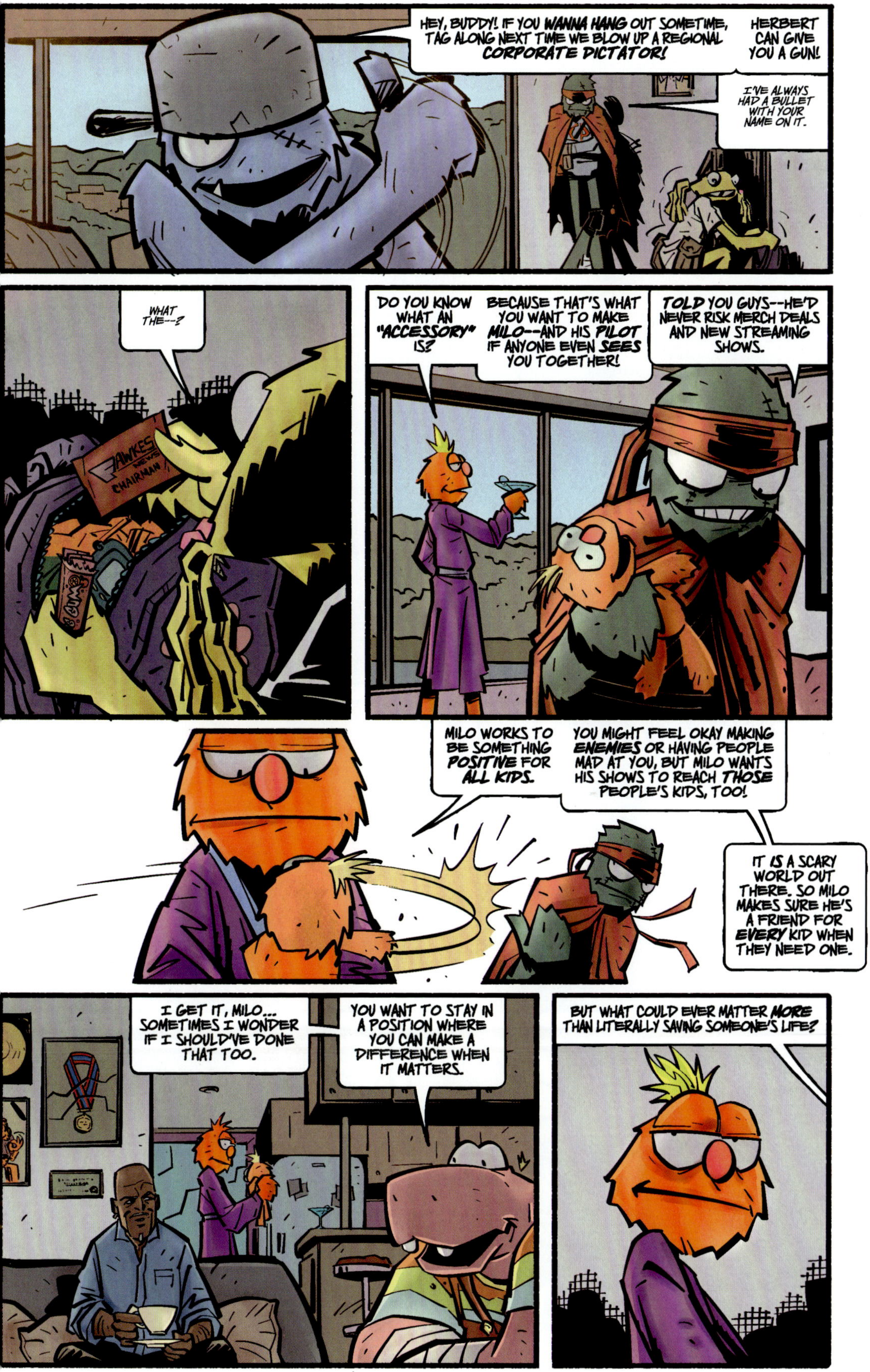
HEY, BUDDY! IF YOU WANNA HANG OUT SOMETIME, TAG ALONG NEXT TIME WE BLOW UP A REGIONAL CORPORATE DICTATOR!
HERBERT CAN GIVE YOU A GUN!
I'VE ALWAYS HAD A BULLET WITH YOUR NAME ON IT.
WHAT THE--?
HAWKES NEWS CHAIRMAN
DO YOU KNOW WHAT AN "ACCESSORY" IS?
BECAUSE THAT'S WHAT YOU WANT TO MAKE MILO--AND HIS PILOT IF ANYONE EVEN SEES YOU TOGETHER!
TOLD YOU GUYS--HE'D NEVER RISK MERCH DEALS AND NEW STREAMING SHOWS.
MILO WORKS TO BE SOMETHING POSITIVE FOR ALL KIDS.
YOU MIGHT FEEL OKAY MAKING ENEMIES OR HAVING PEOPLE MAD AT YOU, BUT MILO WANTS HIS SHOWS TO REACH THOSE PEOPLE'S KIDS, TOO!
IT IS A SCARY WORLD OUT THERE. SO MILO MAKES SURE HE'S A FRIEND FOR EVERY KID WHEN THEY NEED ONE.
I GET IT, MILO... SOMETIMES I WONDER IF I SHOULD'VE DONE THAT TOO.
YOU WANT TO STAY IN A POSITION WHERE YOU CAN MAKE A DIFFERENCE WHEN IT MATTERS.
BUT WHAT COULD EVER MATTER MORE THAN LITERALLY SAVING SOMEONE'S LIFE?

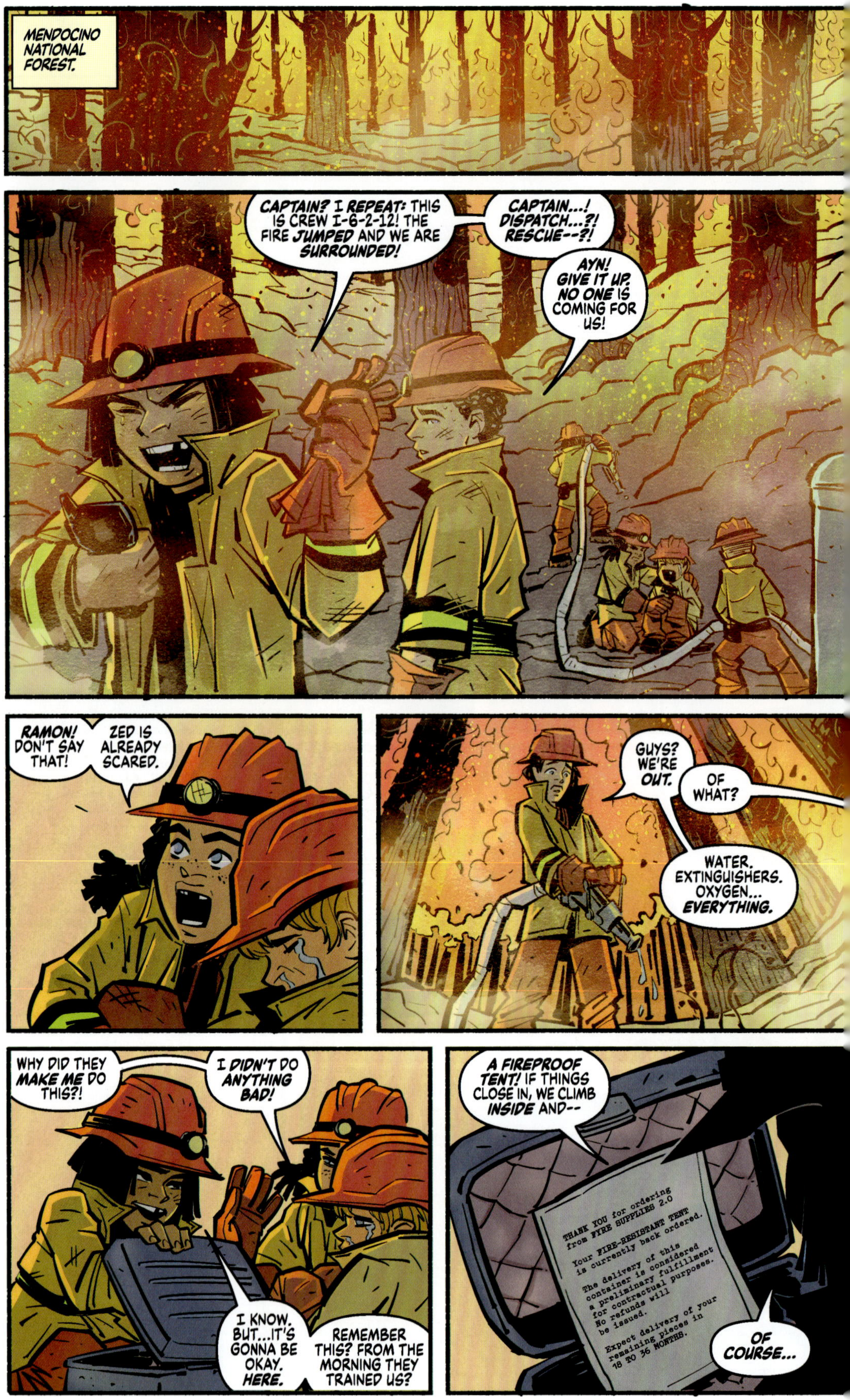
MENDOCINO NATIONAL FOREST.
CAPTAIN? I REPEAT: THIS IS CREW I-6-2-12! THE FIRE JUMPED AND WE ARE SURROUNDED!
CAPTAIN...! DISPATCH...?! RESCUE--?!
AYN! GIVE IT UP. NO ONE IS COMING FOR US!
RAMON! DON'T SAY THAT!
ZED IS ALREADY SCARED.
GUYS? WE'RE OUT.
OF WHAT?
WATER. EXTINGUISHERS. OXYGEN... EVERYTHING.
WHY DID THEY MAKE ME DO THIS?!
I DIDN'T DO ANYTHING BAD!
I KNOW. BUT...IT'S GONNA BE OKAY. HERE.
REMEMBER THIS? FROM THE MORNING THEY TRAINED US?
A FIREPROOF TENT! IF THINGS CLOSE IN, WE CLIMB INSIDE AND--
THANK YOU for ordering from FYRE SUPPLIES 2.0
Your FIRE-RESISTANT TENT is currently back ordered.
The delivery of this container is considered a preliminary fulfillment for contractual purposes. No refunds will be issued.
Expect delivery of your remaining pieces in 18 TO 36 MONTHS.
OF COURSE...

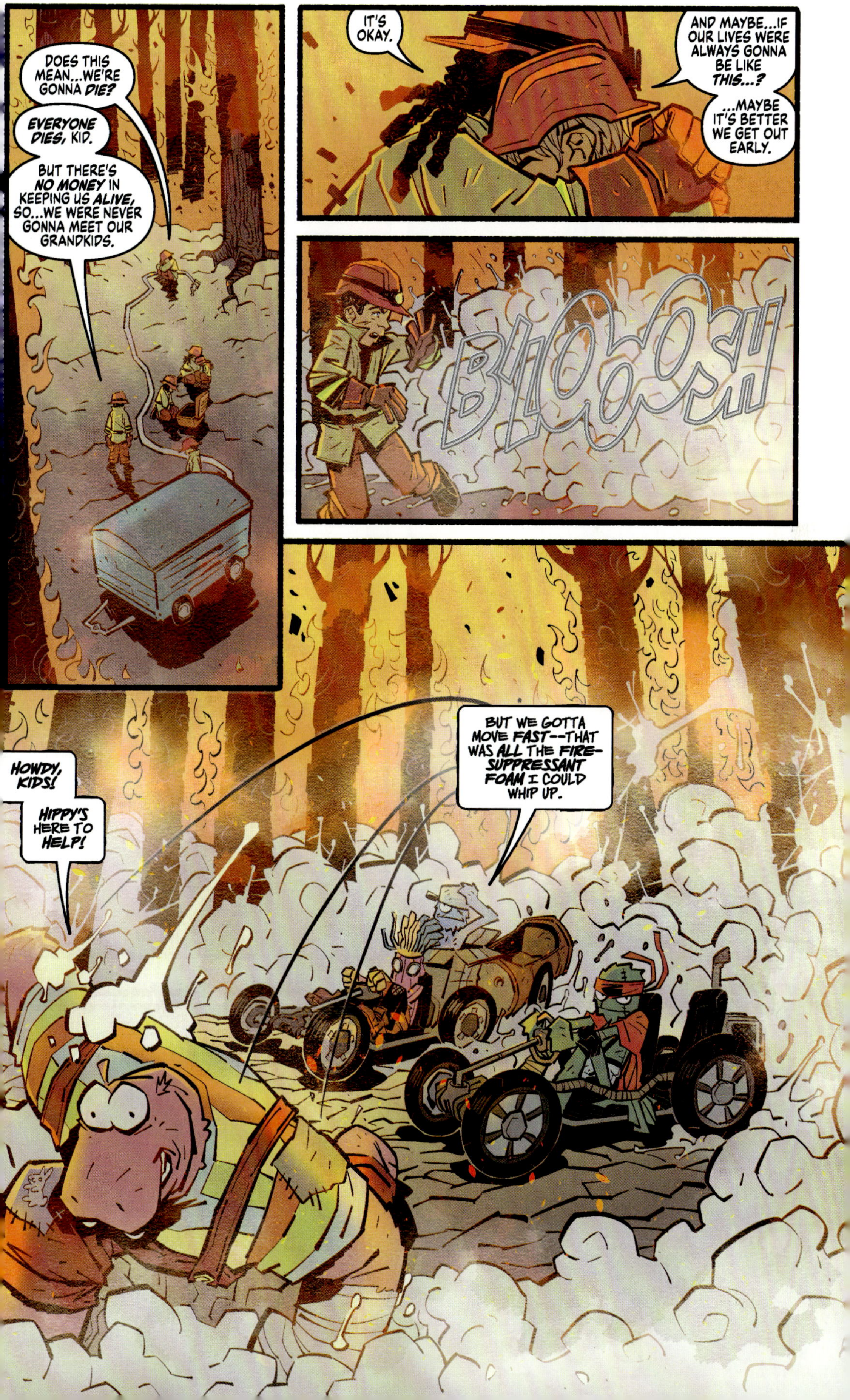
DOES THIS MEAN...WE'RE GONNA DIE?
EVERYONE DIES, KID.
BUT THERE'S NO MONEY IN KEEPING US ALIVE, SO...WE WERE NEVER GONNA MEET OUR GRANDKIDS.
IT'S OKAY.
AND MAYBE...IF OUR LIVES WERE ALWAYS GONNA BE LIKE THIS...?
...MAYBE IT'S BETTER WE GET OUT EARLY.
BLOOOSH
HOWDY, KIDS!
HIPPY'S HERE TO HELP!
BUT WE GOTTA MOVE FAST--THAT WAS ALL THE FIRE-SUPPRESSANT FOAM I COULD WHIP UP.

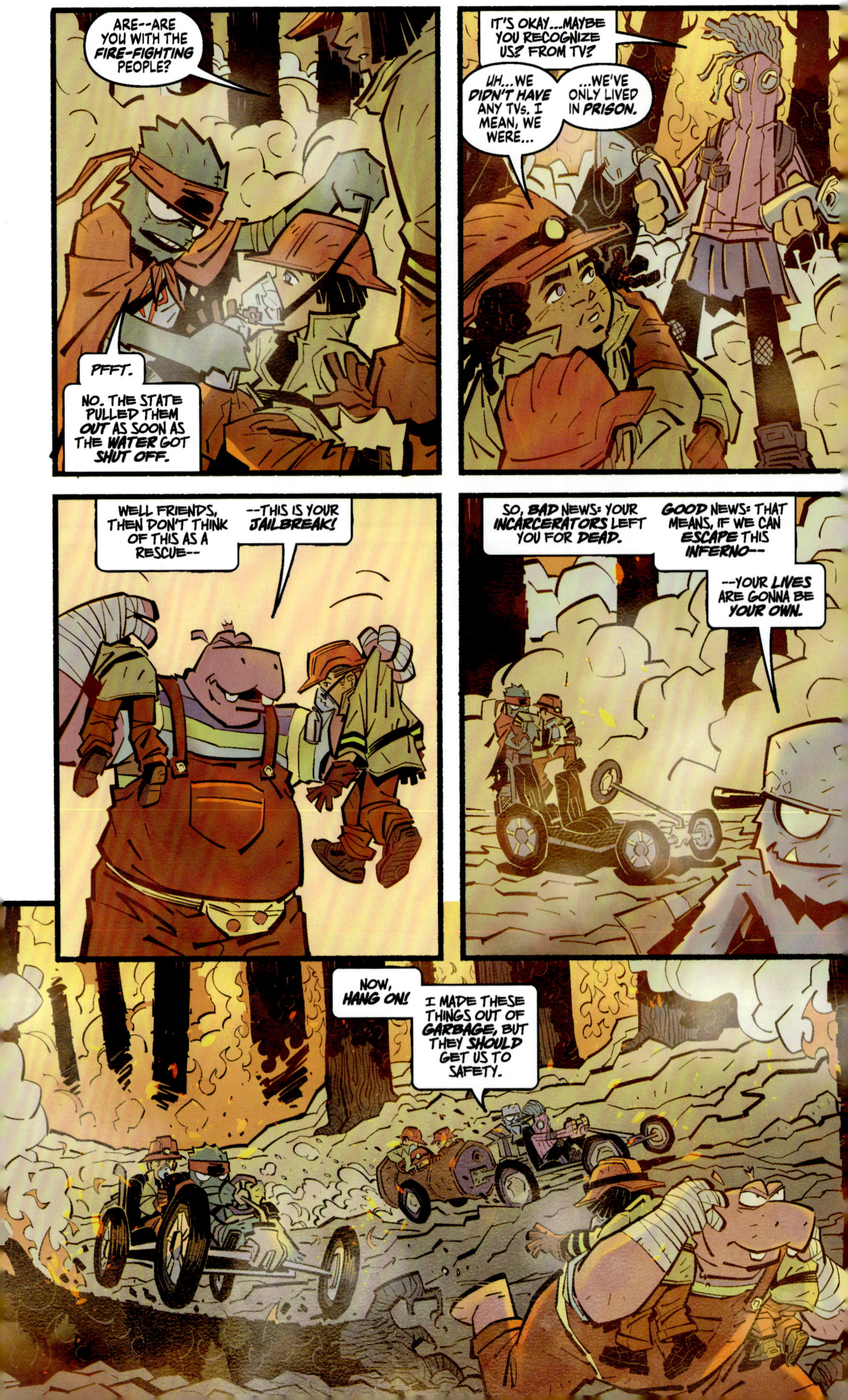
ARE--ARE YOU WITH THE FIRE-FIGHTING PEOPLE?
PFFT.
NO. THE STATE PULLED THEM OUT AS SOON AS THE WATER GOT SHUT OFF.
IT'S OKAY...MAYBE YOU RECOGNIZE US? FROM TV?
UH...WE DIDN'T HAVE ANY TVs. I MEAN, WE WERE...
...WE'VE ONLY LIVED IN PRISON.
WELL FRIENDS, THEN DON'T THINK OF THIS AS A RESCUE--
--THIS IS YOUR JAILBREAK!
SO, BAD NEWS: YOUR INCARCERATORS LEFT YOU FOR DEAD.
GOOD NEWS: THAT MEANS, IF WE CAN ESCAPE THIS INFERNO--
--YOUR LIVES ARE GONNA BE YOUR OWN.
NOW, HANG ON!
I MADE THESE THINGS OUT OF GARBAGE, BUT THEY SHOULD GET US TO SAFETY.

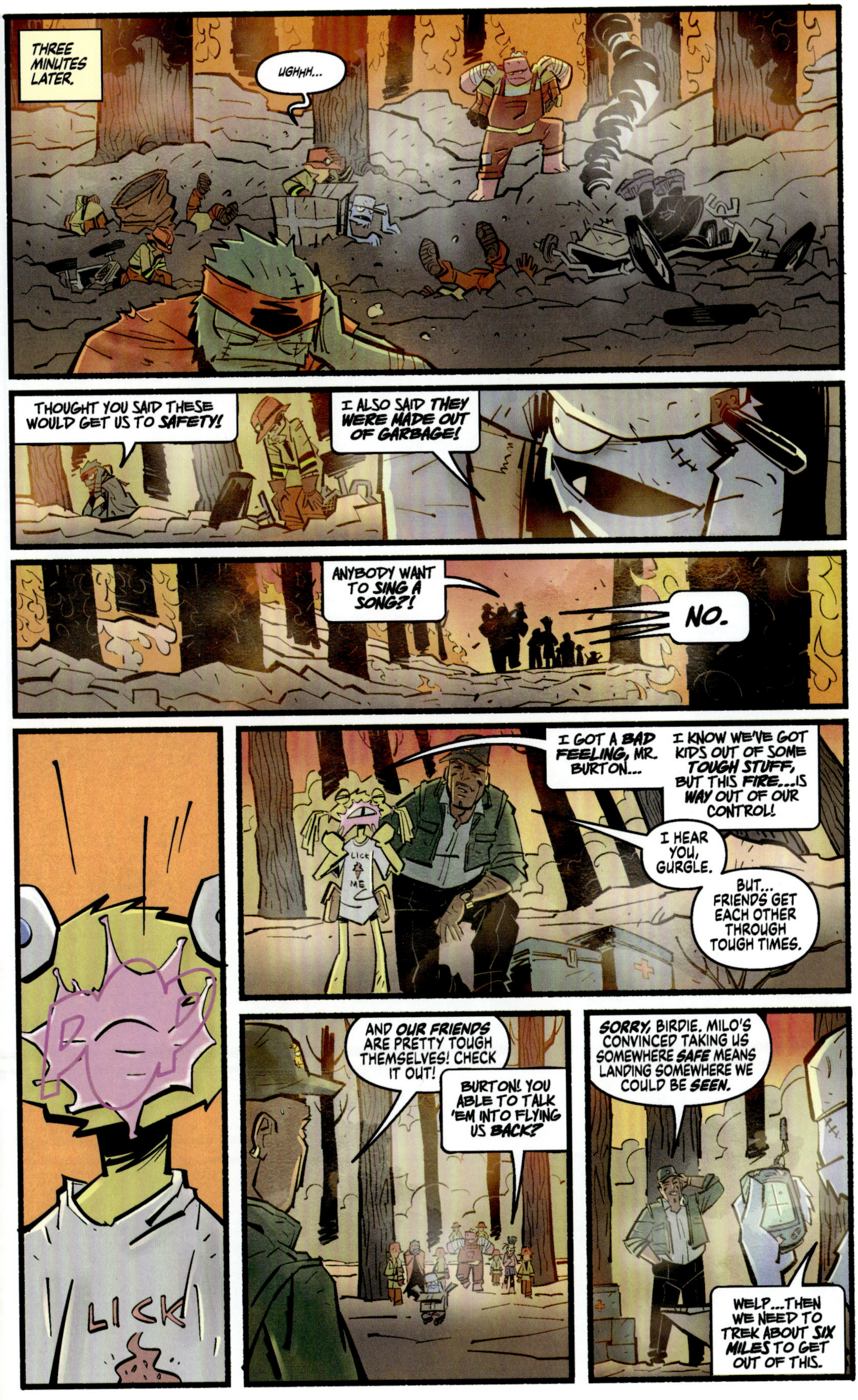
THREE MINUTES LATER.
UGHHH...
THOUGHT YOU SAID THESE WOULD GET US TO SAFETY!
I ALSO SAID THEY WERE MADE OUT OF GARBAGE!
ANYBODY WANT TO SING A SONG?!
NO.
POP
I GOT A BAD FEELING, MR. BURTON...
I KNOW WE'VE GOT KIDS OUT OF SOME TOUGH STUFF, BUT THIS FIRE...IS WAY OUT OF OUR CONTROL!
I HEAR YOU, GURGLE.
BUT... FRIENDS GET EACH OTHER THROUGH TOUGH TIMES.
LICK ME
AND OUR FRIENDS ARE PRETTY TOUGH THEMSELVES! CHECK IT OUT!
BURTON! YOU ABLE TO TALK 'EM INTO FLYING US BACK?
SORRY, BIRDIE. MILO'S CONVINCED TAKING US SOMEWHERE SAFE MEANS LANDING SOMEWHERE WE COULD BE SEEN.
WELP...THEN WE NEED TO TREK ABOUT SIX MILES TO GET OUT OF THIS.
LICK

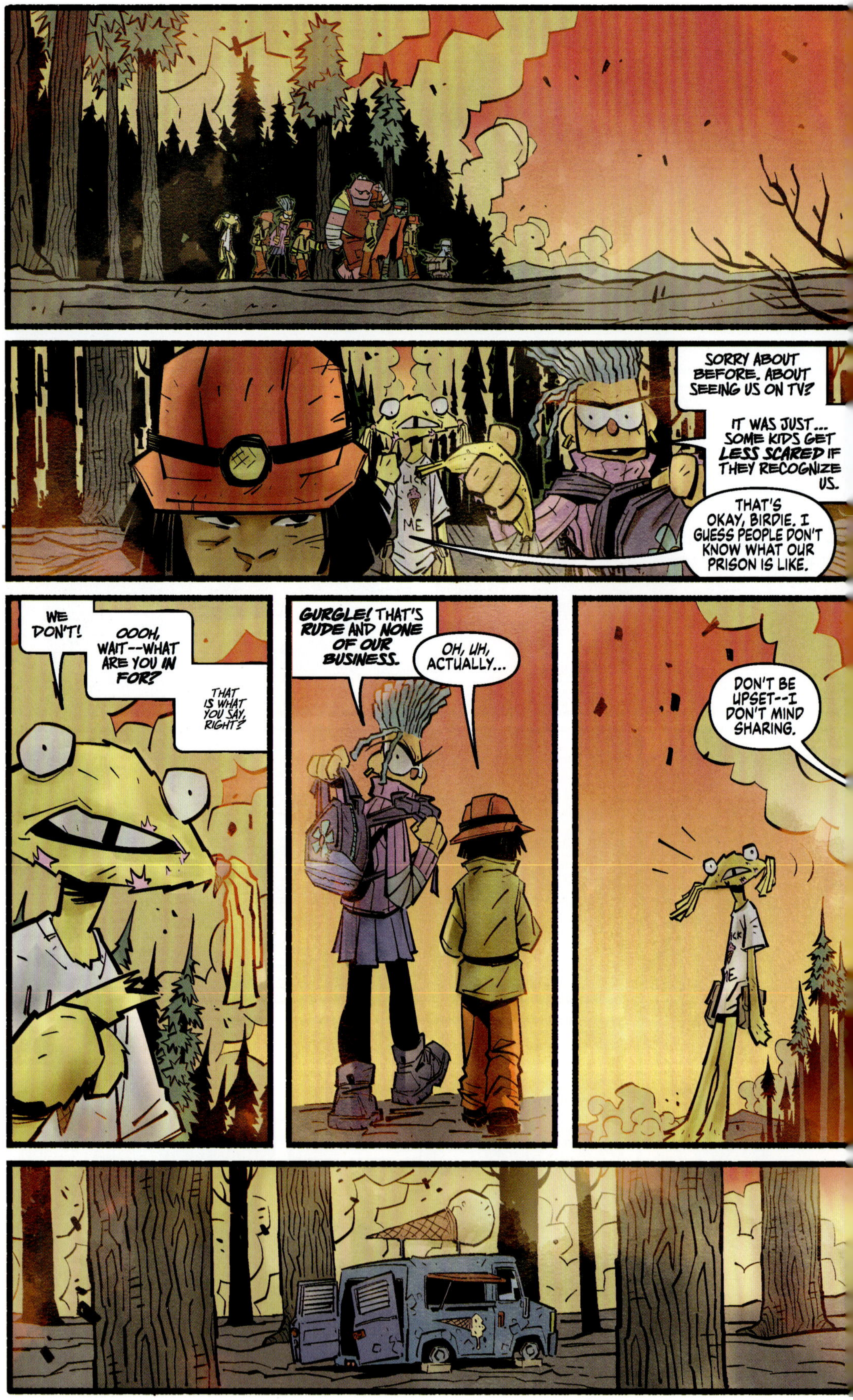
SORRY ABOUT BEFORE. ABOUT SEEING US ON TV?
IT WAS JUST... SOME KIDS GET LESS SCARED IF THEY RECOGNIZE US.
THAT'S OKAY, BIRDIE. I GUESS PEOPLE DON'T KNOW WHAT OUR PRISON IS LIKE.
WE DON'T!
OOOH, WAIT--WHAT ARE YOU IN FOR?
THAT IS WHAT YOU SAY, RIGHT?
GURGLE! THAT'S RUDE AND NONE OF OUR BUSINESS.
OH, UH, ACTUALLY...
DON'T BE UPSET--I DON'T MIND SHARING.

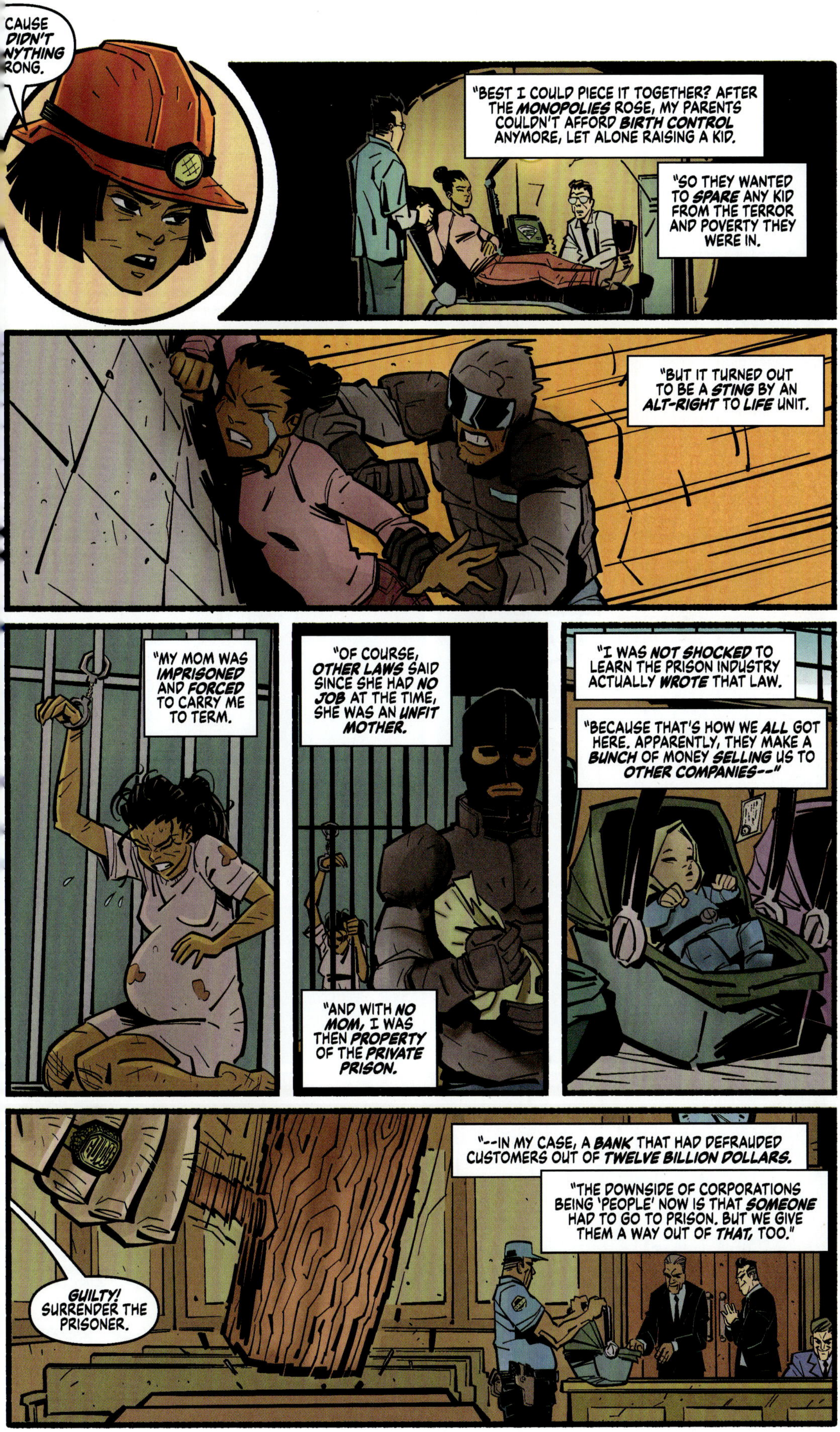
CAUSE DIDN'T NYTHING RONG.
"BEST I COULD PIECE IT TOGETHER? AFTER THE MONOPOLIES ROSE, MY PARENTS COULDN'T AFFORD BIRTH CONTROL ANYMORE, LET ALONE RAISING A KID.
"SO THEY WANTED TO SPARE ANY KID FROM THE TERROR AND POVERTY THEY WERE IN.
"BUT IT TURNED OUT TO BE A STING BY AN ALT-RIGHT TO LIFE UNIT.
"MY MOM WAS IMPRISONED AND FORCED TO CARRY ME TO TERM.
"OF COURSE, OTHER LAWS SAID SINCE SHE HAD NO JOB AT THE TIME, SHE WAS AN UNFIT MOTHER.
"AND WITH NO MOM, I WAS THEN PROPERTY OF THE PRIVATE PRISON.
"I WAS NOT SHOCKED TO LEARN THE PRISON INDUSTRY ACTUALLY WROTE THAT LAW.
"BECAUSE THAT'S HOW WE ALL GOT HERE. APPARENTLY, THEY MAKE A BUNCH OF MONEY SELLING US TO OTHER COMPANIES--"
"--IN MY CASE, A BANK THAT HAD DEFRAUDED CUSTOMERS OUT OF TWELVE BILLION DOLLARS.
"THE DOWNSIDE OF CORPORATIONS BEING 'PEOPLE' NOW IS THAT SOMEONE HAD TO GO TO PRISON. BUT WE GIVE THEM A WAY OUT OF THAT, TOO."
GUILTY! SURRENDER THE PRISONER.

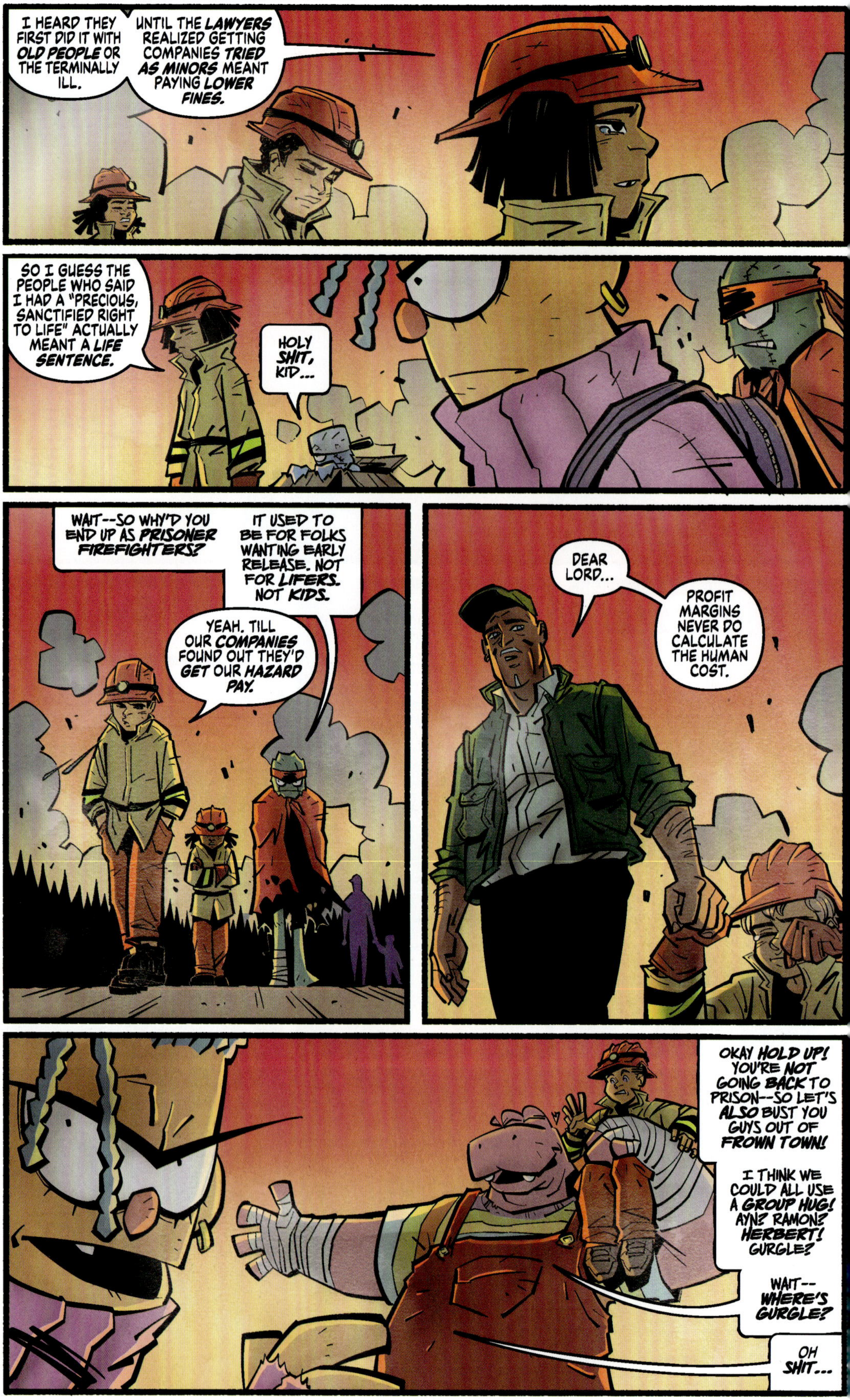
I HEARD THEY FIRST DID IT WITH OLD PEOPLE OR THE TERMINALLY ILL.
UNTIL THE LAWYERS REALIZED GETTING COMPANIES TRIED AS MINORS MEANT PAYING LOWER FINES.
SO I GUESS THE PEOPLE WHO SAID I HAD A "PRECIOUS, SANCTIFIED RIGHT TO LIFE" ACTUALLY MEANT A LIFE SENTENCE.
HOLY SHIT, KID...
WAIT--SO WHY'D YOU END UP AS PRISONER FIREFIGHTERS?
IT USED TO BE FOR FOLKS WANTING EARLY RELEASE. NOT FOR LIFERS. NOT KIDS.
YEAH. TILL OUR COMPANIES FOUND OUT THEY'D GET OUR HAZARD PAY.
DEAR LORD...
PROFIT MARGINS NEVER DO CALCULATE THE HUMAN COST.
OKAY HOLD UP! YOU'RE NOT GOING BACK TO PRISON--SO LET'S ALSO BUST YOU GUYS OUT OF FROWN TOWN!
I THINK WE COULD ALL USE A GROUP HUG! AYN? RAMON? HERBERT! GURGLE?
WAIT-- WHERE'S GURGLE?
OH SHIT...

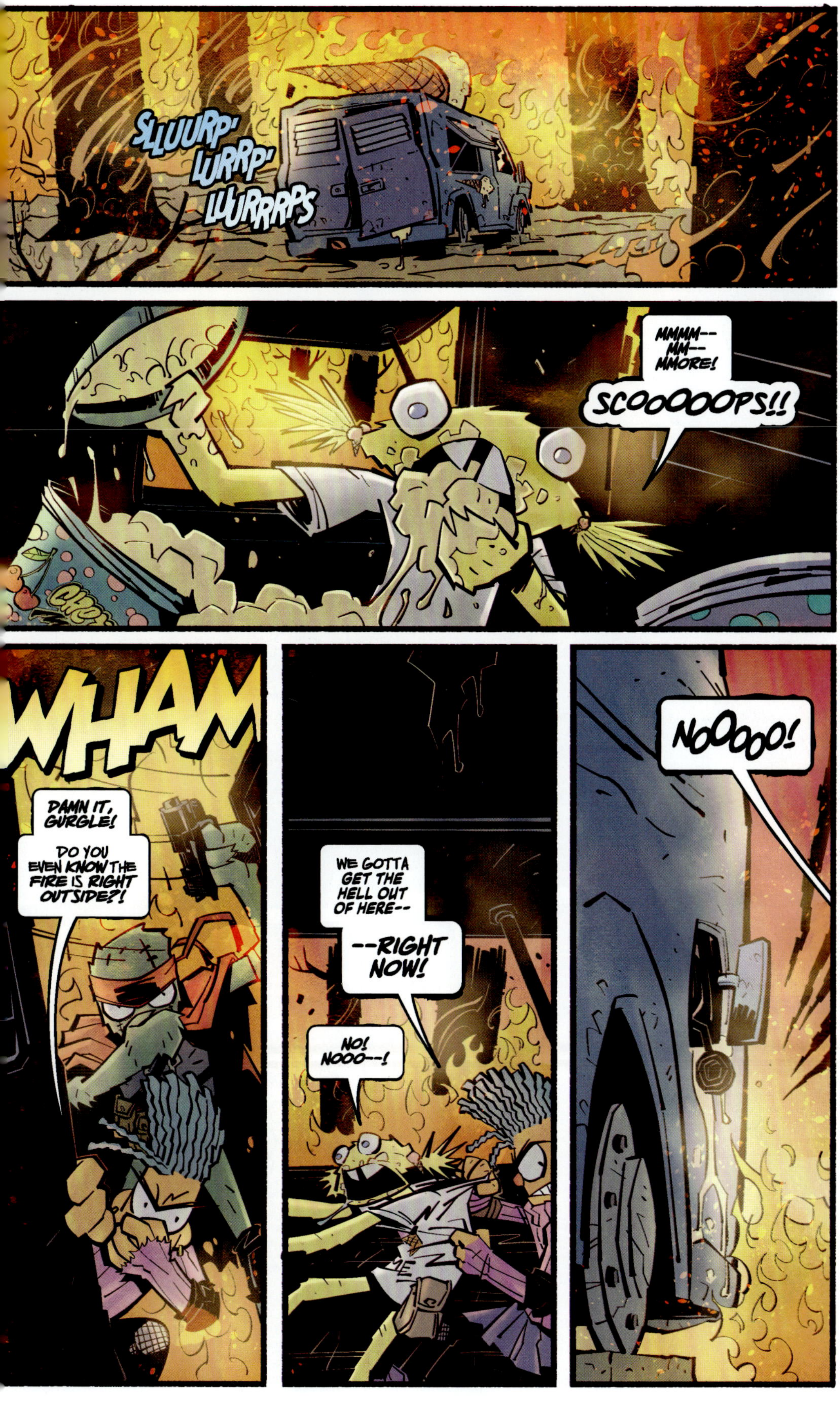
SLLUURP' LURRP' LUURRRPS
MMMM-- MM-- MMORE!
SCOOOOOOPS!!
WHAM
DAMN IT, GURGLE!
DO YOU EVEN KNOW THE FIRE IS RIGHT OUTSIDE?!
WE GOTTA GET THE HELL OUT OF HERE--
--RIGHT NOW!
NO! NOOO--!
NOOOOO!

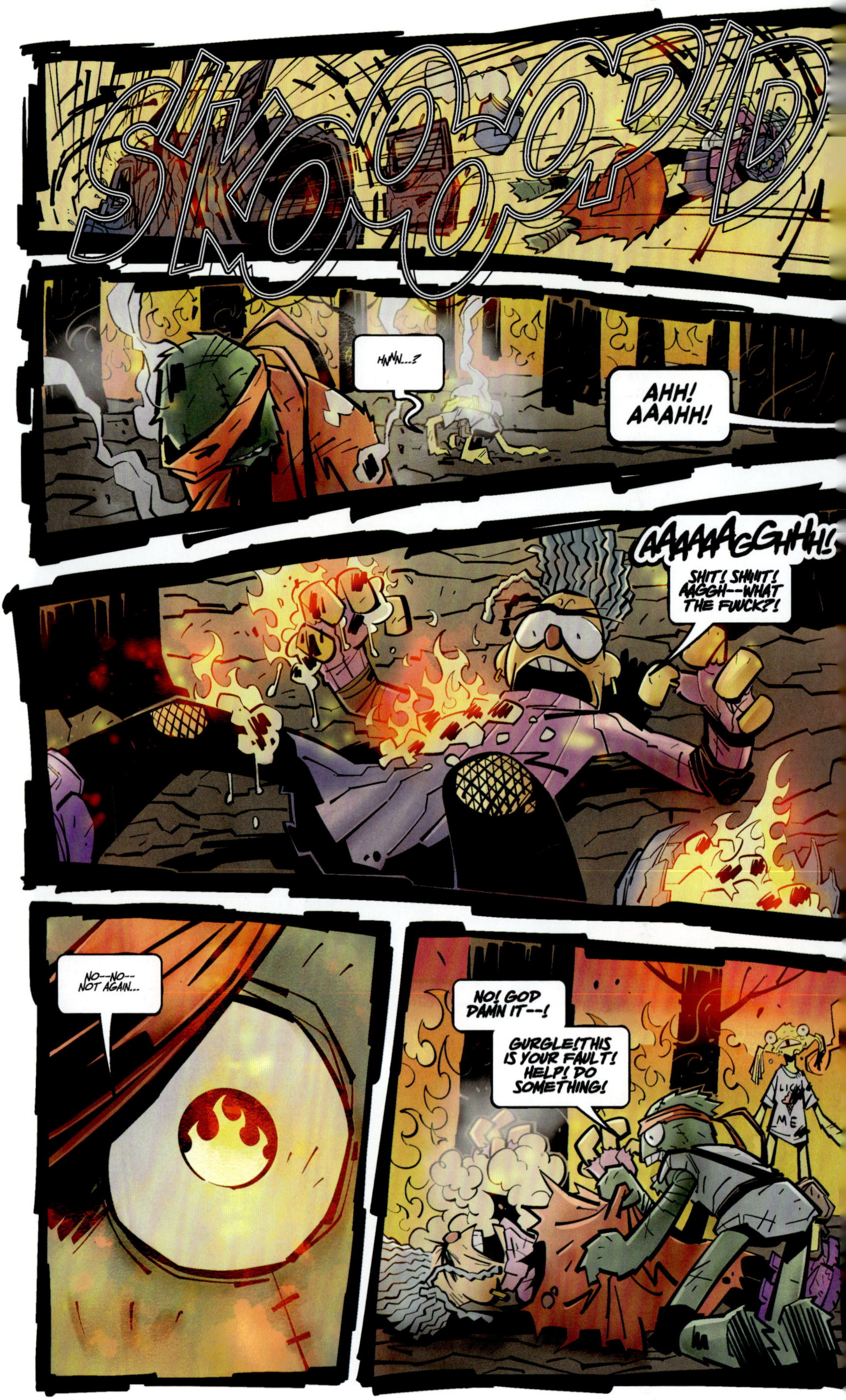
SHKOOOOOOOD
HNNN...?
AHH! AAAHH!
AAAAAAGGHHH!
SHIT! SHIIIT! AAGGH--WHAT THE FUUCK?!
NO--NO-- NOT AGAIN...
NO! GOD DAMN IT--!
GURGLE! THIS IS YOUR FAULT! HELP! DO SOMETHING!
LICK ME

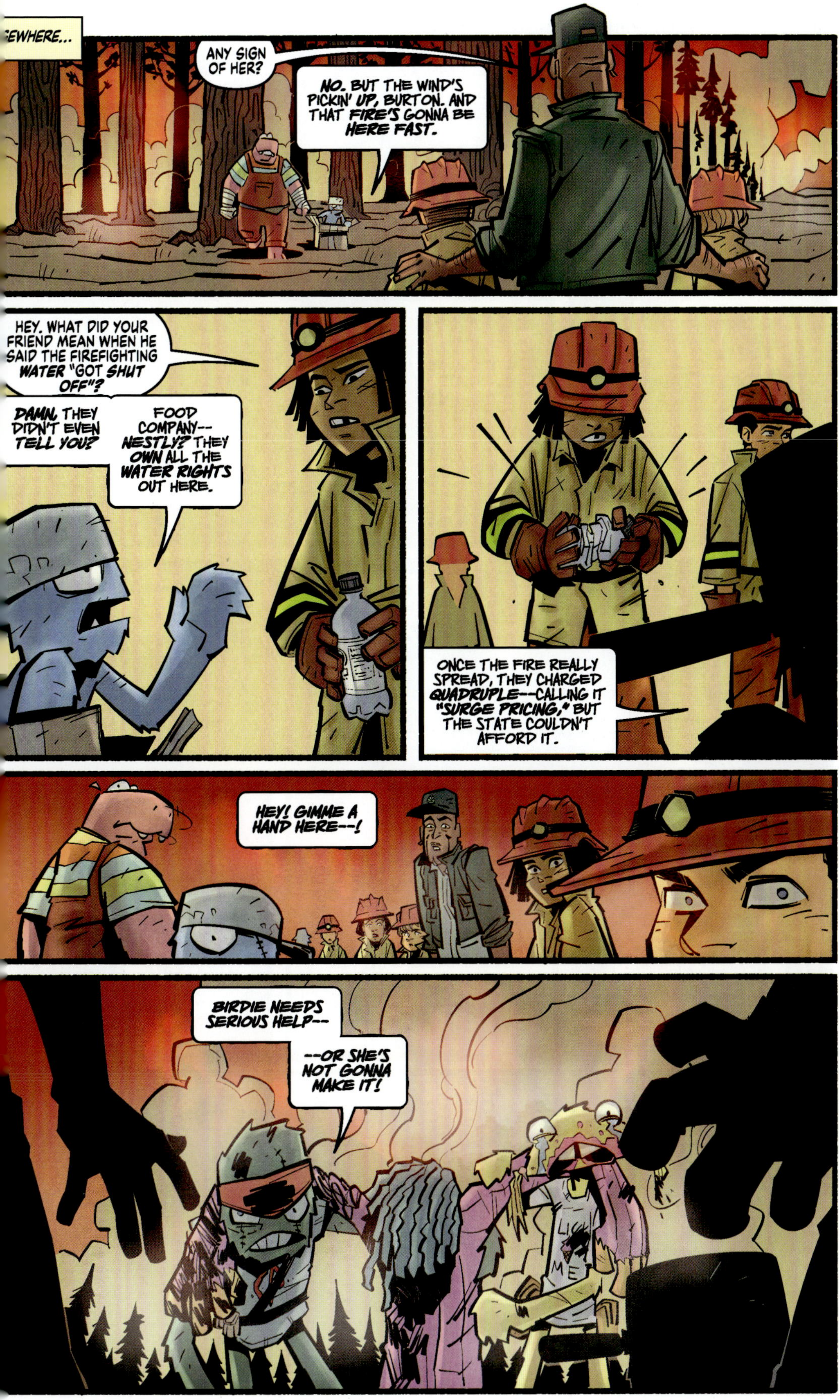
...EWHERE...
ANY SIGN OF HER?
NO. BUT THE WIND'S PICKIN' UP, BURTON. AND THAT FIRE'S GONNA BE HERE FAST.
HEY. WHAT DID YOUR FRIEND MEAN WHEN HE SAID THE FIREFIGHTING WATER "GOT SHUT OFF"?
DAMN. THEY DIDN'T EVEN TELL YOU?
FOOD COMPANY-- NESTLY? THEY OWN ALL THE WATER RIGHTS OUT HERE.
ONCE THE FIRE REALLY SPREAD, THEY CHARGED QUADRUPLE--CALLING IT "SURGE PRICING," BUT THE STATE COULDN'T AFFORD IT.
HEY! GIMME A HAND HERE--!
BIRDIE NEEDS SERIOUS HELP--
--OR SHE'S NOT GONNA MAKE IT!

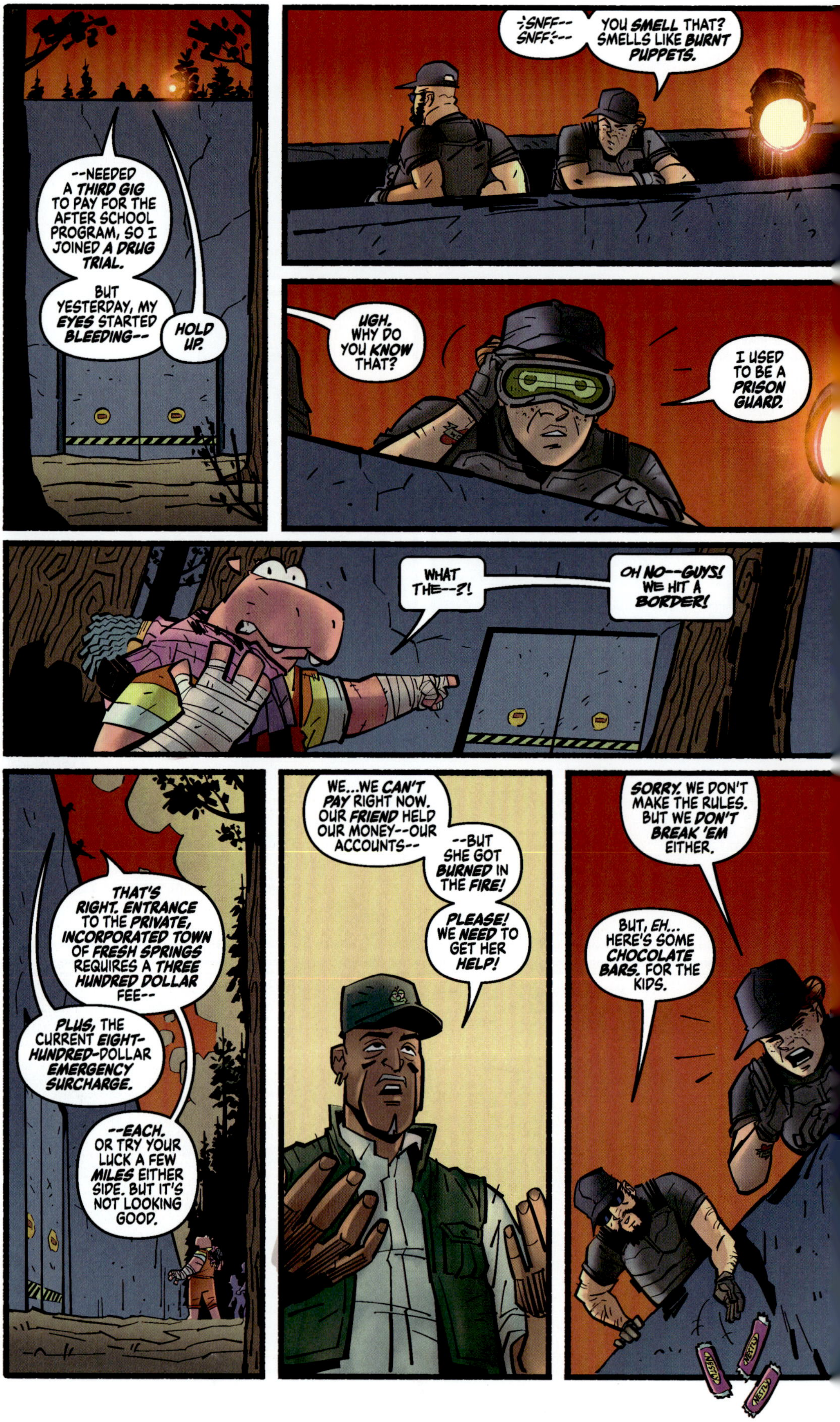
--NEEDED A THIRD GIG TO PAY FOR THE AFTER SCHOOL PROGRAM, SO I JOINED A DRUG TRIAL.
BUT YESTERDAY, MY EYES STARTED BLEEDING--
HOLD UP.
SNFF--SNFF--
YOU SMELL THAT? SMELLS LIKE BURNT PUPPETS.
UGH. WHY DO YOU KNOW THAT?
I USED TO BE A PRISON GUARD.
WHAT THE--?!
OH NO--GUYS! WE HIT A BORDER!
THAT'S RIGHT. ENTRANCE TO THE PRIVATE, INCORPORATED TOWN OF FRESH SPRINGS REQUIRES A THREE HUNDRED DOLLAR FEE--
PLUS, THE CURRENT EIGHT-HUNDRED-DOLLAR EMERGENCY SURCHARGE.
--EACH. OR TRY YOUR LUCK A FEW MILES EITHER SIDE. BUT IT'S NOT LOOKING GOOD.
WE...WE CAN'T PAY RIGHT NOW. OUR FRIEND HELD OUR MONEY--OUR ACCOUNTS--
--BUT SHE GOT BURNED IN THE FIRE!
PLEASE! WE NEED TO GET HER HELP!
SORRY. WE DON'T MAKE THE RULES. BUT WE DON'T BREAK 'EM EITHER.
BUT, EH... HERE'S SOME CHOCOLATE BARS. FOR THE KIDS.

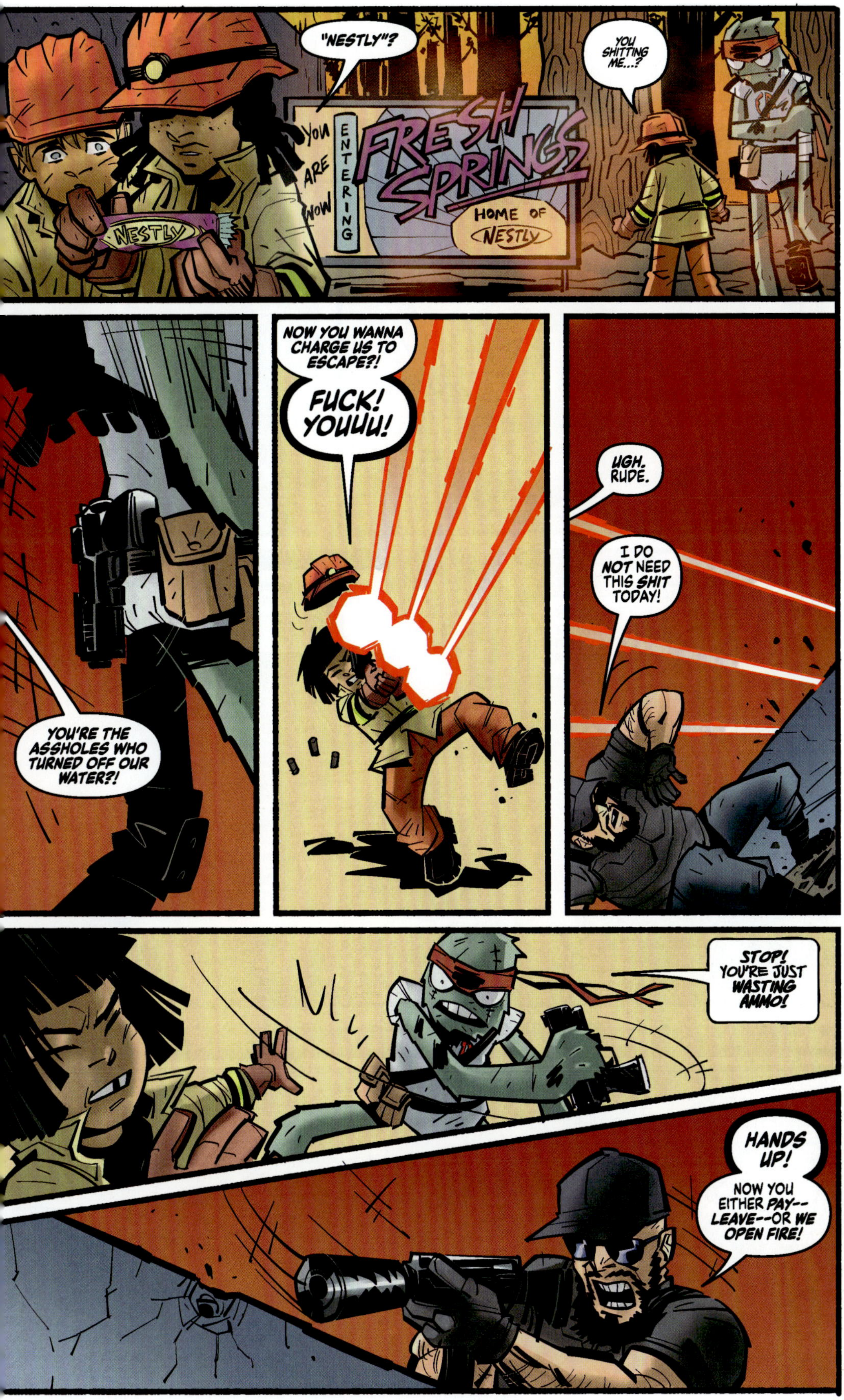
"NESTLY"?
YOU ARE NOW ENTERING FRESH SPRINGS
HOME OF NESTLY
NESTLY
YOU SHITTING ME...?
YOU'RE THE ASSHOLES WHO TURNED OFF OUR WATER?!
NOW YOU WANNA CHARGE US TO ESCAPE?!
FUCK! YOUUU!
UGH. RUDE.
I DO NOT NEED THIS SHIT TODAY!
STOP! YOU'RE JUST WASTING AMMO!
HANDS UP!
NOW YOU EITHER PAY-- LEAVE--OR WE OPEN FIRE!

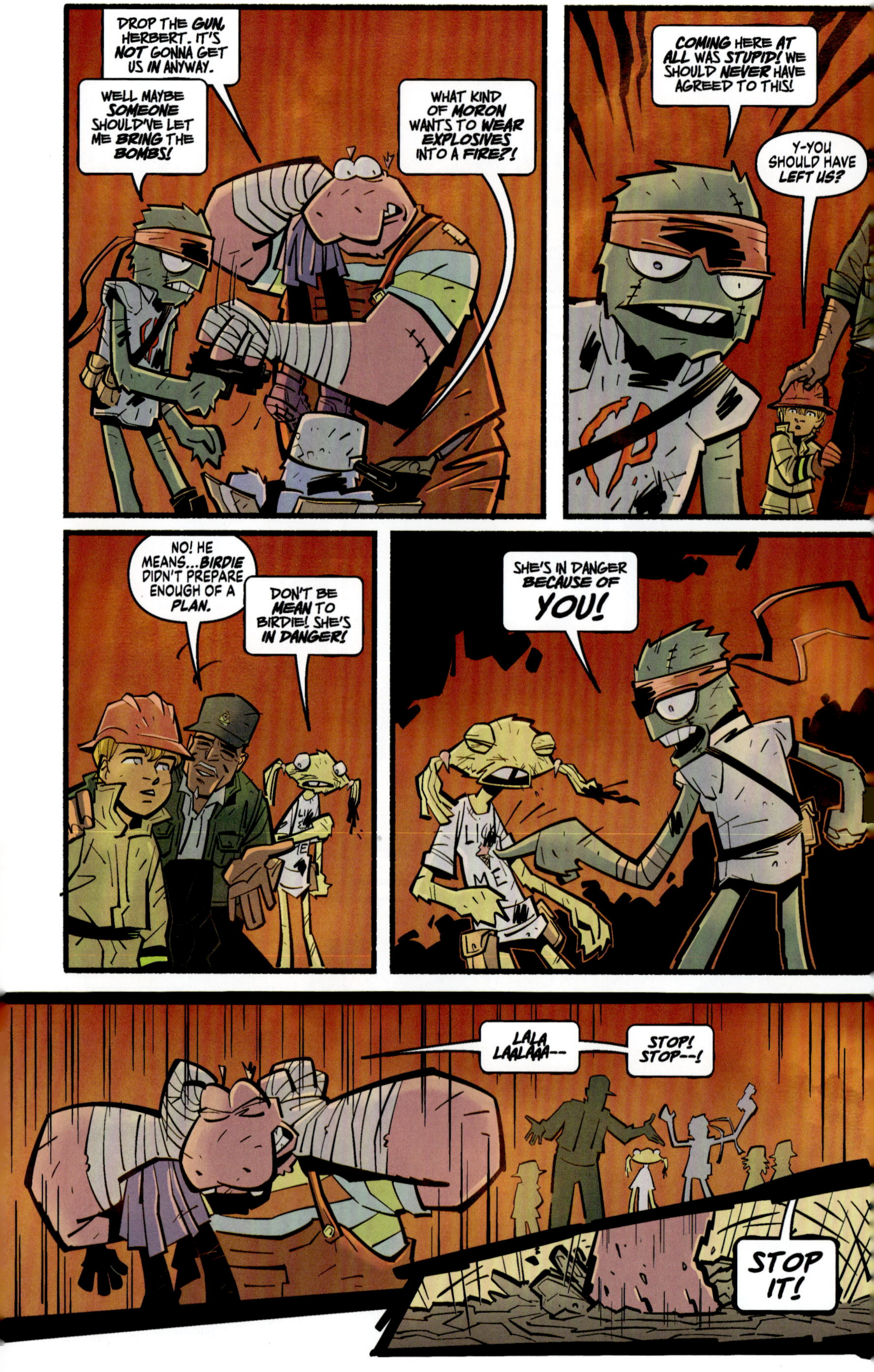
DROP THE GUN, HERBERT. IT'S NOT GONNA GET US IN ANYWAY.
WELL MAYBE SOMEONE SHOULD'VE LET ME BRING THE BOMBS!
WHAT KIND OF MORON WANTS TO WEAR EXPLOSIVES INTO A FIRE?!
COMING HERE AT ALL WAS STUPID! WE SHOULD NEVER HAVE AGREED TO THIS!
Y-YOU SHOULD HAVE LEFT US?
NO! HE MEANS...BIRDIE DIDN'T PREPARE ENOUGH OF A PLAN.
DON'T BE MEAN TO BIRDIE! SHE'S IN DANGER!
SHE'S IN DANGER BECAUSE OF YOU!
LALA LAALAAA--
STOP! STOP--!
STOP IT!

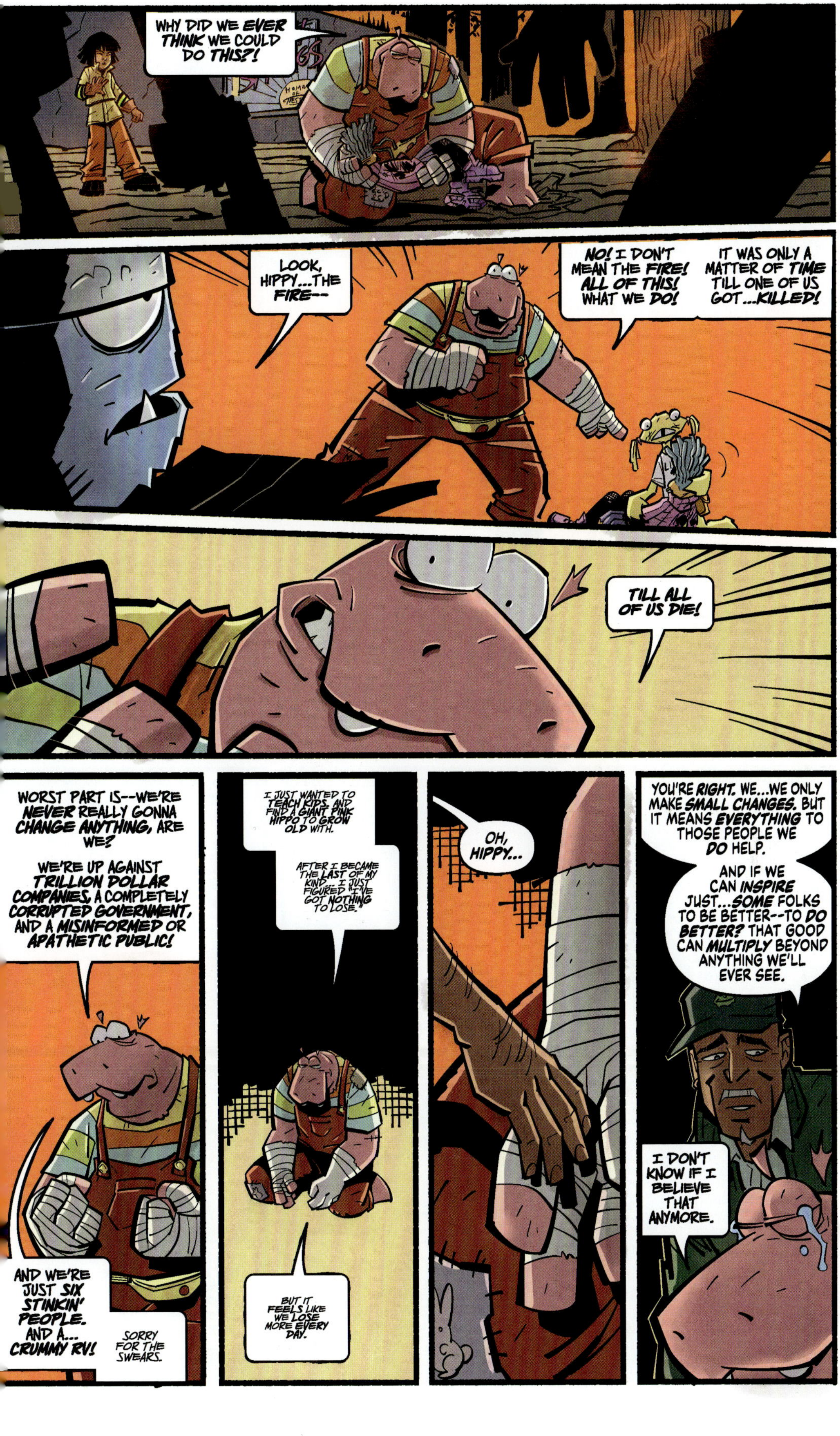
WHY DID WE EVER THINK WE COULD DO THIS?!
LOOK, HIPPY...THE FIRE--
NO! I DON'T MEAN THE FIRE! ALL OF THIS! WHAT WE DO!
IT WAS ONLY A MATTER OF TIME TILL ONE OF US GOT...KILLED!
TILL ALL OF US DIE!
WORST PART IS--WE'RE NEVER REALLY GONNA CHANGE ANYTHING, ARE WE?
WE'RE UP AGAINST TRILLION DOLLAR COMPANIES, A COMPLETELY CORRUPTED GOVERNMENT, AND A MISINFORMED OR APATHETIC PUBLIC!
AND WE'RE JUST SIX STINKIN' PEOPLE. AND A... CRUMMY RV!
SORRY FOR THE SWEARS.
I JUST WANTED TO TEACH KIDS. AND FIND A GIANT PINK HIPPO TO GROW OLD WITH.
AFTER I BECAME THE LAST OF MY KIND... I JUST FIGURED "I'VE GOT NOTHING TO LOSE."
BUT IT FEELS LIKE WE LOSE MORE EVERY DAY.
OH, HIPPY...
YOU'RE RIGHT. WE...WE ONLY MAKE SMALL CHANGES. BUT IT MEANS EVERYTHING TO THOSE PEOPLE WE DO HELP.
AND IF WE CAN INSPIRE JUST...SOME FOLKS TO BE BETTER--TO DO BETTER? THAT GOOD CAN MULTIPLY BEYOND ANYTHING WE'LL EVER SEE.
I DON'T KNOW IF I BELIEVE THAT ANYMORE.

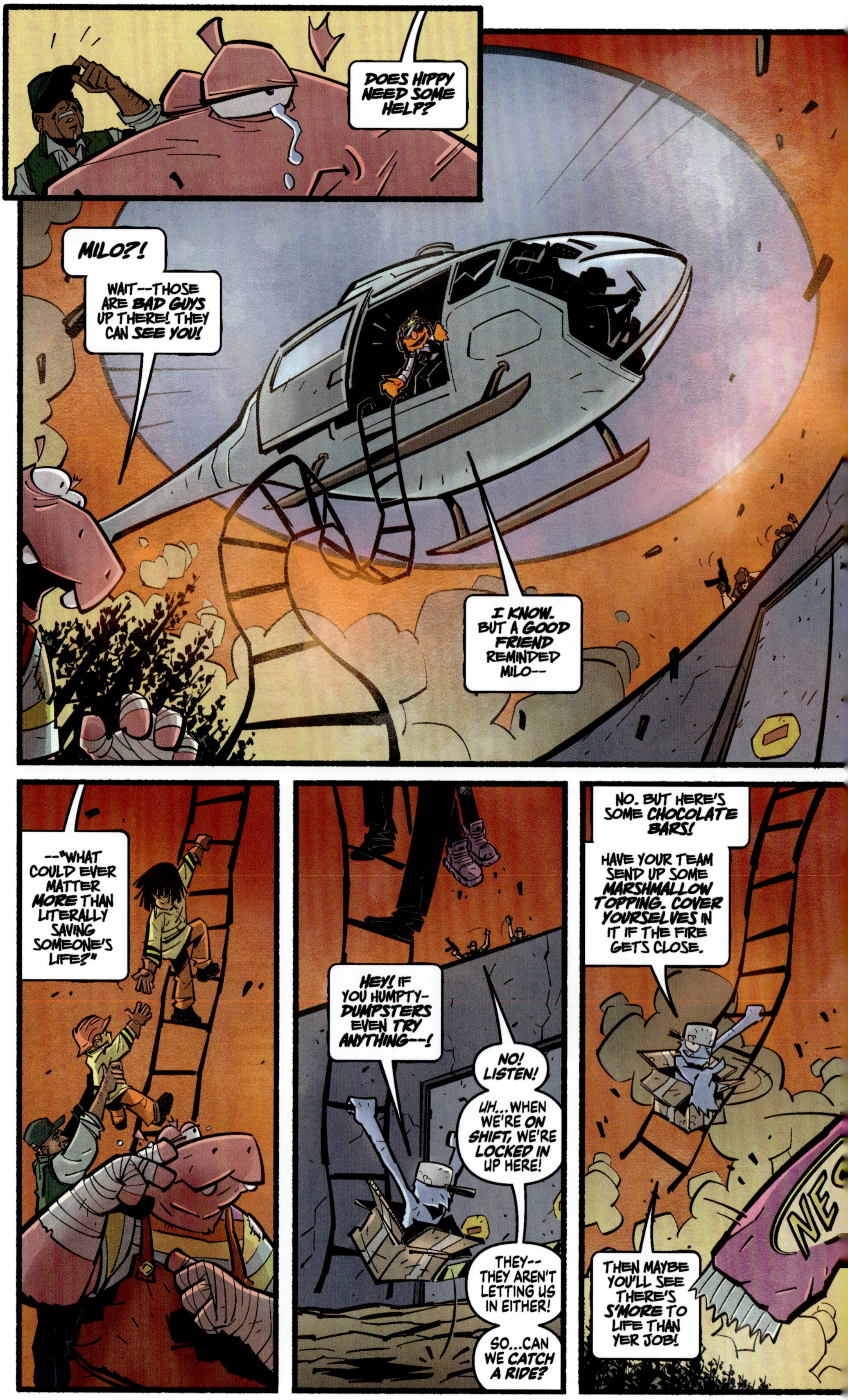
DOES HIPPY NEED SOME HELP?
MILO?!
WAIT--THOSE ARE BAD GUYS UP THERE! THEY CAN SEE YOU!
I KNOW. BUT A GOOD FRIEND REMINDED MILO--
--"WHAT COULD EVER MATTER MORE THAN LITERALLY SAVING SOMEONE'S LIFE?"
HEY! IF YOU HUMPTY-DUMPSTERS EVEN TRY ANYTHING--!
NO! LISTEN!
UH...WHEN WE'RE ON SHIFT, WE'RE LOCKED IN UP HERE!
THEY--THEY AREN'T LETTING US IN EITHER!
SO...CAN WE CATCH A RIDE?
NO. BUT HERE'S SOME CHOCOLATE BARS!
HAVE YOUR TEAM SEND UP SOME MARSHMALLOW TOPPING. COVER YOURSELVES IN IT IF THE FIRE GETS CLOSE.
THEN MAYBE YOU'LL SEE THERE'S S'MORE TO LIFE THAN YER JOB!

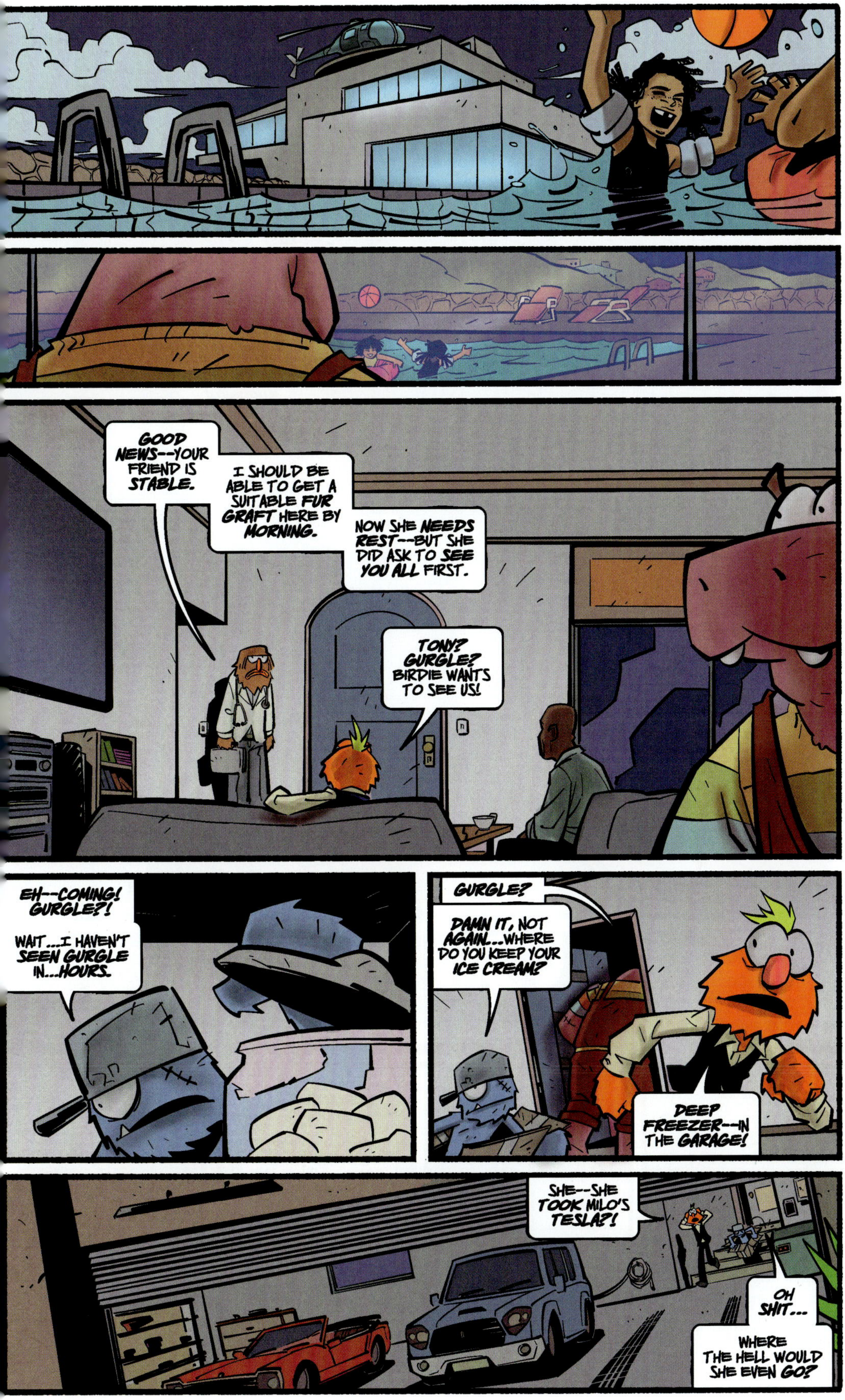
GOOD NEWS--YOUR FRIEND IS STABLE.
I SHOULD BE ABLE TO GET A SUITABLE FUR GRAFT HERE BY MORNING.
NOW SHE NEEDS REST--BUT SHE DID ASK TO SEE YOU ALL FIRST.
TONY? GURGLE? BIRDIE WANTS TO SEE US!
EH--COMING! GURGLE?!
WAIT...I HAVEN'T SEEN GURGLE IN...HOURS.
GURGLE?
DAMN IT, NOT AGAIN...WHERE DO YOU KEEP YOUR ICE CREAM?
DEEP FREEZER--IN THE GARAGE!
SHE--SHE TOOK MILO'S TESLA?!
OH SHIT...
WHERE THE HELL WOULD SHE EVEN GO?

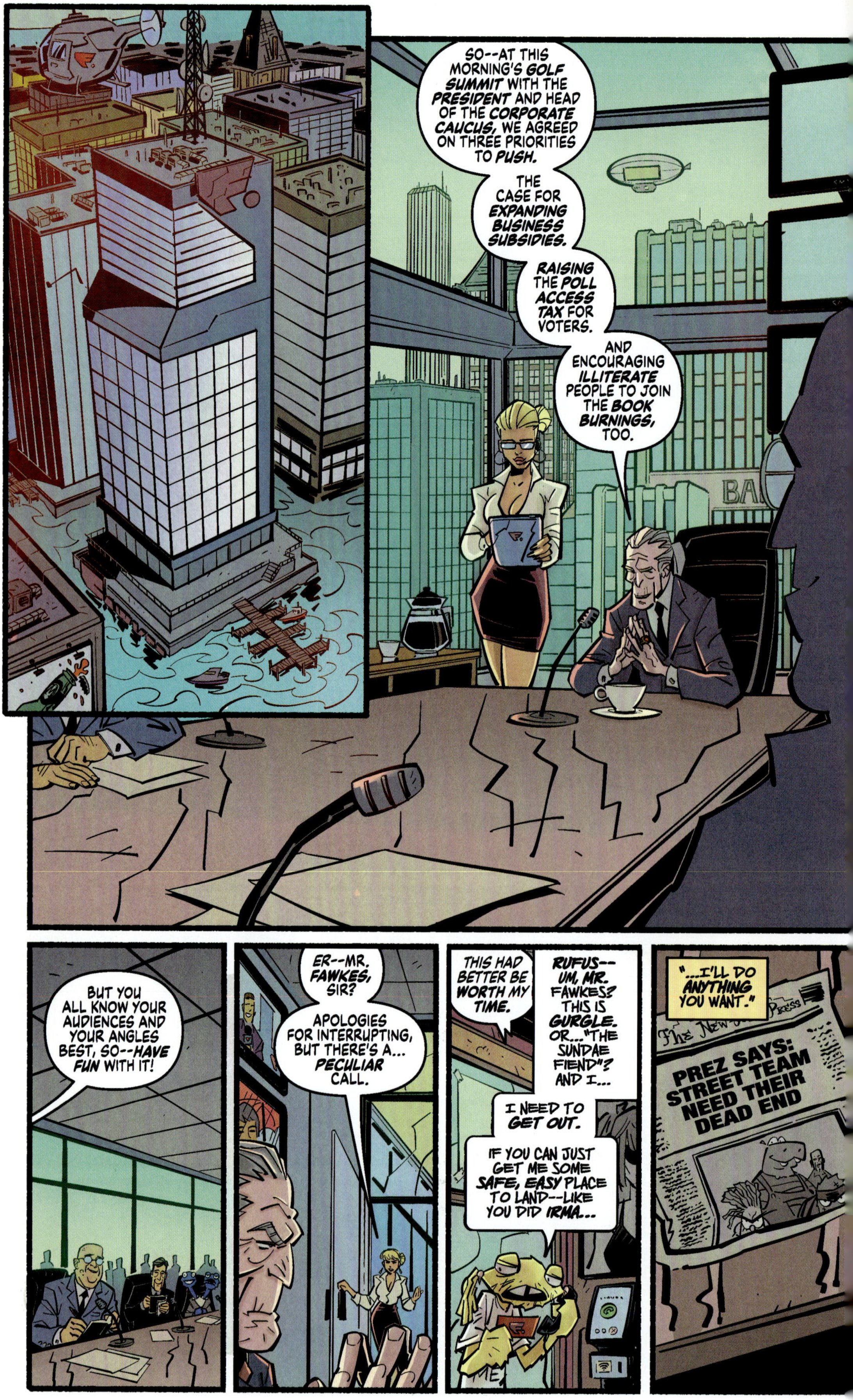
SO--AT THIS MORNING'S GOLF SUMMIT WITH THE PRESIDENT AND HEAD OF THE CORPORATE CAUCUS, WE AGREED ON THREE PRIORITIES TO PUSH.
THE CASE FOR EXPANDING BUSINESS SUBSIDIES.
RAISING THE POLL ACCESS TAX FOR VOTERS.
AND ENCOURAGING ILLITERATE PEOPLE TO JOIN THE BOOK BURNINGS, TOO.
BUT YOU ALL KNOW YOUR AUDIENCES AND YOUR ANGLES BEST, SO--HAVE FUN WITH IT!
ER--MR. FAWKES, SIR?
APOLOGIES FOR INTERRUPTING, BUT THERE'S A... PECULIAR CALL.
THIS HAD BETTER BE WORTH MY TIME.
RUFUS--UM, MR. FAWKES? THIS IS GURGLE. OR..."THE SUNDAE FIEND"? AND I...
I NEED TO GET OUT.
IF YOU CAN JUST GET ME SOME SAFE, EASY PLACE TO LAND--LIKE YOU DID IRMA...
"...I'LL DO ANYTHING YOU WANT."
PREZ SAYS: STREET TEAM NEED THEIR DEAD END

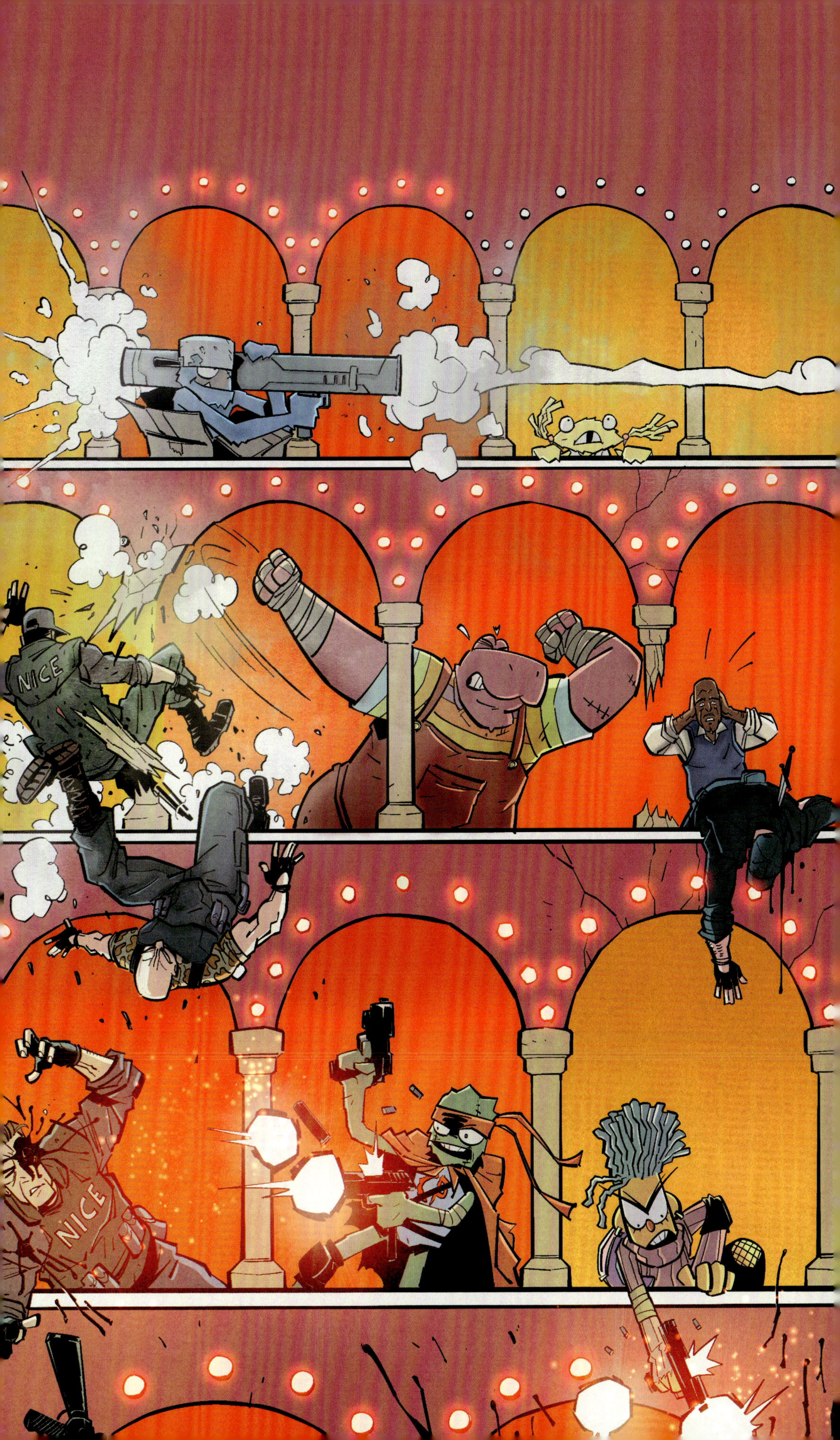
NICE
NICE

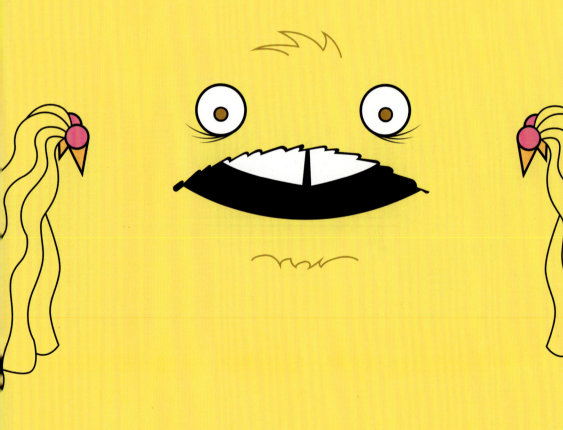

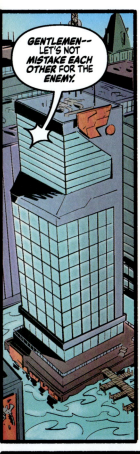

GENTLEMEN-- LET'S NOT MISTAKE EACH OTHER FOR THE ENEMY.

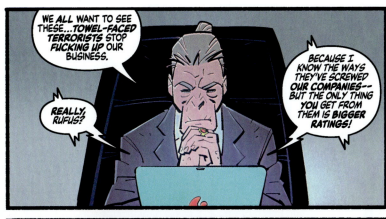

WE ALL WANT TO SEE THESE...TOWEL-FACED TERRORISTS STOP FUCKING UP OUR BUSINESS.

REALLY, RUFUS?

BECAUSE I KNOW THE WAYS THEY'VE SCREWED OUR COMPANIES-- BUT THE ONLY THING YOU GET FROM THEM IS BIGGER RATINGS!

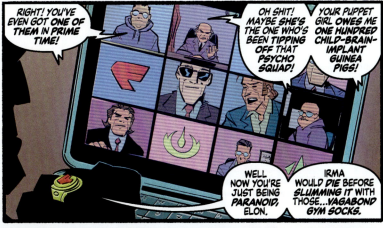

RIGHT! YOU'VE EVEN GOT ONE OF THEM IN PRIME TIME!

OH SHIT! MAYBE SHE'S THE ONE WHO'S BEEN TIPPING OFF THAT PSYCHO SQUAD!

YOUR PUPPET GIRL OWES ME ONE HUNDRED CHILD-BRAIN-IMPLANT GUINEA PIGS!

WELL NOW YOU'RE JUST BEING PARANOID, ELON.

IRMA WOULD DIE BEFORE SLUMMING IT WITH THOSE...VAGABOND GYM SOCKS.

WELL, THEN, WHY THE HELL DID PUBLIC SUPPORT OF OUR GUNZ-4-TOTS LEGISLATION GO DOWN AFTER THEY ATTACKED US?!

YEAH! AND HOW COME THE STORY OF THEM BLOWIN' UP MY TOTALLY COOL CHARITY KID AUCTION GETS THE INTERNET SAYING I'M THE "BAD GUY"?!

AW'RIGHT. I HEAR YOU. WE'VE BEEN A BIT TOO FAIR, TOO BALANCED.

AMERICA WILL HAVE NO DOUBT WHO ITS ENEMIES ARE.

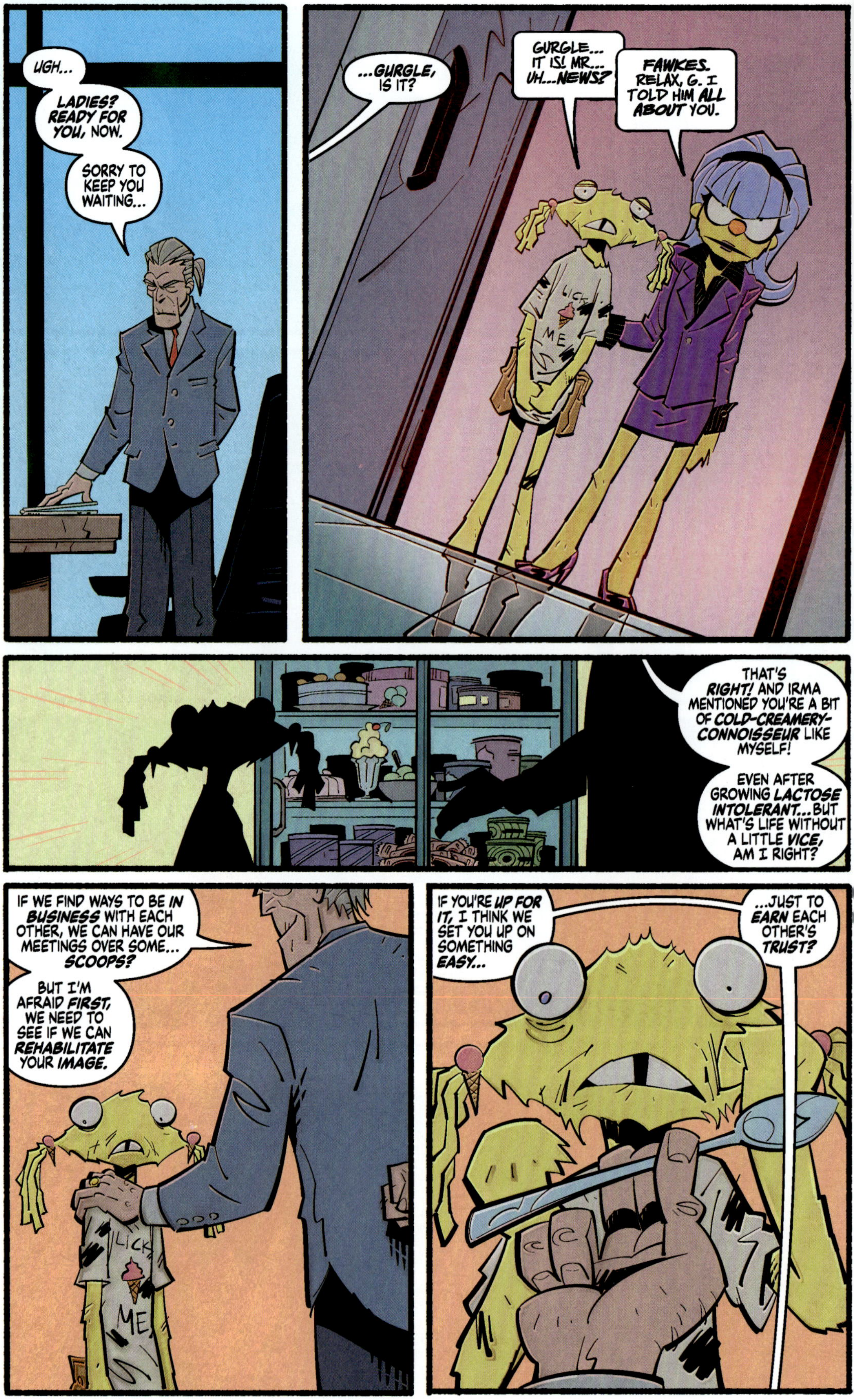
UGH...
LADIES? READY FOR YOU, NOW.
SORRY TO KEEP YOU WAITING...
...GURGLE, IS IT?
GURGLE... IT IS! MR... UH...NEWS?
FAWKES. RELAX, G. I TOLD HIM ALL ABOUT YOU.
LICK ME
THAT'S RIGHT! AND IRMA MENTIONED YOU'RE A BIT OF COLD-CREAMERY-CONNOISSEUR LIKE MYSELF!
EVEN AFTER GROWING LACTOSE INTOLERANT...BUT WHAT'S LIFE WITHOUT A LITTLE VICE, AM I RIGHT?
IF WE FIND WAYS TO BE IN BUSINESS WITH EACH OTHER, WE CAN HAVE OUR MEETINGS OVER SOME... SCOOPS?
BUT I'M AFRAID FIRST, WE NEED TO SEE IF WE CAN REHABILITATE YOUR IMAGE.
LICK ME
IF YOU'RE UP FOR IT, I THINK WE SET YOU UP ON SOMETHING EASY...
...JUST TO EARN EACH OTHER'S TRUST?

DON'T LET ANYONE TELL YOU IT'S "RACIST" TO ACKNOWLEDGE THE TRUTH--

I REMEMBER A TIME, NOT SO LONG AGO, SOME OF THESE "PEOPLE" INSISTED IT WAS OKAY FOR THEM TO PARADE AROUND WITHOUT ANY CLOTHES!

DOES THAT FOREIGN JUNGLE THEY CAME FROM SIMPLY NOT SHARE OUR BASIC MORAL VALUES?

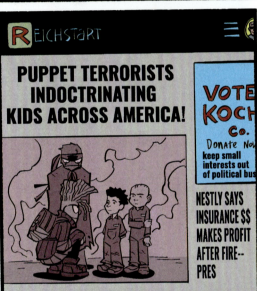

REICHSTART

PUPPET TERRORISTS INDOCTRINATING KIDS ACROSS AMERICA!

VOTE KOCH Co.

Donate No keep small interests out of political bus

NESTLY SAYS INSURANCE $$ MAKES PROFIT AFTER FIRE-- PRES

THEY'VE BEEN OBSESSED WITH CHILDREN SINCE THEY WASHED UP HERE!

GROOMING THEM! BRAINWASHING THEM WITH COMMUNIST IDEOLOGY!

I EVEN HEARD-- AFTER THEY WERE SHUT DOWN--AGENTS FOUND SECRET TUNNELS UNDER THE TV STUDIO, THEME RESTAURANTS, AND THEIR AMUSEMENT PARK!

MY OTHER TRUCK IS A GUN

THESE COLORS DON'T RUN THEY'RE LOADED

WRA

BABY ON BOARD

SOCK PUPPETS GO HOME

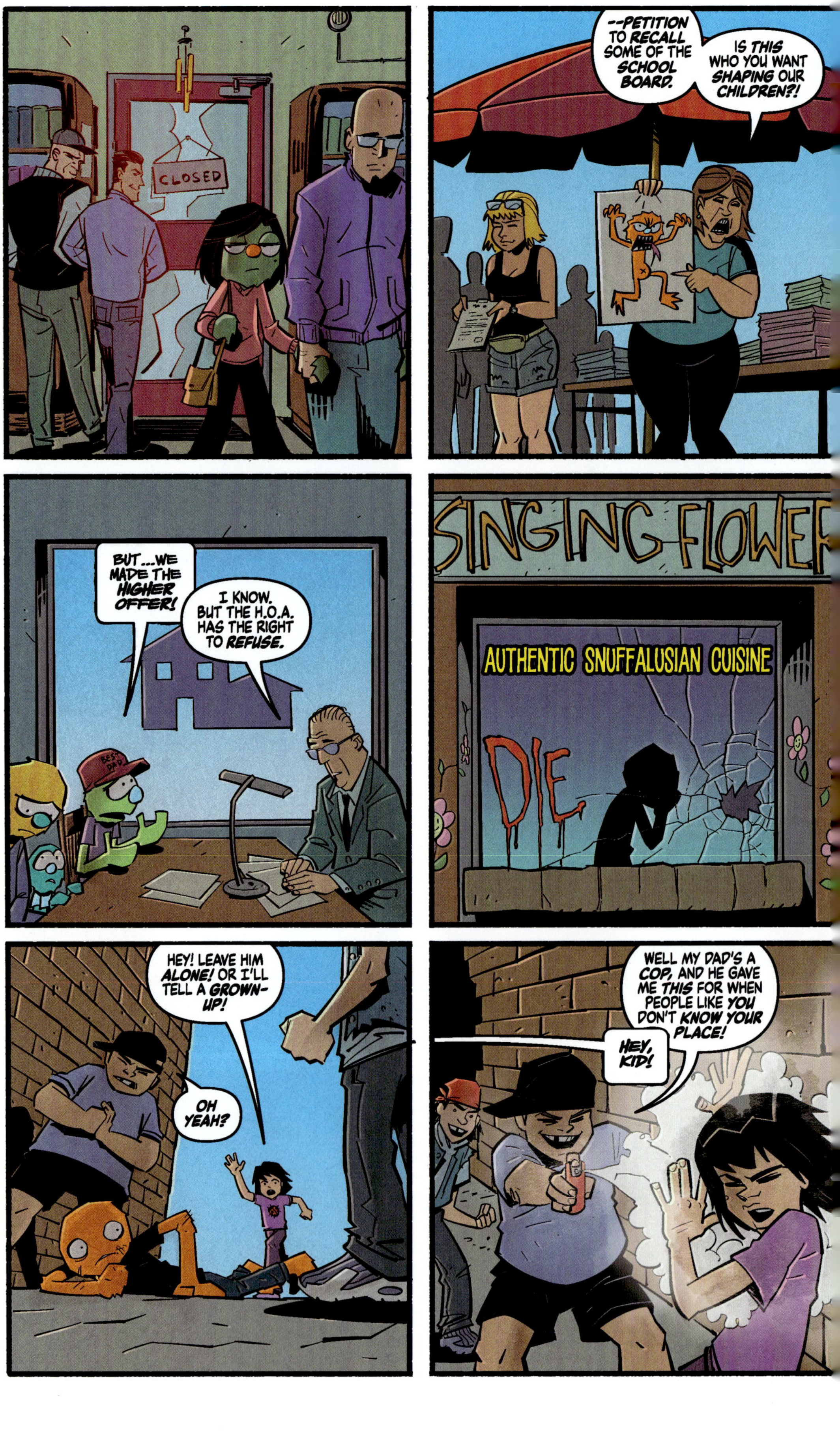
CLOSED
--PETITION TO RECALL SOME OF THE SCHOOL BOARD.
IS THIS WHO YOU WANT SHAPING OUR CHILDREN?!
BUT...WE MADE THE HIGHER OFFER!
I KNOW. BUT THE H.O.A. HAS THE RIGHT TO REFUSE.
BEST DAD
SINGING FLOWER
AUTHENTIC SNUFFALUSIAN CUISINE
DIE
HEY! LEAVE HIM ALONE! OR I'LL TELL A GROWN-UP!
OH YEAH?
WELL MY DAD'S A COP, AND HE GAVE ME THIS FOR WHEN PEOPLE LIKE YOU DON'T KNOW YOUR PLACE!
HEY, KID!

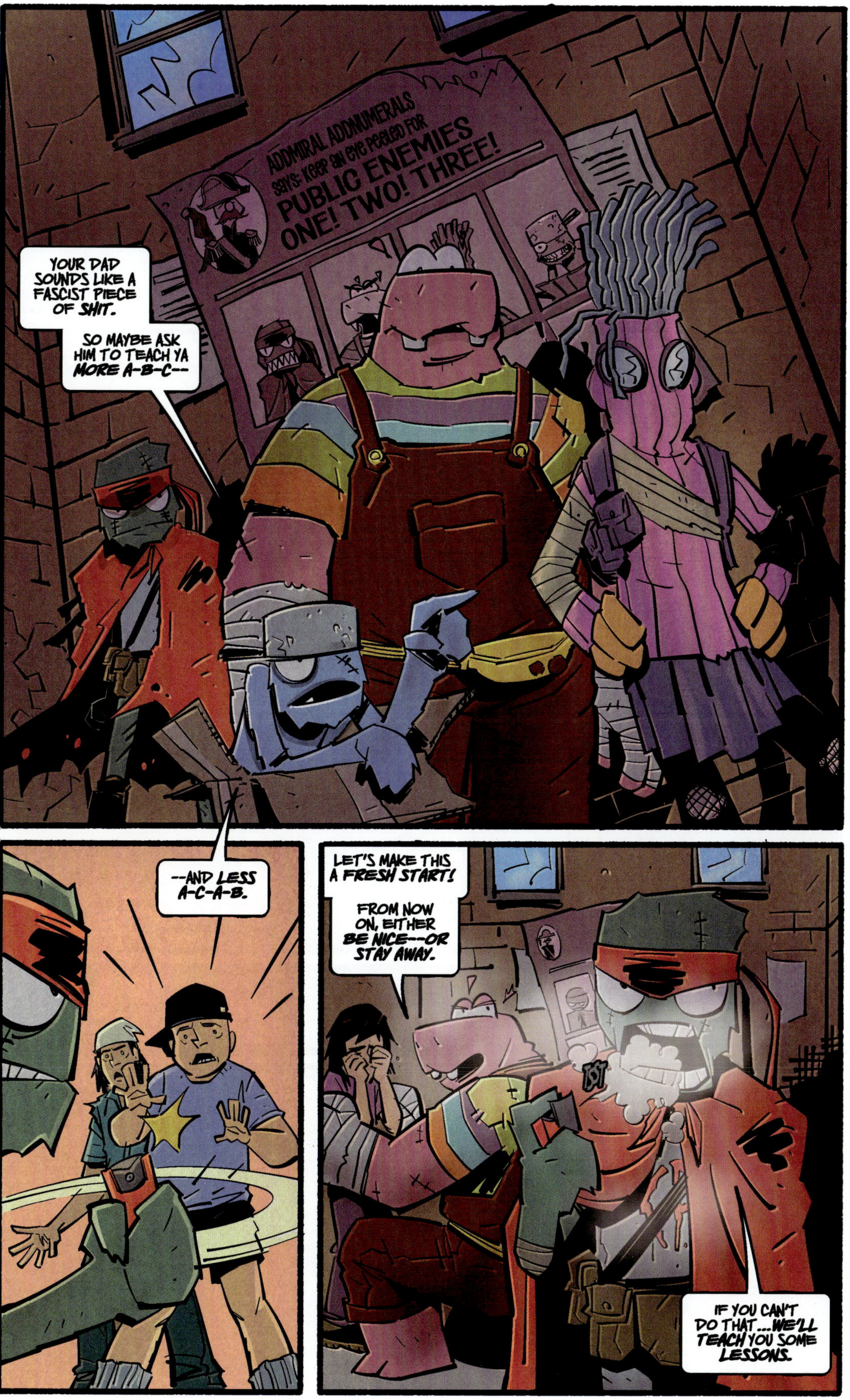
ADDMIRAL ADDNUMERALS says: keep an eye peeled for PUBLIC ENEMIES ONE! TWO! THREE!
YOUR DAD SOUNDS LIKE A FASCIST PIECE OF SHIT.
SO MAYBE ASK HIM TO TEACH YA MORE A-B-C--
--AND LESS A-C-A-B.
LET'S MAKE THIS A FRESH START!
FROM NOW ON, EITHER BE NICE--OR STAY AWAY.
IF YOU CAN'T DO THAT...WE'LL TEACH YOU SOME LESSONS.

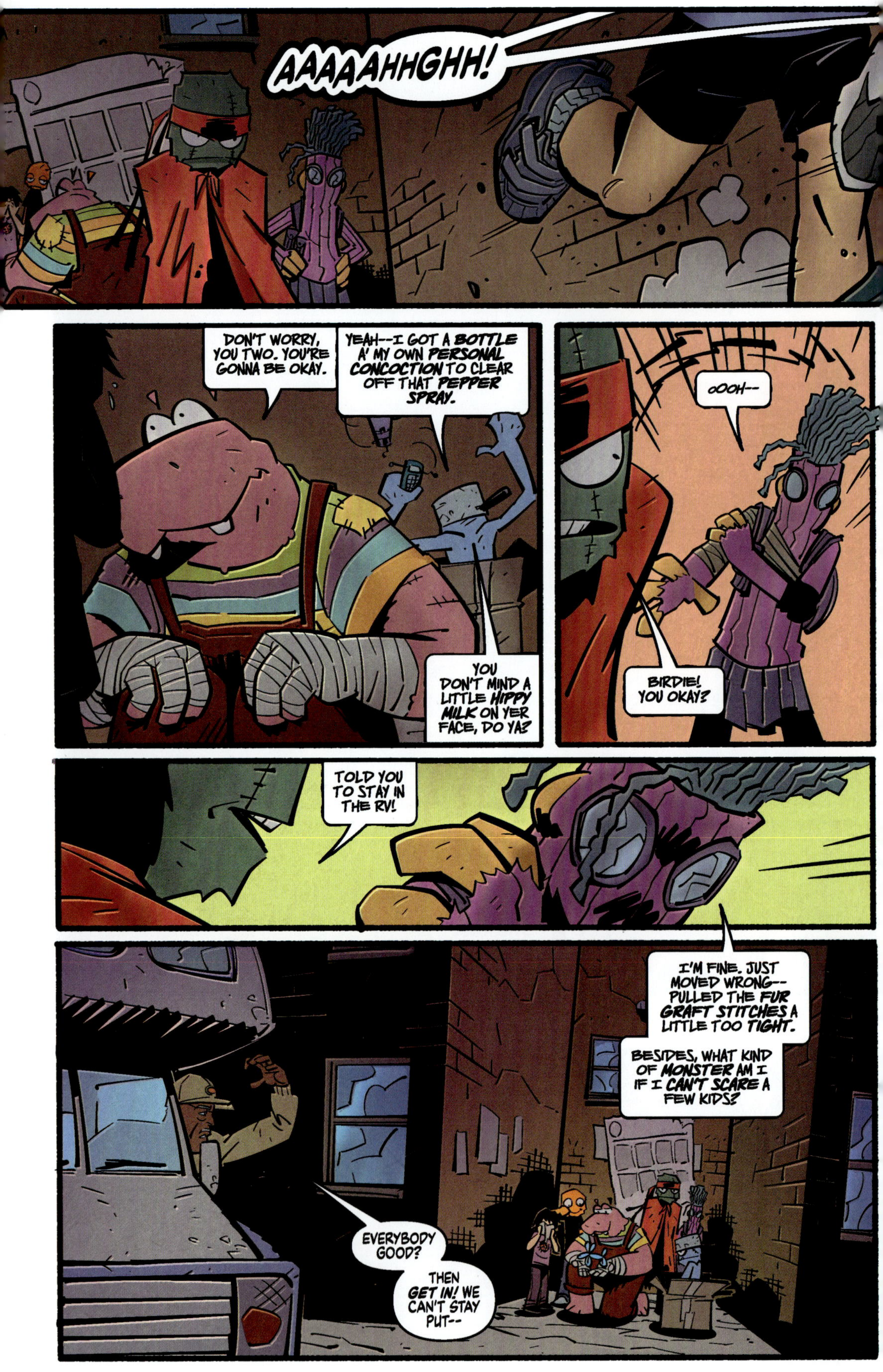
AAAAAHHGHH!
DON'T WORRY, YOU TWO. YOU'RE GONNA BE OKAY.
YEAH--I GOT A BOTTLE A' MY OWN PERSONAL CONCOCTION TO CLEAR OFF THAT PEPPER SPRAY.
YOU DON'T MIND A LITTLE HIPPY MILK ON YER FACE, DO YA?
OOOH--
BIRDIE! YOU OKAY?
TOLD YOU TO STAY IN THE RV!
I'M FINE. JUST MOVED WRONG-- PULLED THE FUR GRAFT STITCHES A LITTLE TOO TIGHT.
BESIDES, WHAT KIND OF MONSTER AM I IF I CAN'T SCARE A FEW KIDS?
EVERYBODY GOOD?
THEN GET IN! WE CAN'T STAY PUT--

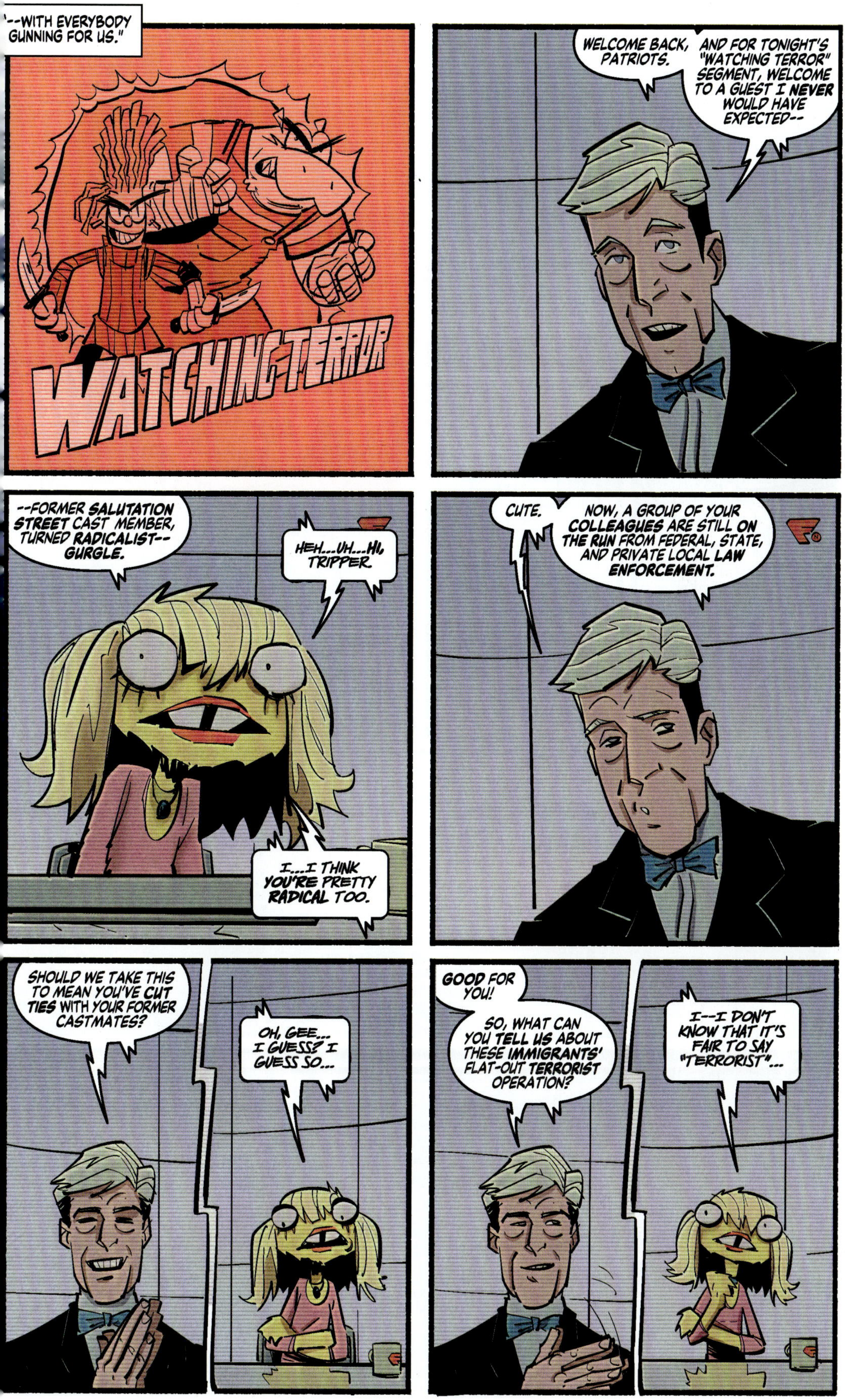
"--WITH EVERYBODY GUNNING FOR US."
WATCHING TERROR
WELCOME BACK, PATRIOTS.
AND FOR TONIGHT'S "WATCHING TERROR" SEGMENT, WELCOME TO A GUEST I NEVER WOULD HAVE EXPECTED--
--FORMER SALUTATION STREET CAST MEMBER, TURNED RADICALIST-- GURGLE.
HEH...UH...HI, TRIPPER.
I...I THINK YOU'RE PRETTY RADICAL TOO.
CUTE.
NOW, A GROUP OF YOUR COLLEAGUES ARE STILL ON THE RUN FROM FEDERAL, STATE, AND PRIVATE LOCAL LAW ENFORCEMENT.
SHOULD WE TAKE THIS TO MEAN YOU'VE CUT TIES WITH YOUR FORMER CASTMATES?
OH, GEE... I GUESS? I GUESS SO...
GOOD FOR YOU!
SO, WHAT CAN YOU TELL US ABOUT THESE IMMIGRANTS' FLAT-OUT TERRORIST OPERATION?
I--I DON'T KNOW THAT IT'S FAIR TO SAY "TERRORIST"...

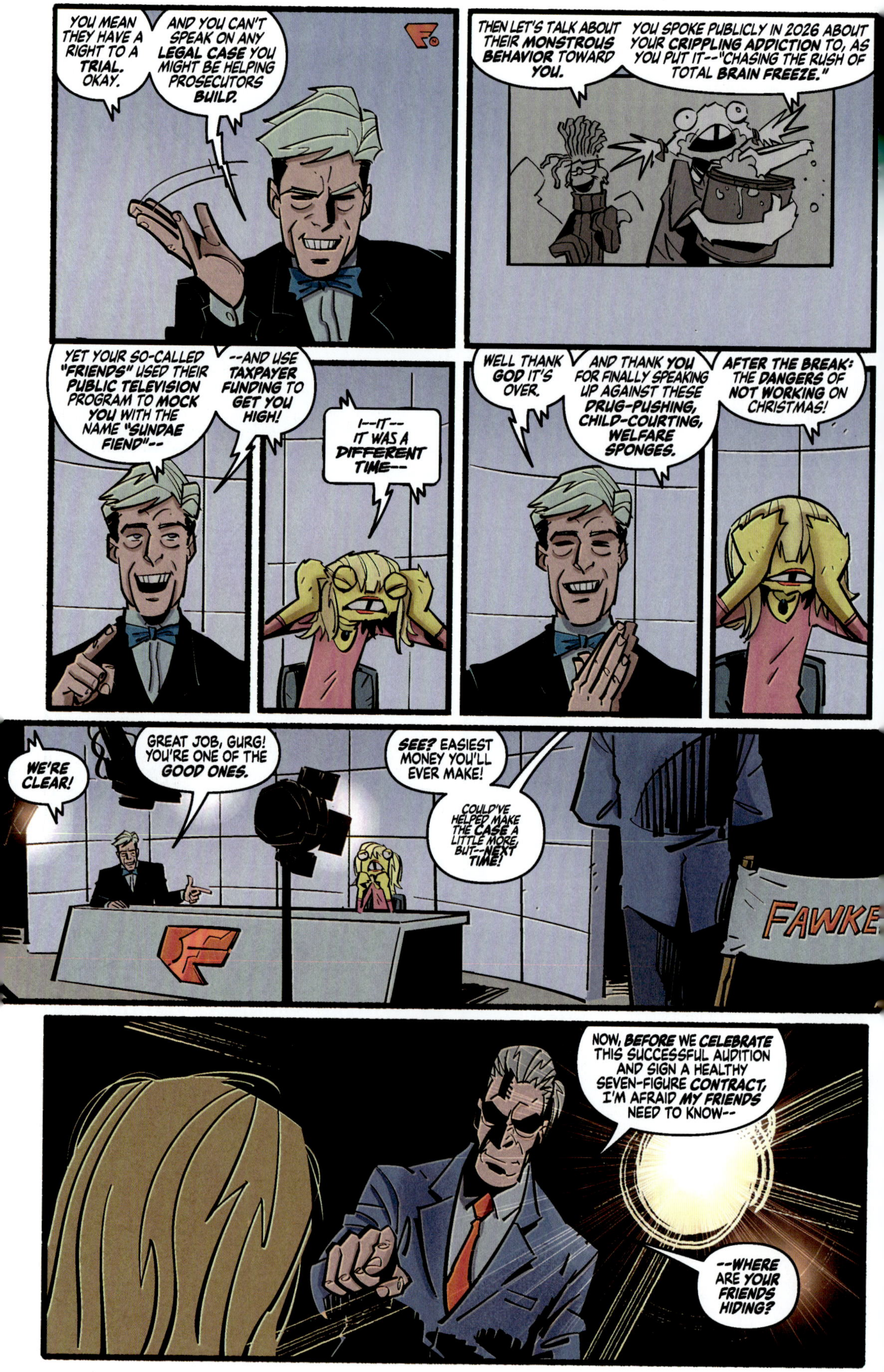
YOU MEAN THEY HAVE A RIGHT TO A TRIAL. OKAY.
AND YOU CAN'T SPEAK ON ANY LEGAL CASE YOU MIGHT BE HELPING PROSECUTORS BUILD.
THEN LET'S TALK ABOUT THEIR MONSTROUS BEHAVIOR TOWARD YOU.
YOU SPOKE PUBLICLY IN 2026 ABOUT YOUR CRIPPLING ADDICTION TO, AS YOU PUT IT--"CHASING THE RUSH OF TOTAL BRAIN FREEZE."
YET YOUR SO-CALLED "FRIENDS" USED THEIR PUBLIC TELEVISION PROGRAM TO MOCK YOU WITH THE NAME "SUNDAE FIEND"--
--AND USE TAXPAYER FUNDING TO GET YOU HIGH!
I--IT--IT WAS A DIFFERENT TIME--
WELL THANK GOD IT'S OVER.
AND THANK YOU FOR FINALLY SPEAKING UP AGAINST THESE DRUG-PUSHING, CHILD-COURTING, WELFARE SPONGES.
AFTER THE BREAK: THE DANGERS OF NOT WORKING ON CHRISTMAS!
WE'RE CLEAR!
GREAT JOB, GURG! YOU'RE ONE OF THE GOOD ONES.
SEE? EASIEST MONEY YOU'LL EVER MAKE!
COULD'VE HELPED MAKE THE CASE A LITTLE MORE, BUT--NEXT TIME!
FAWKE
NOW, BEFORE WE CELEBRATE THIS SUCCESSFUL AUDITION AND SIGN A HEALTHY SEVEN-FIGURE CONTRACT, I'M AFRAID MY FRIENDS NEED TO KNOW--
--WHERE ARE YOUR FRIENDS HIDING?

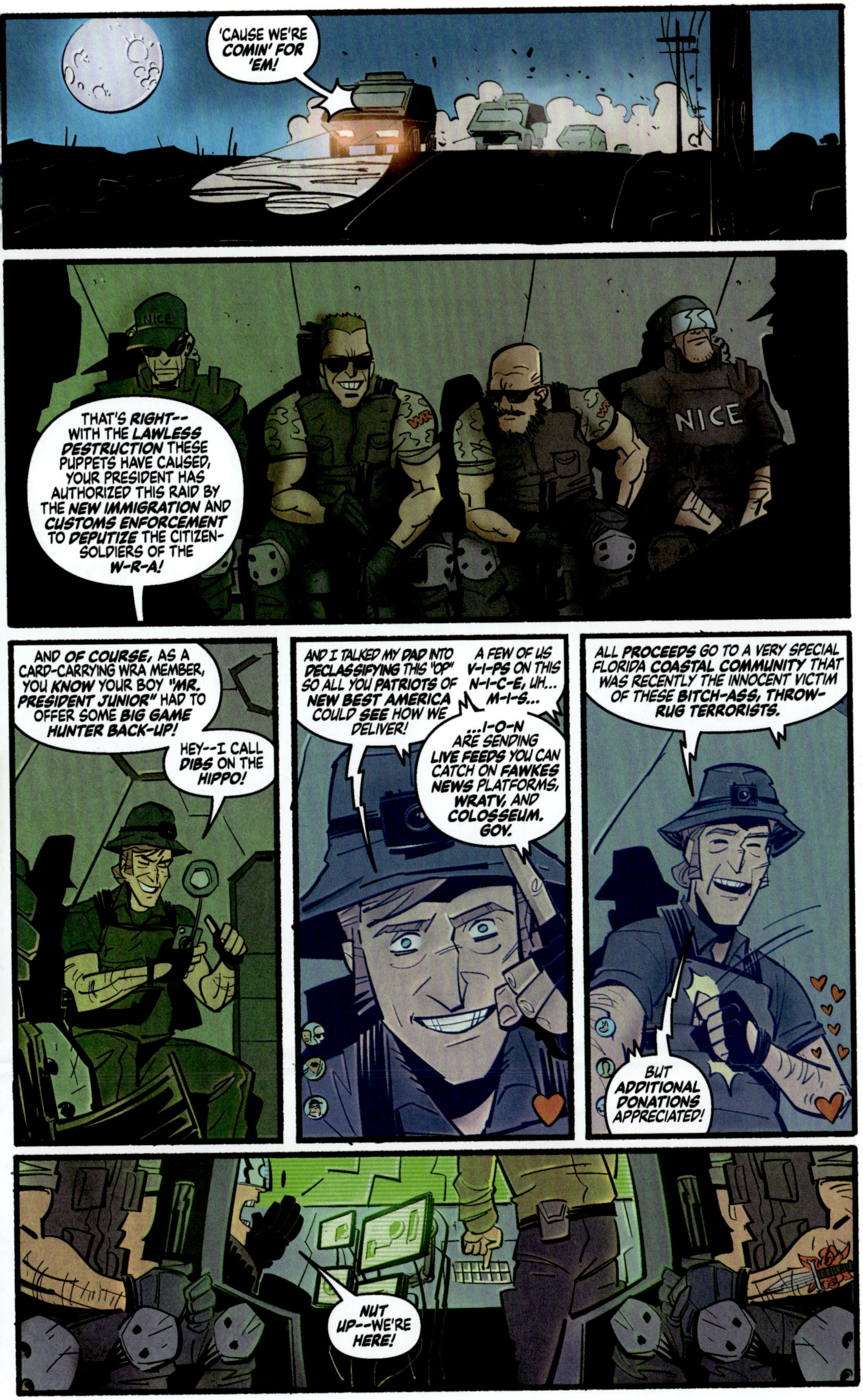
'CAUSE WE'RE COMIN' FOR 'EM!
NICE
THAT'S RIGHT--WITH THE LAWLESS DESTRUCTION THESE PUPPETS HAVE CAUSED, YOUR PRESIDENT HAS AUTHORIZED THIS RAID BY THE NEW IMMIGRATION AND CUSTOMS ENFORCEMENT TO DEPUTIZE THE CITIZEN-SOLDIERS OF THE W-R-A!
AND OF COURSE, AS A CARD-CARRYING WRA MEMBER, YOU KNOW YOUR BOY "MR. PRESIDENT JUNIOR" HAD TO OFFER SOME BIG GAME HUNTER BACK-UP!
HEY--I CALL DIBS ON THE HIPPO!
AND I TALKED MY DAD INTO DECLASSIFYING THIS "OP" SO ALL YOU PATRIOTS OF NEW BEST AMERICA COULD SEE HOW WE DELIVER!
A FEW OF US V-I-PS ON THIS N-I-C-E, UH... M-I-S...
...I-O-N ARE SENDING LIVE FEEDS YOU CAN CATCH ON FAWKES NEWS PLATFORMS, WRATV, AND COLOSSEUM. GOV.
ALL PROCEEDS GO TO A VERY SPECIAL FLORIDA COASTAL COMMUNITY THAT WAS RECENTLY THE INNOCENT VICTIM OF THESE BITCH-ASS, THROW-RUG TERRORISTS.
BUT ADDITIONAL DONATIONS APPRECIATED!
NUT UP--WE'RE HERE!

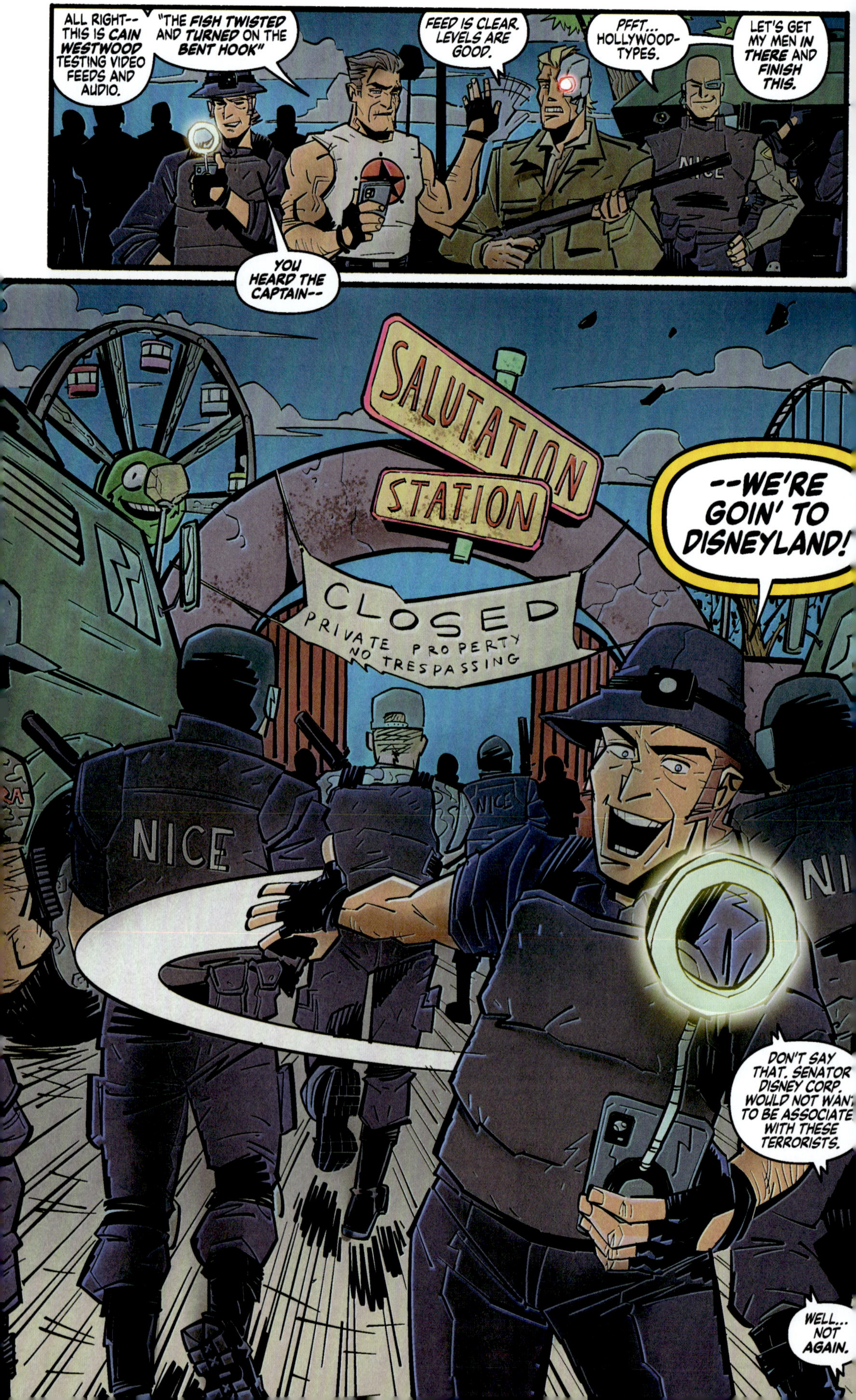

ALL RIGHT-- THIS IS CAIN WESTWOOD TESTING VIDEO FEEDS AND AUDIO.
"THE FISH TWISTED AND TURNED ON THE BENT HOOK"
FEED IS CLEAR. LEVELS ARE GOOD.
PFFT... HOLLYWOOD-TYPES.
LET'S GET MY MEN IN THERE AND FINISH THIS.
NICE
YOU HEARD THE CAPTAIN--
SALUTATION STATION
CLOSED PRIVATE PROPERTY NO TRESPASSING
--WE'RE GOIN' TO DISNEYLAND!
NICE
DON'T SAY THAT. SENATOR DISNEY CORP. WOULD NOT WAN' TO BE ASSOCIATE WITH THESE TERRORISTS.
WELL... NOT AGAIN.

I MEAN IT, BIRDIE!

SECURITY

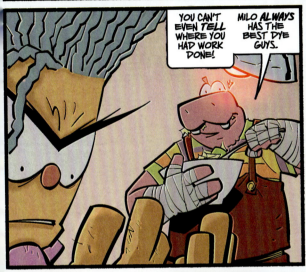

YOU CAN'T EVEN *TELL* WHERE YOU HAD WORK DONE!

MILO *ALWAYS* HAS THE BEST DYE GUYS.

LOOK AT THIS!

THEY HAD *PEOPLE* DRESS UP AS US?

THAT'S *FUR-FACE!*

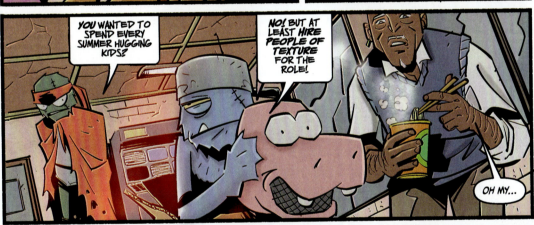

YOU WANTED TO SPEND EVERY SUMMER HUGGING KIDS?

NO! BUT AT LEAST *HIRE* PEOPLE OF *TEXTURE* FOR THE ROLE!

OH MY...

...THIS *IS* PROBLEMATIC.

IRMA & BIRDIE BIG SCISSOR FUN

WHAT THE--?

CHIEF? DID YOU ORDER POWER-ON?

NEGATIVE. FALL BACK TO COVER POSITIONS!

SPELLYA SPELLINGT

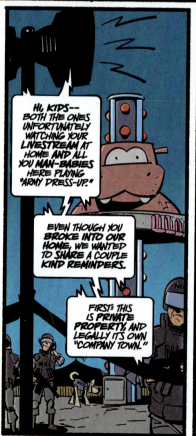

HI, KIDS-- BOTH THE ONES UNFORTUNATELY WATCHING YOUR LIVESTREAM AT HOME AND ALL YOU MAN-BABIES HERE PLAYING "ARMY DRESS-UP."

EVEN THOUGH YOU BROKE INTO OUR HOME, WE WANTED TO SHARE A COUPLE KIND REMINDERS.

FIRST: THIS IS PRIVATE PROPERTY, AND LEGALLY IT'S OWN "COMPANY TOWN."

SO BY YOUR LAWS, YOU HAVE NO RIGHTS EXCEPT ONES WE GRANT.

AND IF YOU'D READ THE SIGN OUT FRONT, YOU'D KNOW--

--THERE'S NO GUNS, NO ENTERING WITHOUT PERMISSION, AND ONE HOLD-OVER FROM THE PREVIOUS OWNERS--

--"BY ENTERING THIS PROPERTY YOU ASSUME ALL LIABILITY FOR ANY ACCIDENTS, INJURIES, OR DEATHS THAT OCCUR."

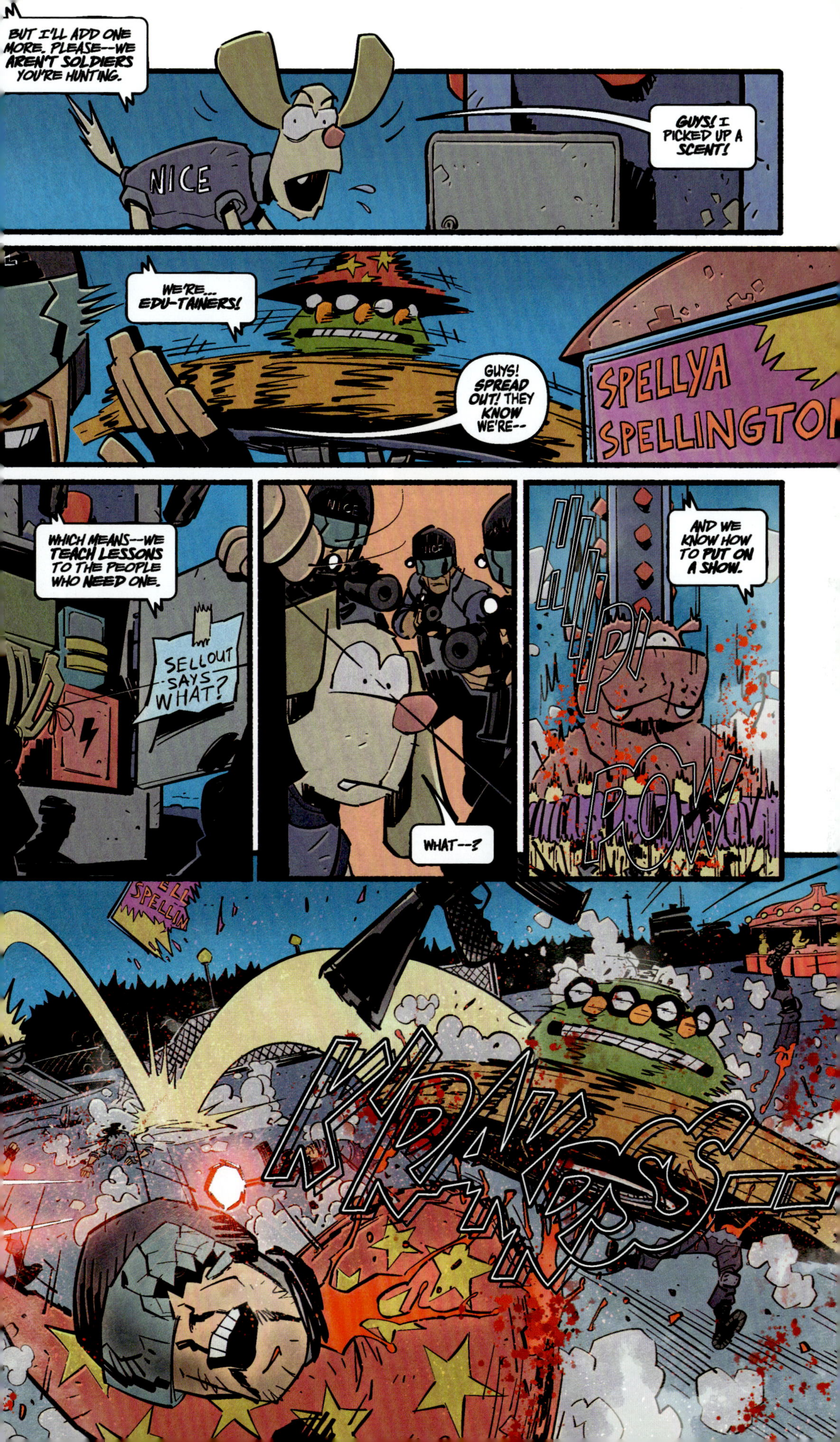
BUT I'LL ADD ONE MORE. PLEASE--WE AREN'T SOLDIERS YOU'RE HUNTING.
NICE
GUYS! I PICKED UP A SCENT!
WE'RE... EDU-TAINERS!
GUYS! SPREAD OUT! THEY KNOW WE'RE--
SPELLYA SPELLINGTON
WHICH MEANS--WE TEACH LESSONS TO THE PEOPLE WHO NEED ONE.
SELLOUT SAYS WHAT?
WHAT--?
AND WE KNOW HOW TO PUT ON A SHOW.
POW
KRAKOOSSH

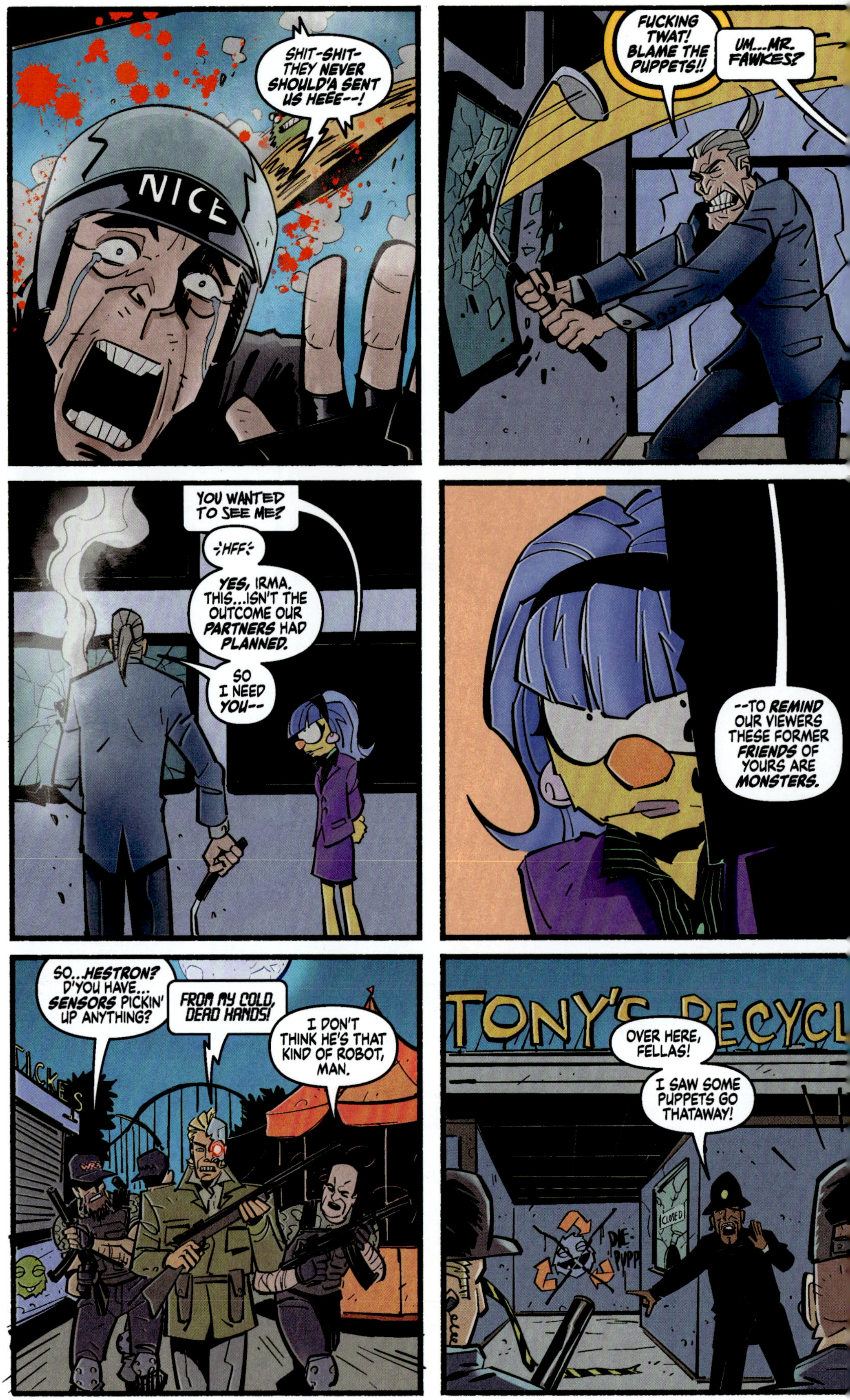
SHIT-SHIT-THEY NEVER SHOULD'A SENT US HEEE--!
NICE
FUCKING TWAT! BLAME THE PUPPETS!!
UM...MR. FAWKES?
YOU WANTED TO SEE ME?
HFF
YES, IRMA. THIS...ISN'T THE OUTCOME OUR PARTNERS HAD PLANNED.
SO I NEED YOU--
--TO REMIND OUR VIEWERS THESE FORMER FRIENDS OF YOURS ARE MONSTERS.
SO...HESTRON? D'YOU HAVE... SENSORS PICKIN' UP ANYTHING?
FROM MY COLD, DEAD HANDS!
I DON'T THINK HE'S THAT KIND OF ROBOT, MAN.
TONY'S RECYCL
OVER HERE, FELLAS!
I SAW SOME PUPPETS GO THATAWAY!
CLOSED

HEY, KIDS! YOU'VE HEARD YOUR PAL TONY TELL YA TO RECYCLE YOUR UNWANTED TRASH--BUT EVER WONDER WHAT HAPPENS TO IT?

FIRST, IT GETS COLLECTED AND SORTED BY MAGNETS AND WORKERS.

TH... ARE RE... OR O...

AW, MAN-- WHAT THE HELL?!

--SNFF-- SNFF--

THAT DOESN'T SMELL LIKE WATE--

OW! AH! IT BURNS!

FPPUUCHH! I-IT WWSS FPPUCHHING AASSIIID!

THEN, THE CLEANED MATERIAL GETS CRUSHED INTO TIGHT BLOCKS FOR SHIPPING.

BUT DON'T WORRY, WE'LL BE GENTLE!

FINALLY, RECYCLABLES GET MELTED DOWN INTO RAW MATERIAL.

BUT I'VE GOT NO USE FOR CONCENTRATED PIECES OF SHIT.

SO CONGRATS! YOU DIED FOR NOTHING.

FROM MY HOT, DEAD HAARNNDDZZ--

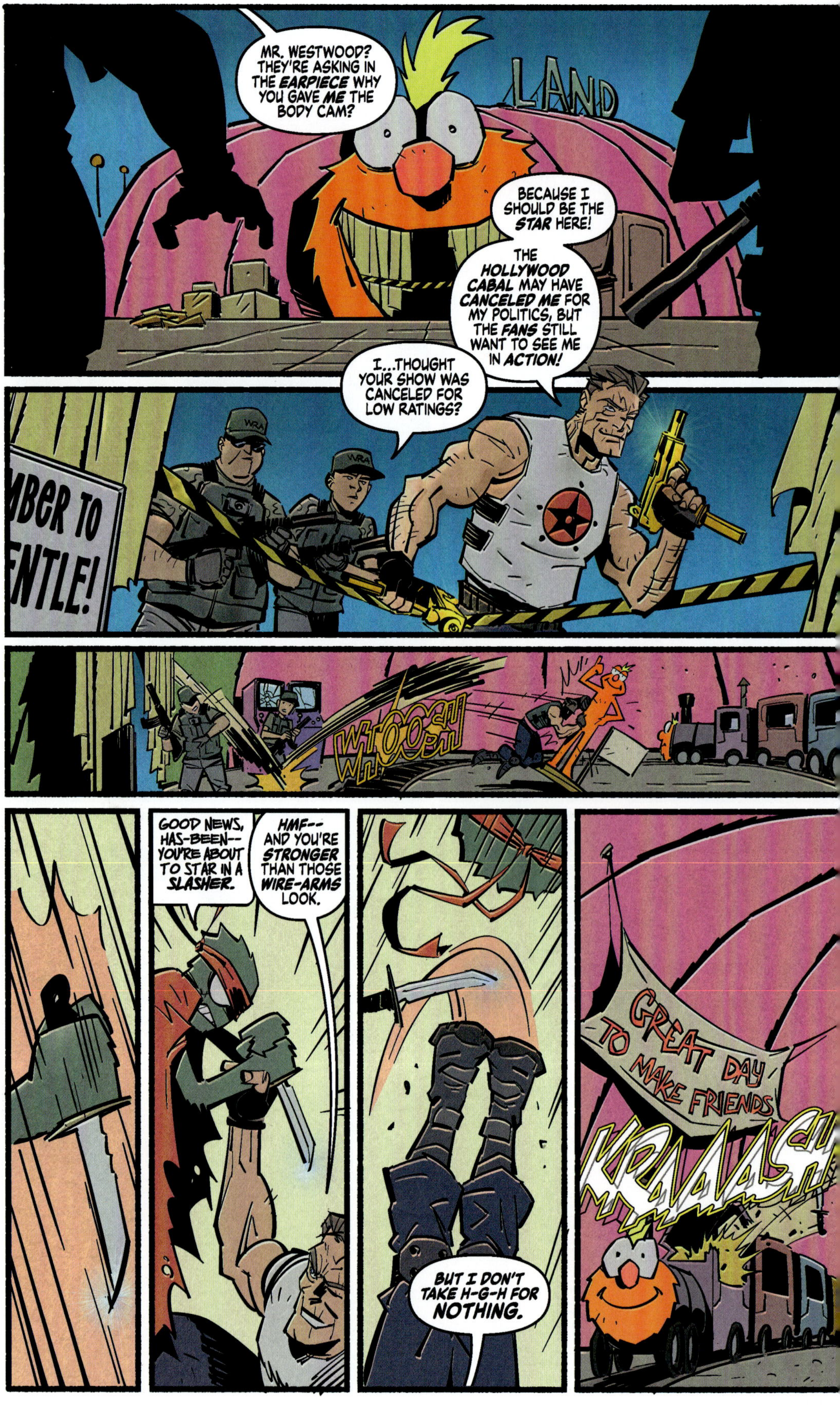
LAND
MR. WESTWOOD? THEY'RE ASKING IN THE ***EARPIECE*** WHY YOU GAVE ***ME*** THE BODY CAM?
BECAUSE I SHOULD BE THE ***STAR*** HERE!
THE ***HOLLYWOOD CABAL*** MAY HAVE ***CANCELED ME*** FOR MY POLITICS, BUT THE ***FANS*** STILL WANT TO SEE ME IN ***ACTION!***
I...THOUGHT YOUR SHOW WAS CANCELED FOR LOW RATINGS?
GOOD NEWS, HAS-BEEN-- YOU'RE ABOUT TO STAR IN A ***SLASHER.***
HMF-- AND YOU'RE ***STRONGER*** THAN THOSE ***WIRE-ARMS*** LOOK.
BUT I DON'T TAKE H-G-H FOR ***NOTHING.***
GREAT DAY TO MAKE FRIENDS

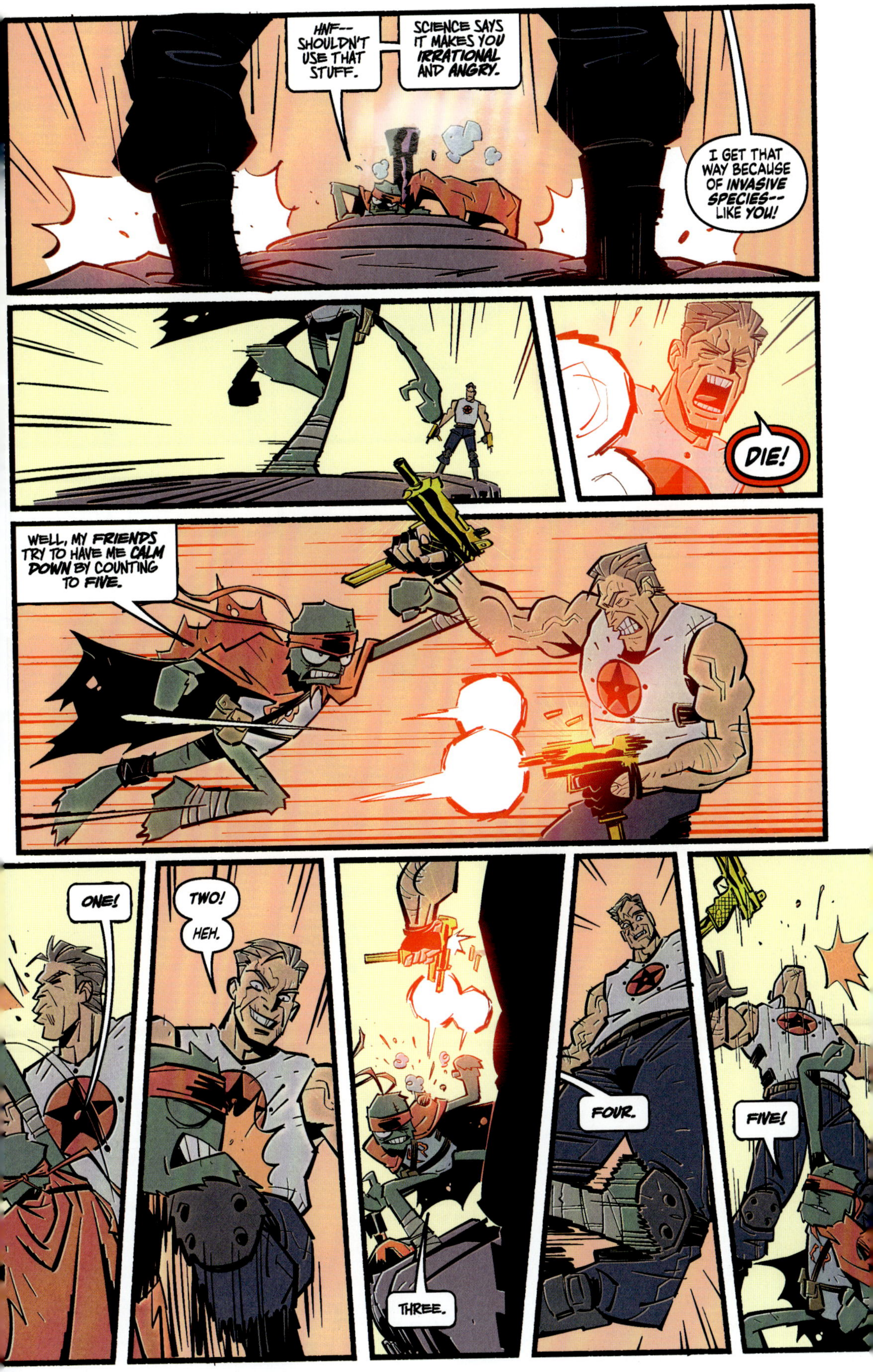
HNF--SHOULDN'T USE THAT STUFF.
SCIENCE SAYS IT MAKES YOU IRRATIONAL AND ANGRY.
I GET THAT WAY BECAUSE OF INVASIVE SPECIES--LIKE YOU!
DIE!
WELL, MY FRIENDS TRY TO HAVE ME CALM DOWN BY COUNTING TO FIVE.
ONE!
TWO!
HEH.
THREE.
FOUR.
FIVE!

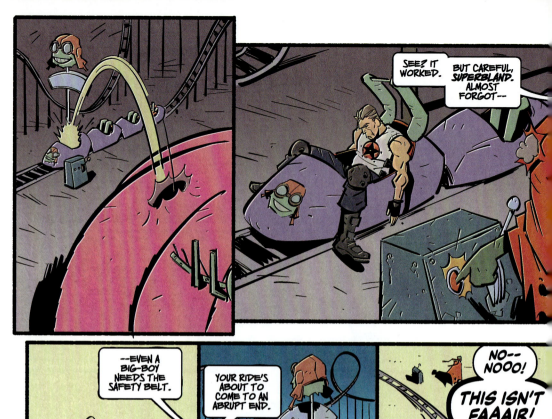

SEE? IT WORKED.

BUT CAREFUL, SUPERBLAND. ALMOST FORGOT--

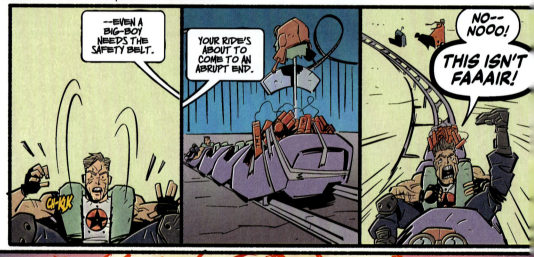

--EVEN A BIG-BOY NEEDS THE SAFETY BELT.

CH-KLK

YOUR RIDE'S ABOUT TO COME TO AN ABRUPT END.

NO-- NOOO!

THIS ISN'T FAAAIR!

FAIRNESS? YOU MUST HAVE ME CONFUSED FOR SOMEONE ELSE.

BOOM

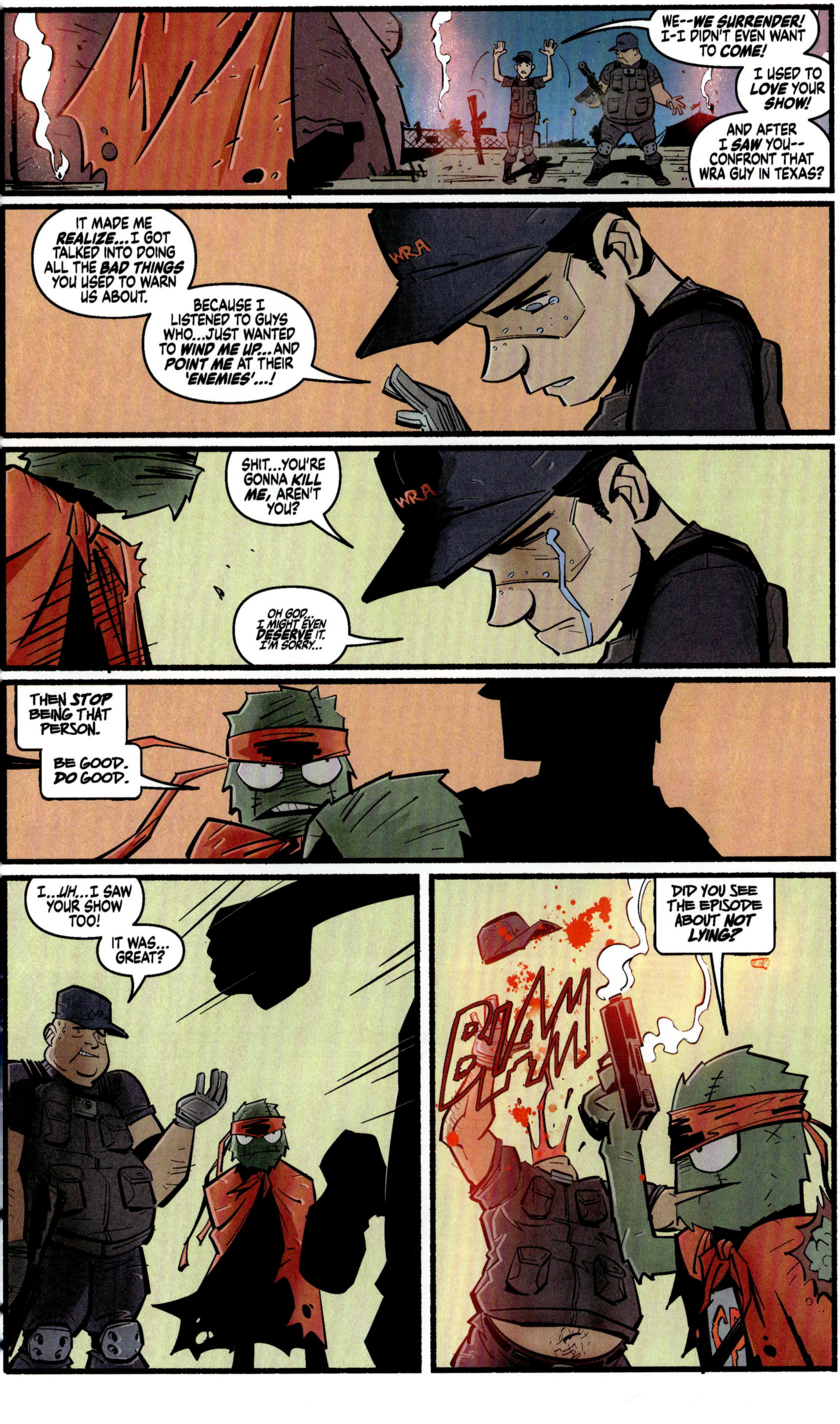

WE--WE SURRENDER! I-I DIDN'T EVEN WANT TO COME!
I USED TO LOVE YOUR SHOW!
AND AFTER I SAW YOU--CONFRONT THAT WRA GUY IN TEXAS?
IT MADE ME REALIZE...I GOT TALKED INTO DOING ALL THE BAD THINGS YOU USED TO WARN US ABOUT.
BECAUSE I LISTENED TO GUYS WHO...JUST WANTED TO WIND ME UP...AND POINT ME AT THEIR 'ENEMIES'...!
WRA
SHIT...YOU'RE GONNA KILL ME, AREN'T YOU?
OH GOD... I MIGHT EVEN DESERVE IT. I'M SORRY...
THEN STOP BEING THAT PERSON.
BE GOOD. DO GOOD.
I..UH...I SAW YOUR SHOW TOO!
IT WAS... GREAT?
DID YOU SEE THE EPISODE ABOUT NOT LYING?
BLAM

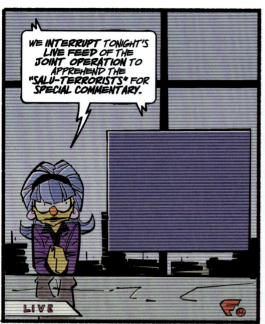

WE INTERRUPT TONIGHT'S LIVE FEED OF THE JOINT OPERATION TO APPREHEND THE "SALU-TERRORISTS" FOR SPECIAL COMMENTARY.

LIVE

SOME VIEWERS ARE POSTING CONCERNS THAT THE TARGETS AREN'T RECEIVING SOME SORT OF...HUMANE TREATMENT THEY IMAGINE SHOULD BE ENTITLED TO.

BUT I...FEEL THE NEED TO SHOW YOU...WE AREN'T DEALING WITH "NORMAL PEOPLE"--

IRMA? WH-WHAT IS THIS?

LIVE

--WE'RE DEALING WITH MONSTERS.

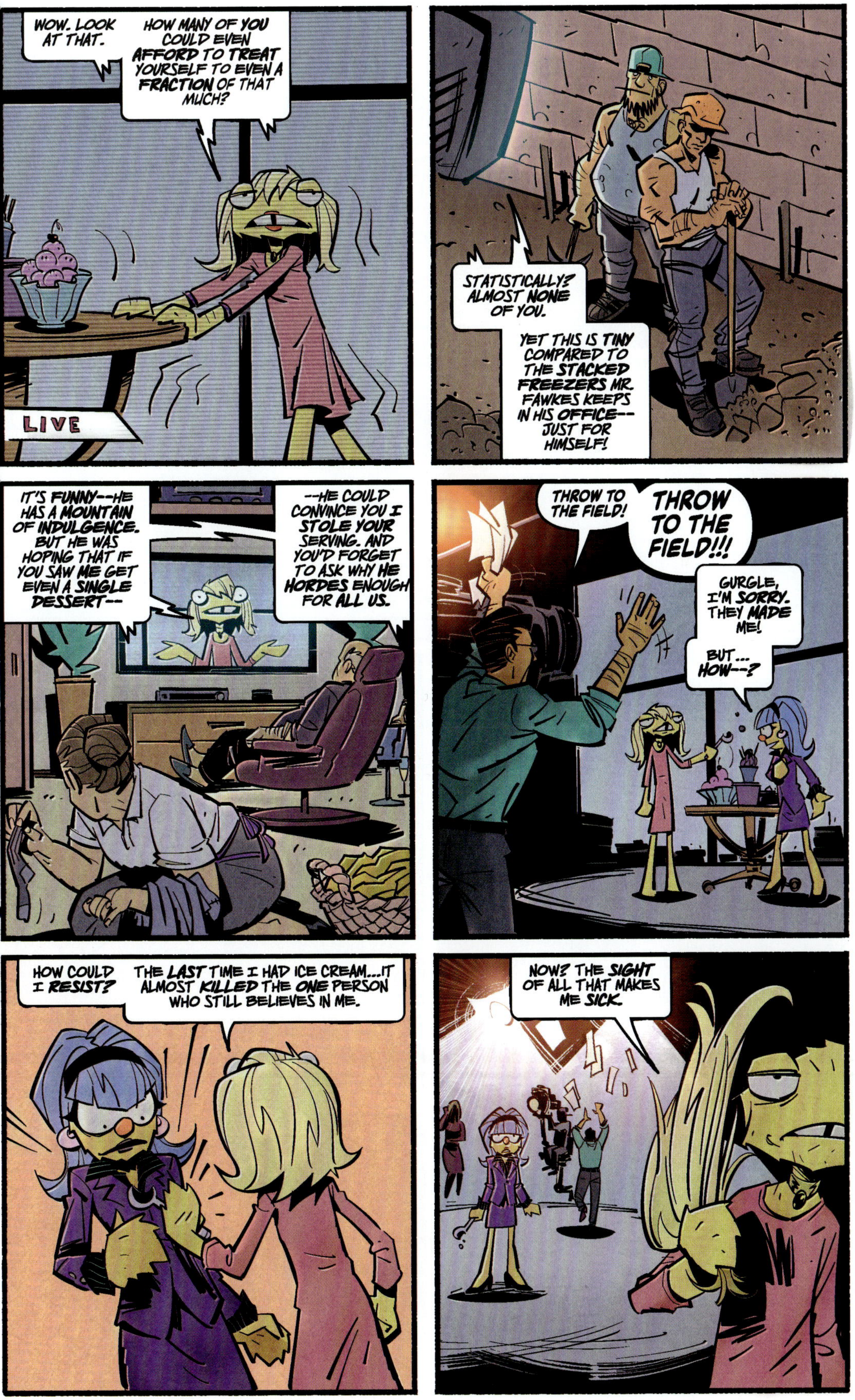
WOW. LOOK AT THAT.
HOW MANY OF YOU COULD EVEN AFFORD TO TREAT YOURSELF TO EVEN A FRACTION OF THAT MUCH?
LIVE
STATISTICALLY? ALMOST NONE OF YOU.
YET THIS IS TINY COMPARED TO THE STACKED FREEZERS MR. FAWKES KEEPS IN HIS OFFICE--JUST FOR HIMSELF!
IT'S FUNNY--HE HAS A MOUNTAIN OF INDULGENCE. BUT HE WAS HOPING THAT IF YOU SAW ME GET EVEN A SINGLE DESSERT--
--HE COULD CONVINCE YOU I STOLE YOUR SERVING. AND YOU'D FORGET TO ASK WHY HE HORDES ENOUGH FOR ALL US.
THROW TO THE FIELD!
THROW TO THE FIELD!!!
GURGLE, I'M SORRY. THEY MADE ME!
BUT... HOW--?
HOW COULD I RESIST?
THE LAST TIME I HAD ICE CREAM...IT ALMOST KILLED THE ONE PERSON WHO STILL BELIEVES IN ME.
NOW? THE SIGHT OF ALL THAT MAKES ME SICK.

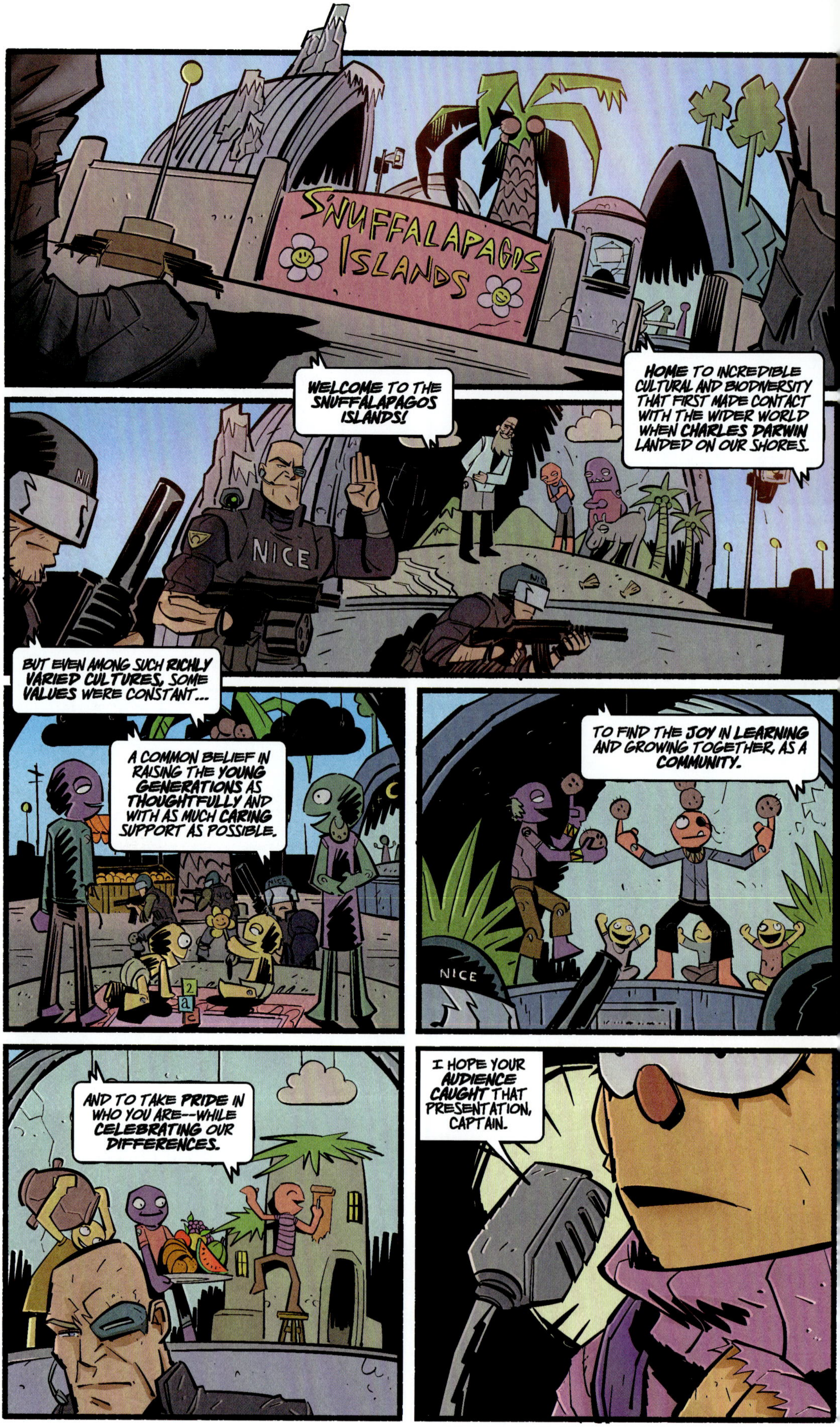
SNUFFALAPAGOS ISLANDS
WELCOME TO THE SNUFFALAPAGOS ISLANDS!
HOME TO INCREDIBLE CULTURAL AND BIODIVERSITY THAT FIRST MADE CONTACT WITH THE WIDER WORLD WHEN CHARLES DARWIN LANDED ON OUR SHORES.
NICE
BUT EVEN AMONG SUCH RICHLY VARIED CULTURES, SOME VALUES WERE CONSTANT...
A COMMON BELIEF IN RAISING THE YOUNG GENERATIONS AS THOUGHTFULLY AND WITH AS MUCH CARING SUPPORT AS POSSIBLE.
TO FIND THE JOY IN LEARNING AND GROWING TOGETHER, AS A COMMUNITY.
NICE
AND TO TAKE PRIDE IN WHO YOU ARE--WHILE CELEBRATING OUR DIFFERENCES.
I HOPE YOUR AUDIENCE CAUGHT THAT PRESENTATION, CAPTAIN.

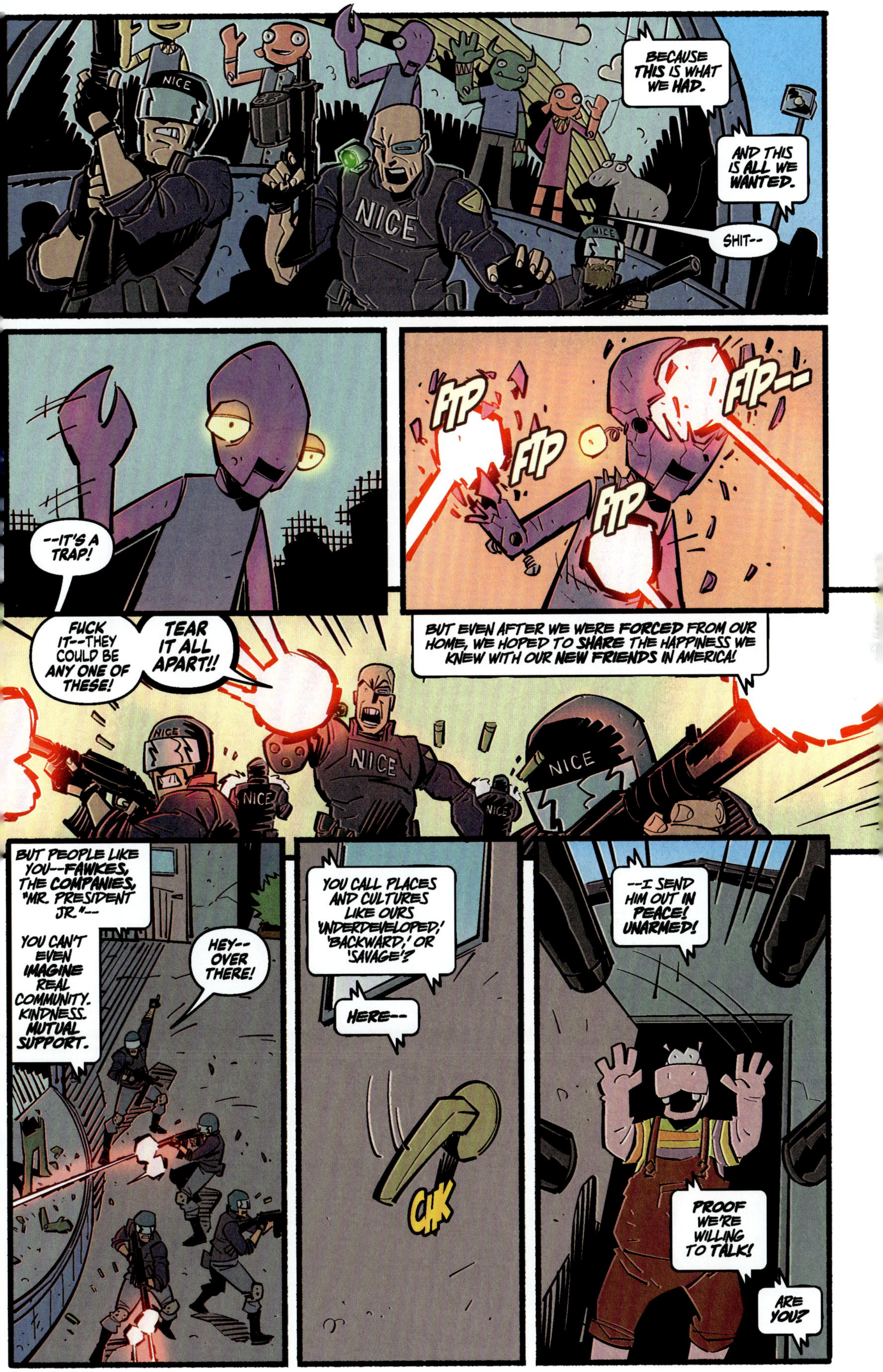
BECAUSE THIS IS WHAT WE HAD.
AND THIS IS ALL WE WANTED.
SHIT--
--IT'S A TRAP!
FTP
FTP
FTP
FTP--
FUCK IT--THEY COULD BE ANY ONE OF THESE!
TEAR IT ALL APART!!
BUT EVEN AFTER WE WERE FORCED FROM OUR HOME, WE HOPED TO SHARE THE HAPPINESS WE KNEW WITH OUR NEW FRIENDS IN AMERICA!
BUT PEOPLE LIKE YOU--FAWKES, THE COMPANIES, "MR. PRESIDENT JR."--
YOU CAN'T EVEN IMAGINE REAL COMMUNITY. KINDNESS. MUTUAL SUPPORT.
HEY--OVER THERE!
YOU CALL PLACES AND CULTURES LIKE OURS 'UNDERDEVELOPED,' 'BACKWARD,' OR 'SAVAGE'?
HERE--
CLIK
--I SEND HIM OUT IN PEACE! UNARMED!
PROOF WE'RE WILLING TO TALK!
ARE YOU?

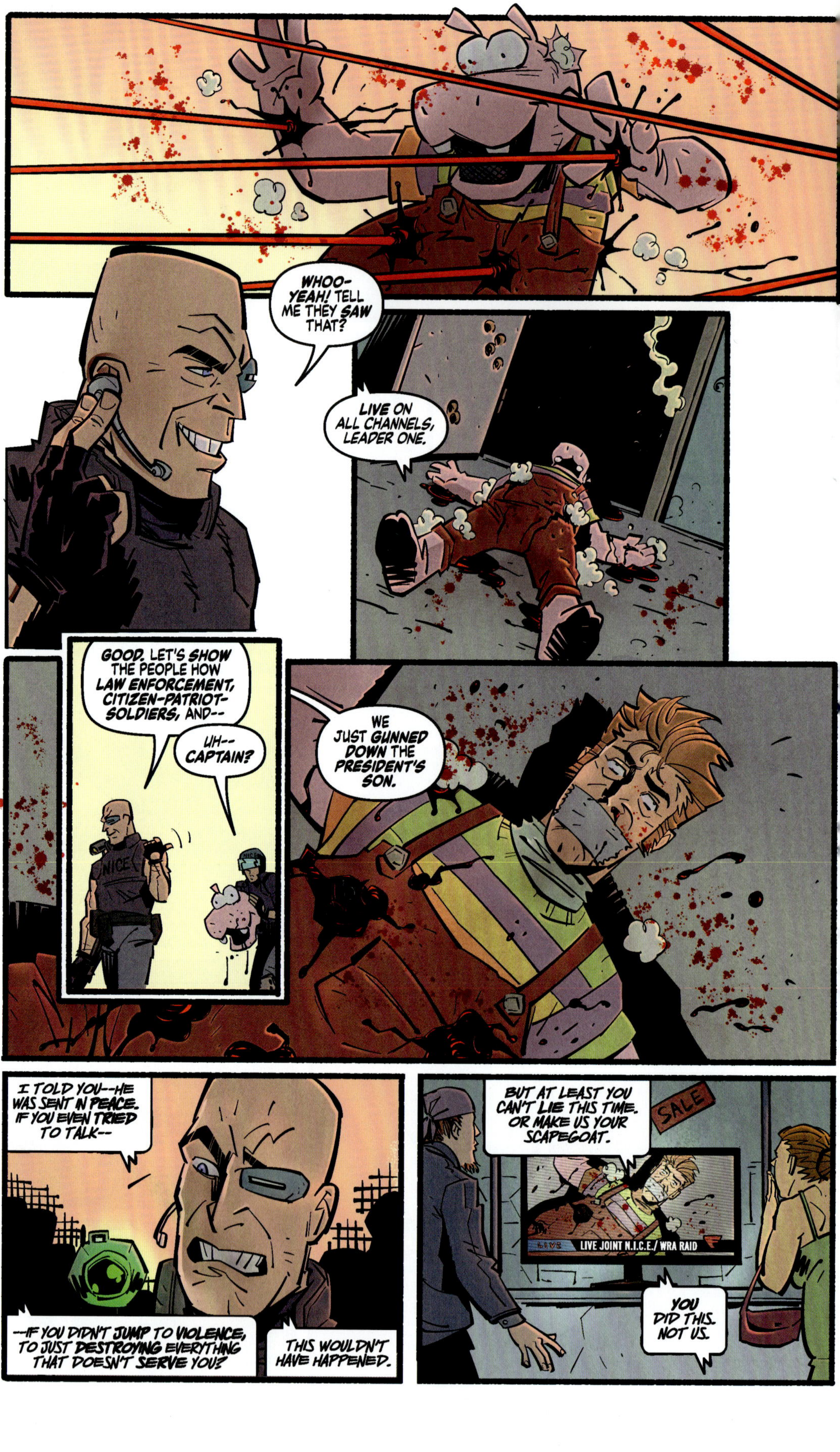
WHOO-YEAH! TELL ME THEY SAW THAT?
LIVE ON ALL CHANNELS, LEADER ONE.
GOOD. LET'S SHOW THE PEOPLE HOW LAW ENFORCEMENT, CITIZEN-PATRIOT-SOLDIERS, AND--
UH-- CAPTAIN?
NICE
WE JUST GUNNED DOWN THE PRESIDENT'S SON.
I TOLD YOU--HE WAS SENT IN PEACE. IF YOU EVEN TRIED TO TALK--
--IF YOU DIDN'T JUMP TO VIOLENCE, TO JUST DESTROYING EVERYTHING THAT DOESN'T SERVE YOU?
THIS WOULDN'T HAVE HAPPENED.
SALE
BUT AT LEAST YOU CAN'T LIE THIS TIME. OR MAKE US YOUR SCAPEGOAT.
LIVE JOINT N.I.C.E./ WRA RAID
YOU DID THIS. NOT US.

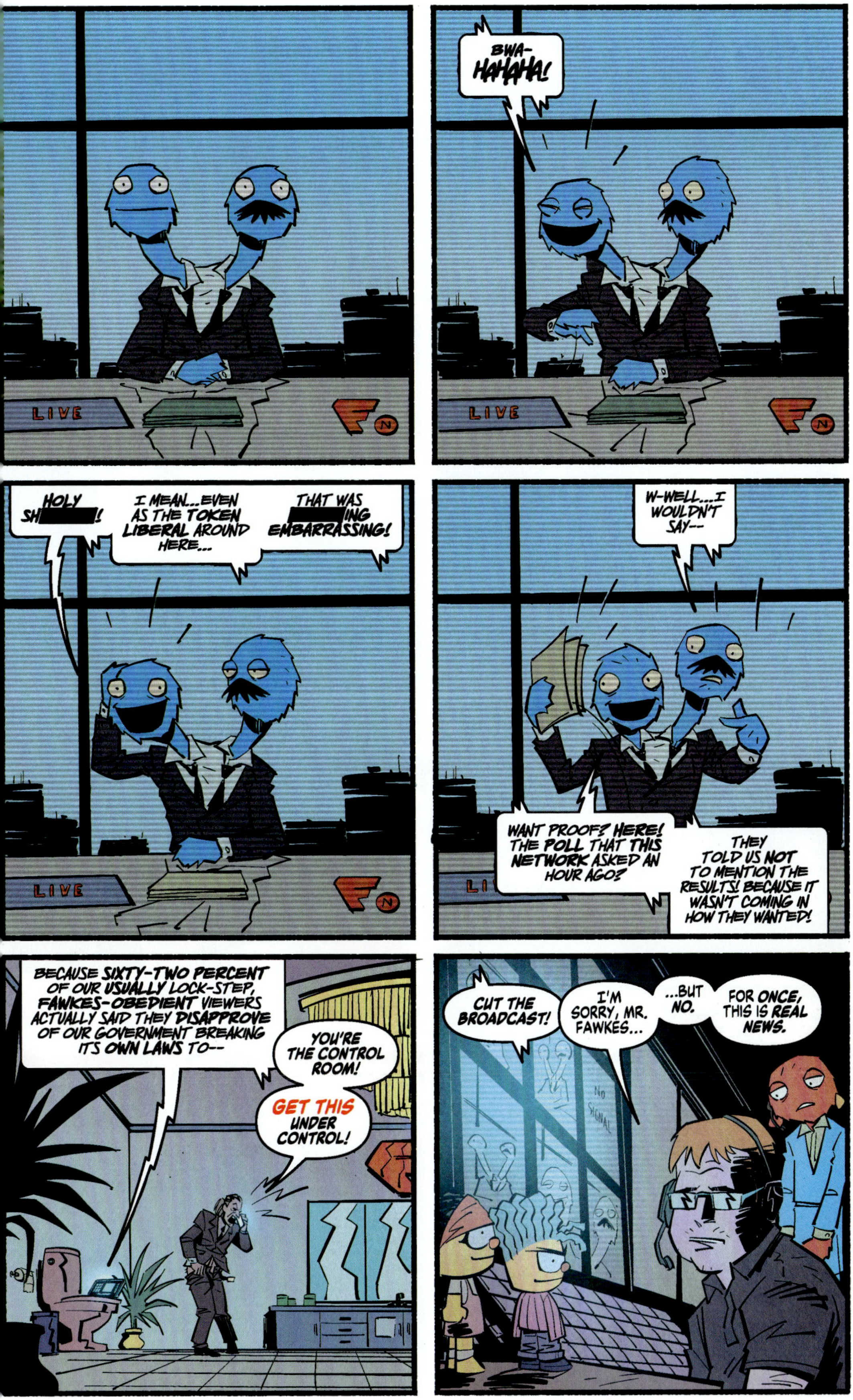
LIVE
BWA-HAHAHA!
LIVE
HOLY SH[redacted]!
I MEAN...EVEN AS THE TOKEN LIBERAL AROUND HERE...
THAT WAS [redacted]ING EMBARRASSING!
LIVE
W-WELL...I WOULDN'T SAY--
WANT PROOF? HERE! THE POLL THAT THIS NETWORK ASKED AN HOUR AGO?
THEY TOLD US NOT TO MENTION THE RESULTS! BECAUSE IT WASN'T COMING IN HOW THEY WANTED!
BECAUSE SIXTY-TWO PERCENT OF OUR USUALLY LOCK-STEP, FAWKES-OBEDIENT VIEWERS ACTUALLY SAID THEY DISAPPROVE OF OUR GOVERNMENT BREAKING ITS OWN LAWS TO--
YOU'RE THE CONTROL ROOM!
GET THIS UNDER CONTROL!
CUT THE BROADCAST!
I'M SORRY, MR. FAWKES...
...BUT NO.
FOR ONCE, THIS IS REAL NEWS.
NO SIGNAL

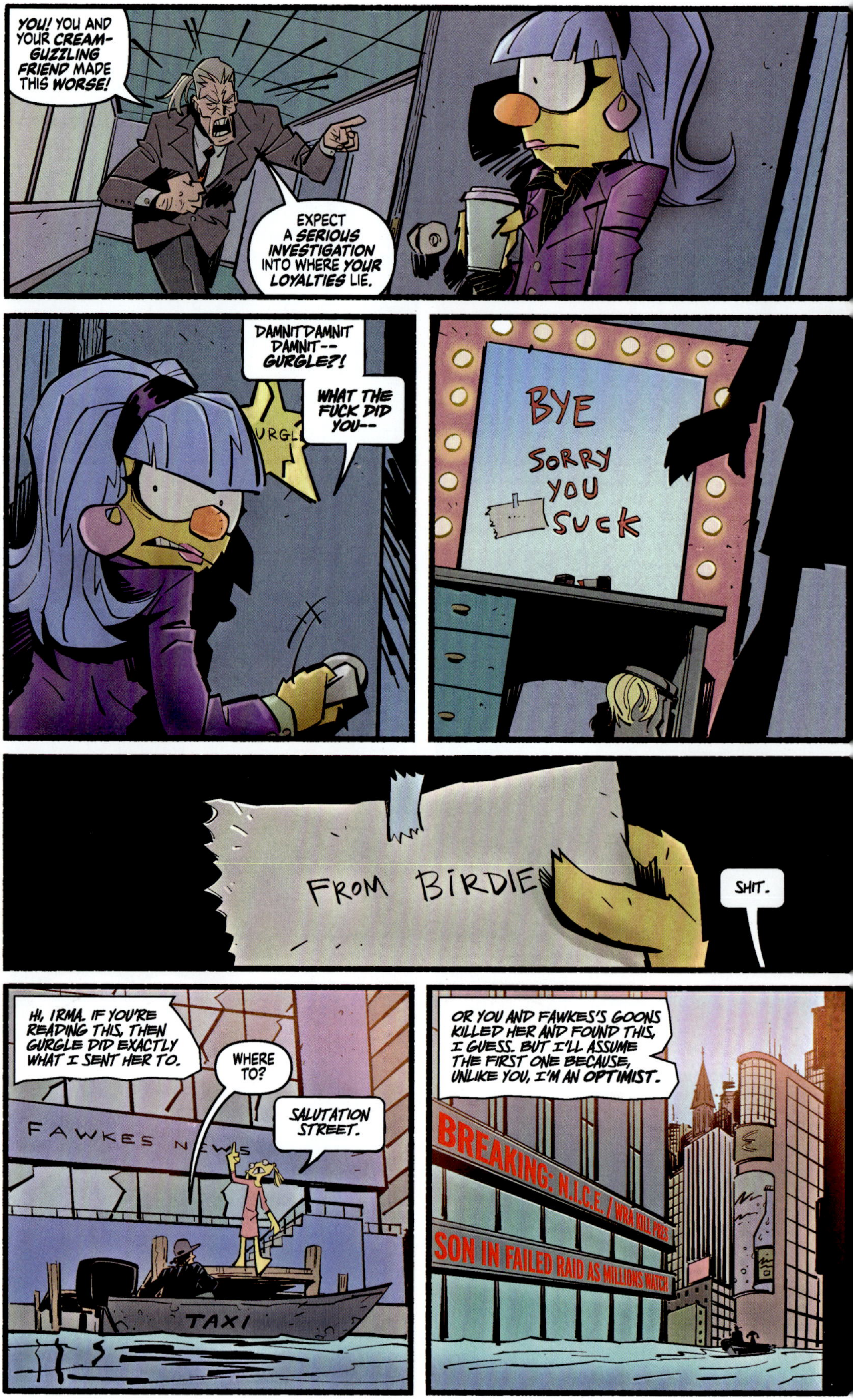
YOU! YOU AND YOUR CREAM-GUZZLING FRIEND MADE THIS WORSE!
EXPECT A SERIOUS INVESTIGATION INTO WHERE YOUR LOYALTIES LIE.
DAMNITDAMNIT DAMNIT-- GURGLE?!
URGL
WHAT THE FUCK DID YOU--
BYE
SORRY YOU SUCK
FROM BIRDIE
SHIT.
HI, IRMA. IF YOU'RE READING THIS, THEN GURGLE DID EXACTLY WHAT I SENT HER TO.
FAWKES NEWS
WHERE TO?
SALUTATION STREET.
TAXI
OR YOU AND FAWKES'S GOONS KILLED HER AND FOUND THIS, I GUESS. BUT I'LL ASSUME THE FIRST ONE BECAUSE, UNLIKE YOU, I'M AN OPTIMIST.
BREAKING: N.I.C.E. / WRA KILL PRES
SON IN FAILED RAID AS MILLIONS WATCH

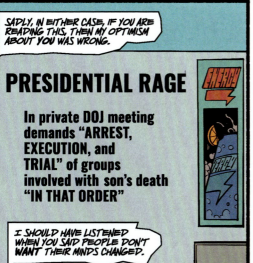

SADLY, IN EITHER CASE, IF YOU ARE READING THIS, THEN MY OPTIMISM ABOUT YOU WAS WRONG.
PRESIDENTIAL RAGE
In private DOJ meeting demands "ARREST, EXECUTION, and TRIAL" of groups involved with son's death "IN THAT ORDER"
ENERGY
I SHOULD HAVE LISTENED WHEN YOU SAID PEOPLE DON'T WANT THEIR MINDS CHANGED.
BUT I'M FINALLY LEARNING MY LESSON--
--SOMETIMES WE NEED TO STOP CARING.
IT'S WASTED ON THE BULLY WHO THINKS IT'S FUNNY TO HURT YOU WHEN YOU TRY TO BE NICE.
SOME PEOPLE ARE A BLACK HOLE.
THEY LIVE TO DEVOUR YOUR ENERGY, TO DESTROY, AND WILL NEVER CHANGE.
WHILE YOU COULD USE THAT ENERGY, INSTEAD, FOR SOMETHING GOOD.
BLAME N.I.C.E
HELP, OR JUST INSPIRE, PEOPLE WHO ARE READY TO MAKE CHANGE FOR THE BETTER.
SO HERE'S MY LAST BIT OF OPTIMISM FOR YOU, IRM:
PUPPETS
I HOPE LOSING... WHATEVER WE HAD DOES FINALLY INSPIRE YOU TO CHANGE.
BUT I WON'T BE COMING BACK TO SEE IT.
WE NEED TO PUT MORE GOOD INTO THE WORLD THAN WE CAN EVER EXPECT IN RETURN.
THERE ARE TOO MANY PEOPLE RACING TO THE BOTTOM.
PUPPETS ARE PEOPLE CORPORATIONS ARE NOT
I'D RATHER HELP THE PEOPLE WHO NEED IT GET TO THE END OF THE STREET.
--B.

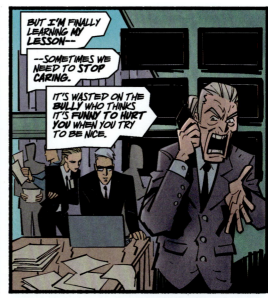

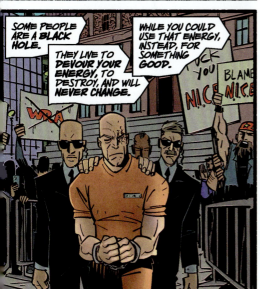

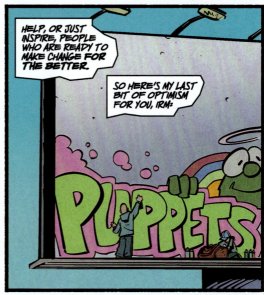

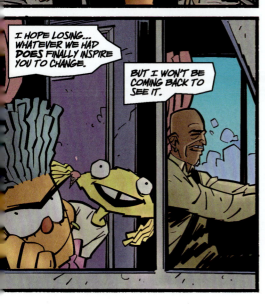

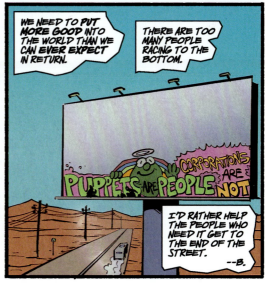

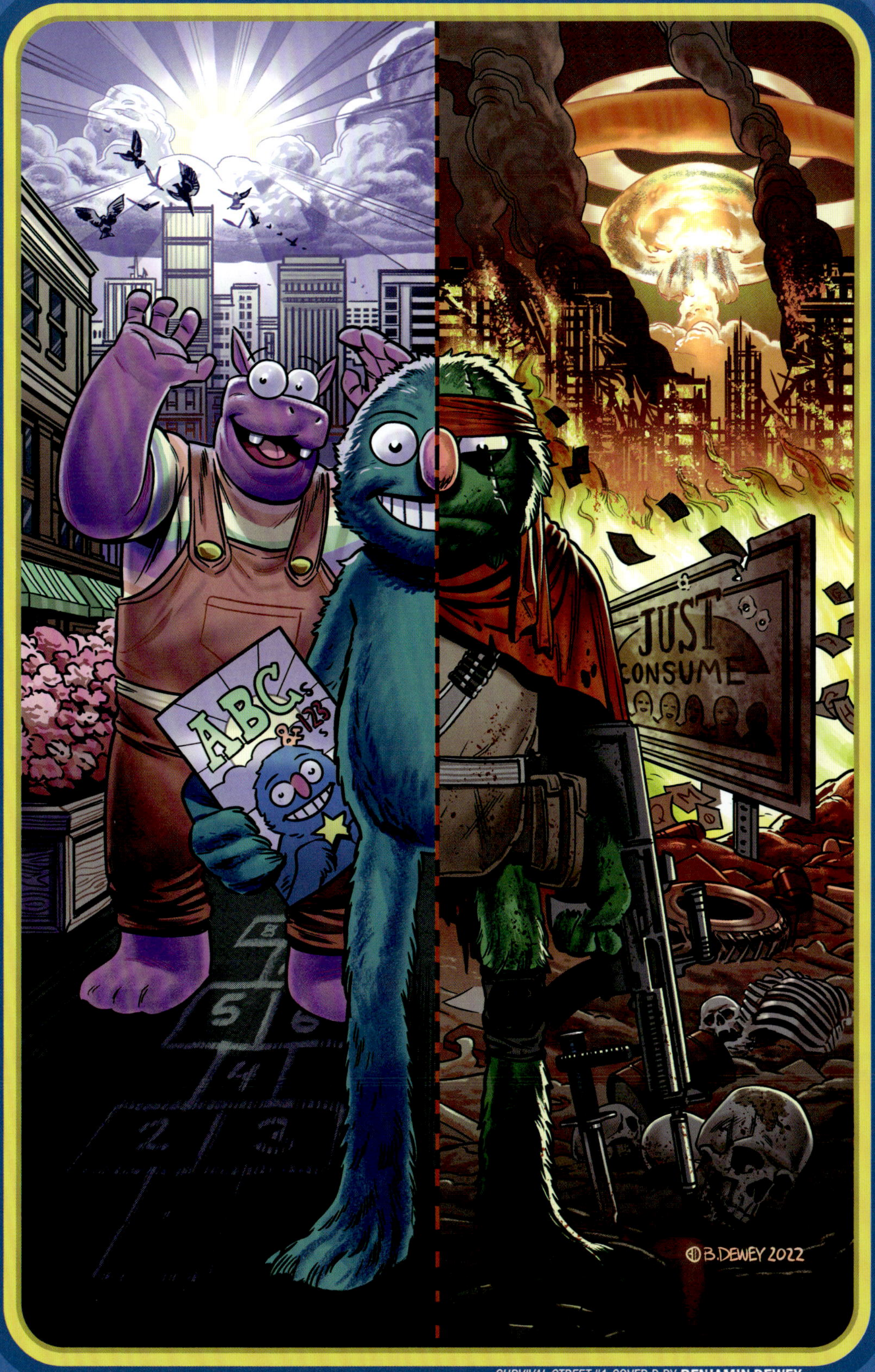
ABCs
&123
JUST
CONSUME
B.DEWEY 2022

SURVIVAL STREET #1 COVER B BY **BENJAMIN DEWEY**

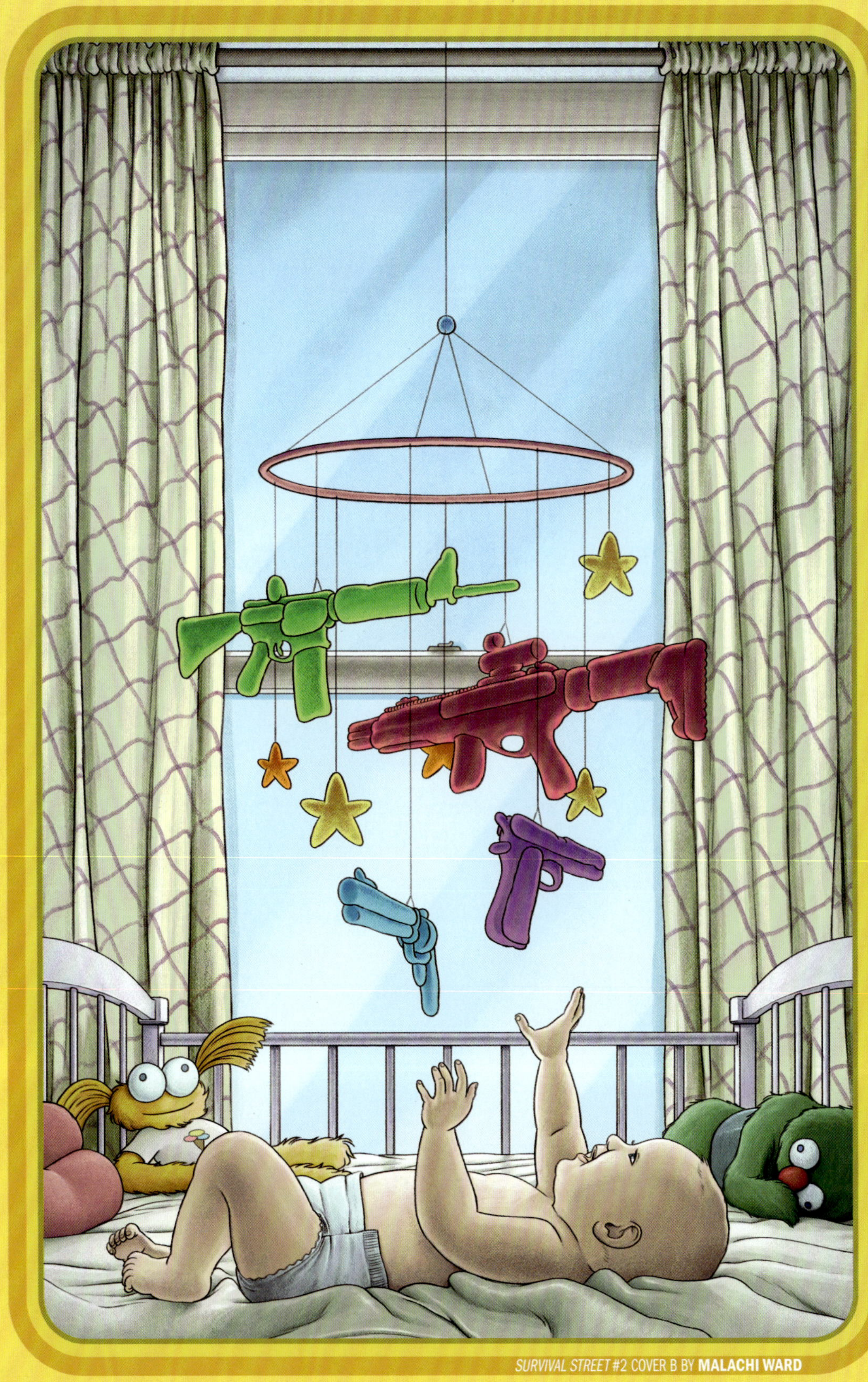

SURVIVAL STREET #2 COVER B BY **MALACHI WARD**

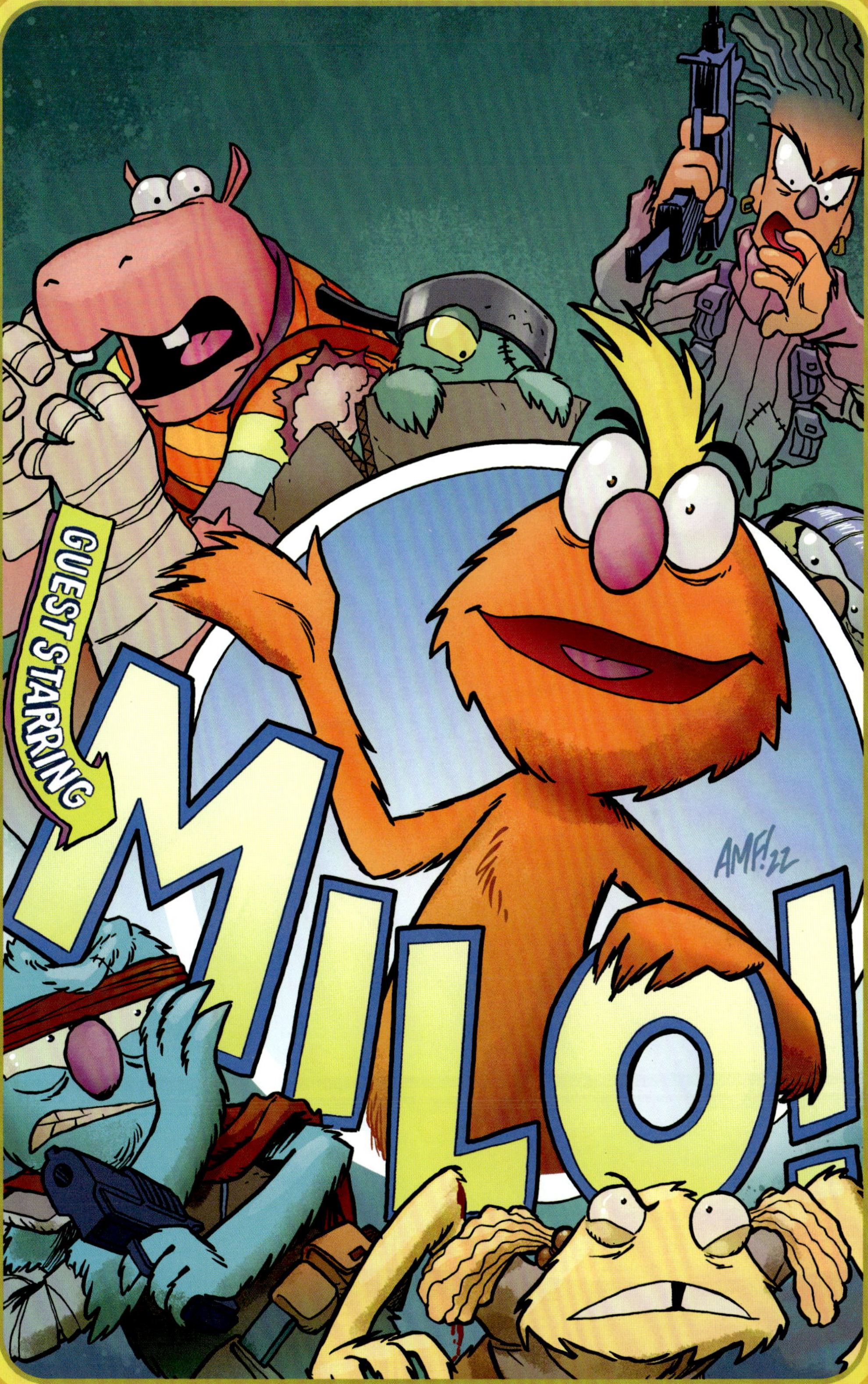
GUEST STARRING
MILO!
AMF! 22

SURVIVAL STREET #3 COVER B BY **TONY FLEECS**

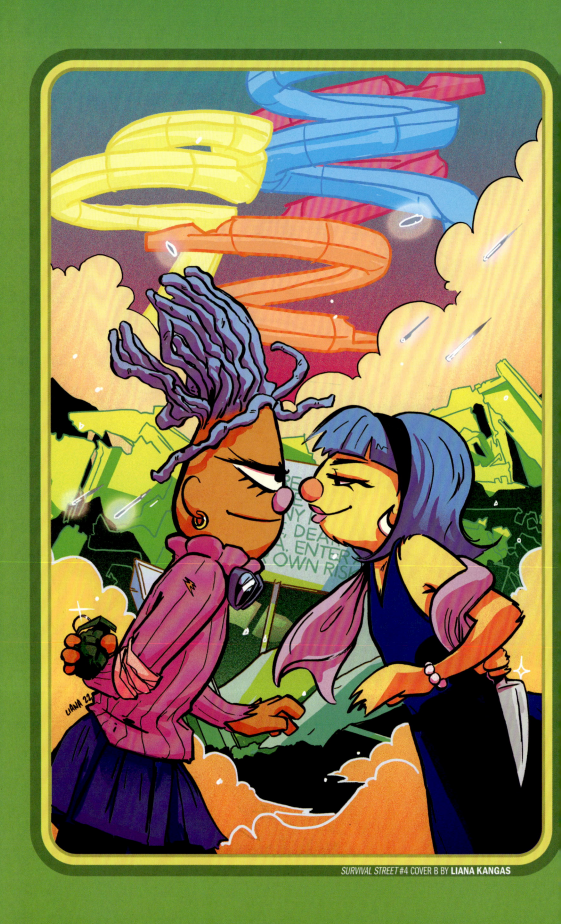

SURVIVAL STREET #4 COVER B BY **LIANA KANGAS**

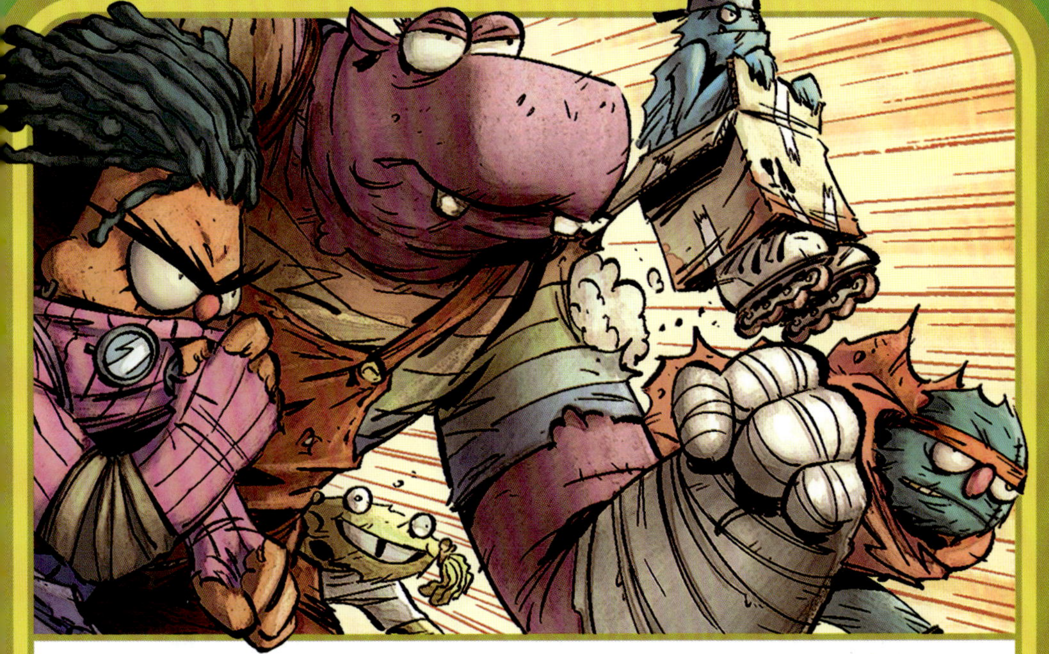

We never wanted to be right.

Okay, *yes*—when we started what became *Survival Street*, we wanted to build a world of stories that let us bite into any and every *real-world* nightmare that was haunting our brains at the moment.

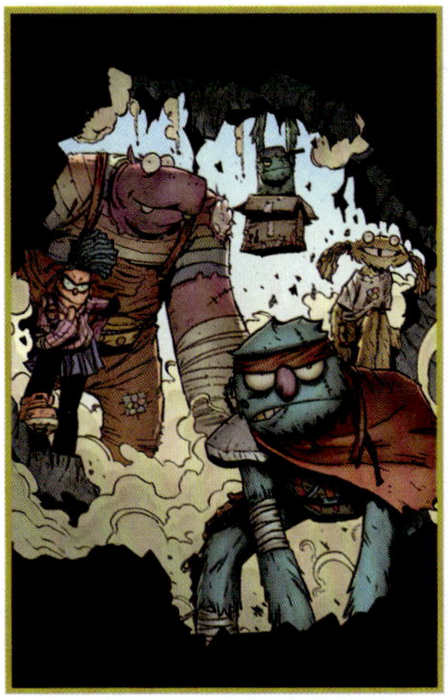

But we swear to you—we always intended it to be *fun* and *funny*. We originally met and collaborated doing live comedy! Humor is how we cope with *everything*. Including but not limited to:

- ☞ Awkward social situations
- ☞ Pain
- ☞ Compliments
- ☞ Corporate dehumanization
- ☞ Creeping fascism
- ☞ Existential dread
- ☞ Thinly veiled marketing

And good satire starts from a real and recognizable place—but the comedy works better when you dial up the absurdity of the issue (without losing the actual idea or principles you're tackling).

You want to push far enough into absurdity for it to be escapist and funny. If it's too close the real debate, people are already sorted or burned out, and it's harder for them to go on *this* ride.

So we wrote *Survival Street* to be a wildly exaggerated, comically grotesque, hyperbolic dystopia where the rich and power hungry were finally able take full control of America and strip-mine it for profit and parts—including the people.

And to match the absurdity of our exaggerated society, we chose heroes that could represent absurd levels of hope, kindness, and everything good we were promised people could be—children's television puppets.

But ever since we plotted these stories last summer—to our horror—*real life* has wildly accelerated straight toward making things we pitched as ridiculous hyperbole the *actual news*. If a sci-fi writer predicts the future, I'm pretty sure you get a technology named after you.

But when your satire starts coming true?

It doesn't feel good.

Of course, we bumped up the stakes, the shamelessness, and disaster capitalism as much as we could to stay ahead of reality and hopefully keep things in the Fun Zone™ for y'all!

But at this point, if you're going to recommend this book to a friend, we'd encourage them to pick it up ASAP.

Because we're increasingly worried that, pretty soon, the only surreal part of the story will be the puppets.

—**JAMES ASMUS** and **JIM FESTANTE**

ART BY **ABYLAY KUSSAINOV** COLORS BY **SERGEI NAZAROV**

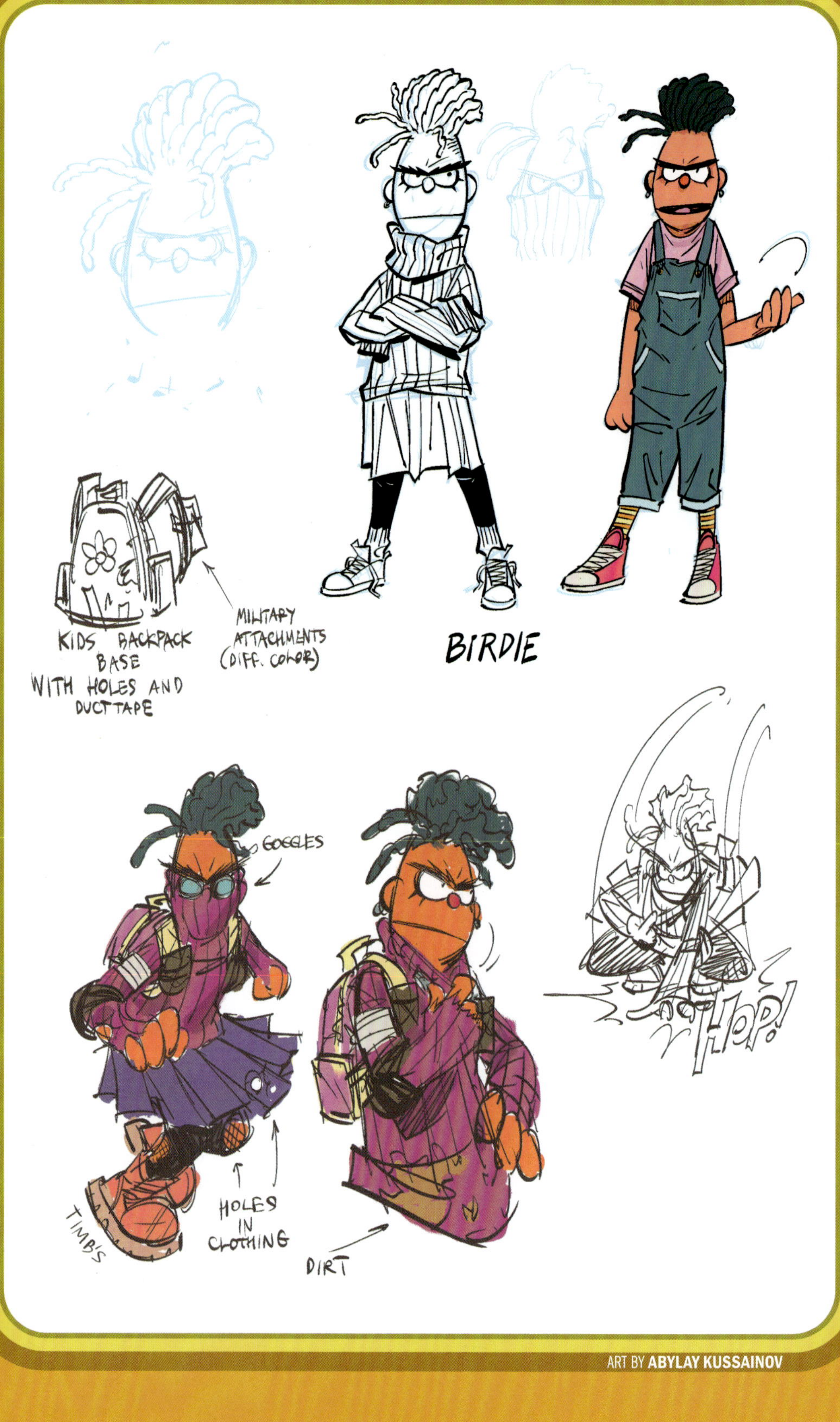
KIDS BACKPACK BASE WITH HOLES AND DUCTTAPE
MILITARY ATTACHMENTS (DIFF. COLOR)
BIRDIE
GOGGLES
HOP!
TIMB'S
HOLES IN CLOTHING
DIRT

ART BY **ABYLAY KUSSAINOV**

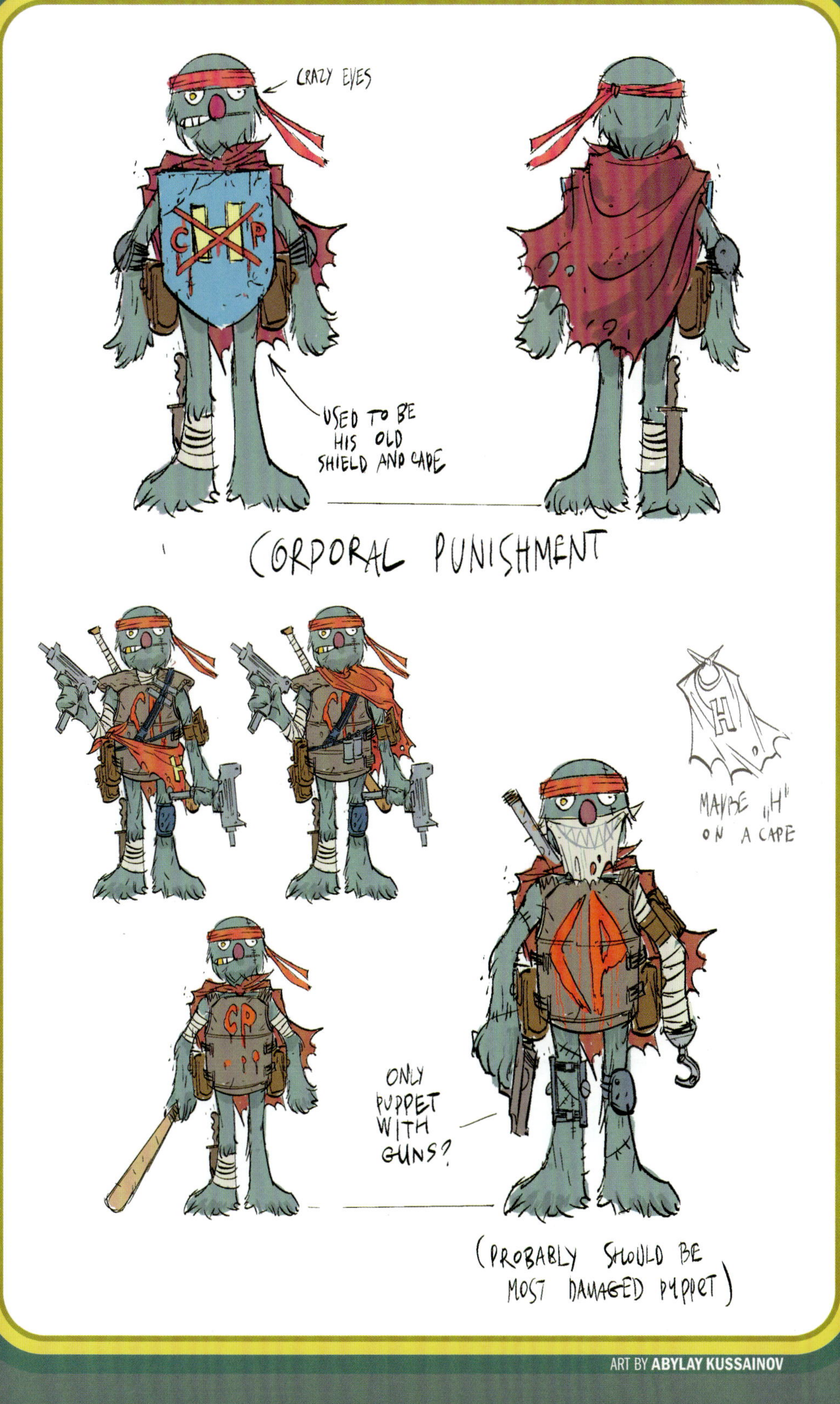
CRAZY EYES
USED TO BE HIS OLD SHIELD AND CAPE
CORPORAL PUNISHMENT
MAYBE "H" ON A CAPE
ONLY PUPPET WITH GUNS?
(PROBABLY SHOULD BE MOST DAMAGED PUPPET)

ART BY **ABYLAY KUSSAINOV**

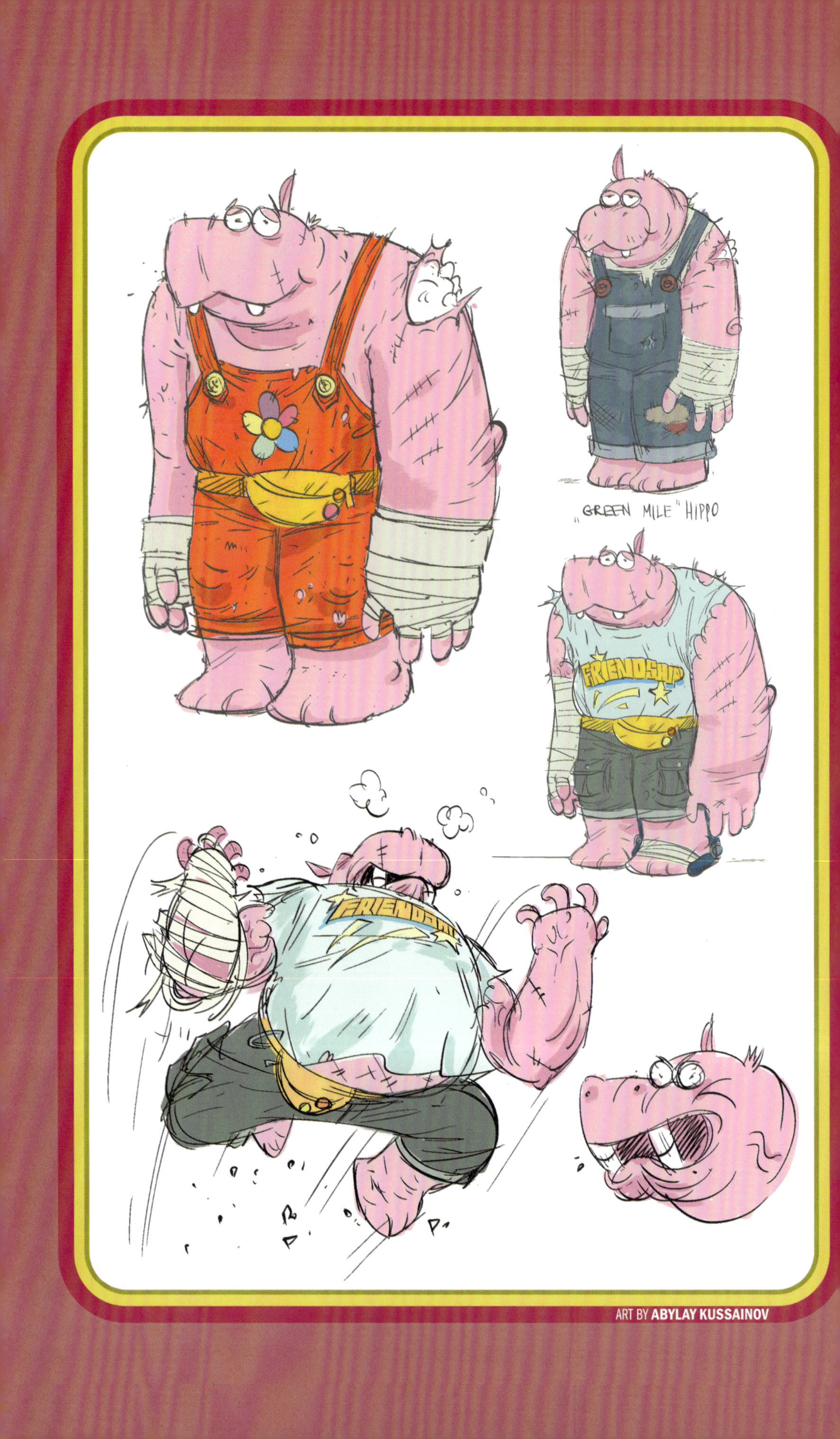

"GREEN MILE" HIPPO
FRIENDSHIP
FRIENDSHIP

ART BY **ABYLAY KUSSAINOV**

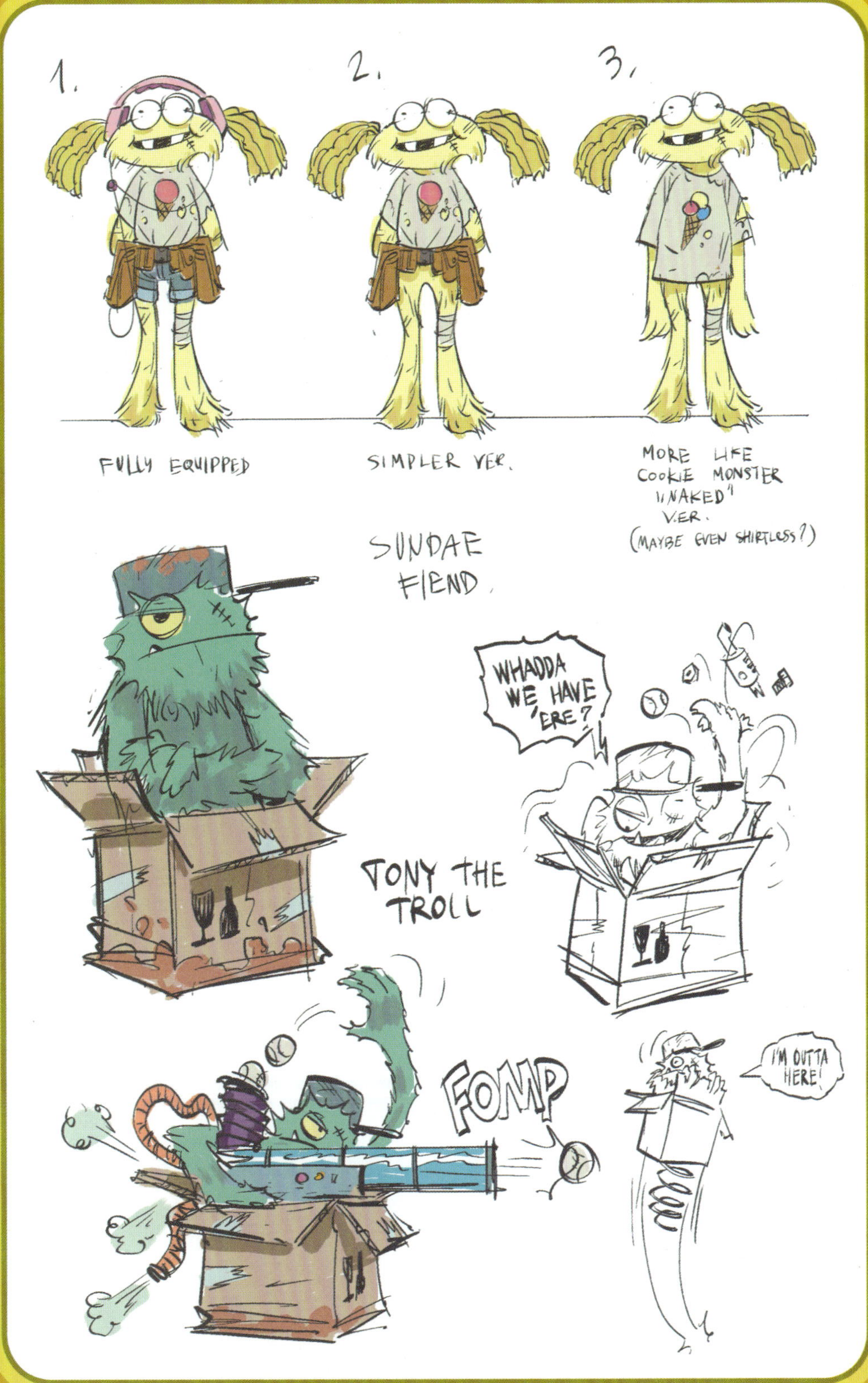
1.
2.
3.
FULLY EQUIPPED
SIMPLER VER.
MORE LIKE COOKIE MONSTER "NAKED" VER.
(MAYBE EVEN SHIRTLESS?)
SUNDAE FIEND.
WHADDA WE HAVE 'ERE?
TONY THE TROLL
FOMP
I'M OUTTA HERE!

ART BY **ABYLAY KUSSAINOV**

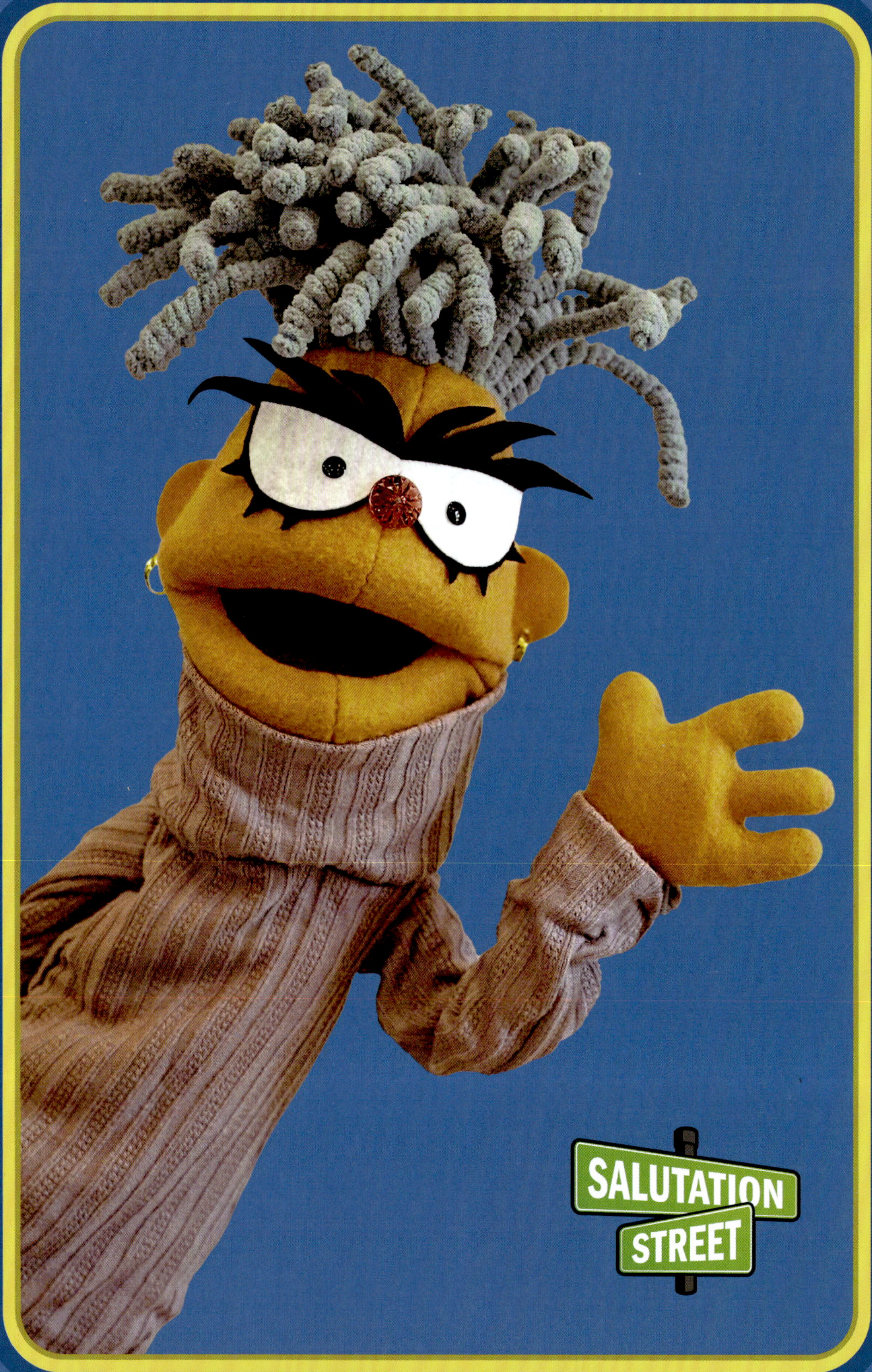
SALUTATION
STREET

BIRDIE PUPPET BY **MARIA ANDREOTTI**